Praise for *A Matter of Faith*

My first reaction in reading *A Matter of Faith* was that I hoped the current students at NCSSM don't get their hands on this book! After all, they might get ideas of how to pick locks, how to raid the cafeteria in the dead of night, and how to have secret romantic liaisons in hidden places on campus. But on further reading and contemplation, I have decided to applaud Brian Morin's effort to honestly explore the concept of growing up with all the pitfalls, tragedies, and personal triumphs involved. Morin bravely records a gripping story that is made intellectually challenging, yet enjoyable, as multiple characters explore issues of friendship, love, loyalty, childhood, adulthood, and parenthood. I urge you to take these issues raised in this book to heart in your own life and work to make this world a better place.

> Joe Liles
> Instructor of Art
> North Carolina School of Science and Mathematics

Brian Morin is a gifted, serious young Southern writer with much to say to people everywhere and of all ages. *A Matter of Faith* is splendidly written and compellingly told.

> Tom Camp
> Author of *With Both Eyes Shut, Everything Looks the Same*, and father of Mary Jean (Camp) Leonardi, '86

To Faith

Sex......Violence.......NCSSM!!!!!!!!!!!
The Southern Novel that William Faulkner wasn't quite ready to write!!!!!
The 'Coming-of-Age' novel that will draw many a nod from S&M'ers of every class.

Chuck Britton
Instructor of Physics
North Carolina School of Science and Mathematics

i was in durham one day last week (in the midst of two workshops) and found your package in my office...unfortunately, the first chance i will get to do anything with it is maybe late july, when i have a few days free...

John "Doc John" Kolena
Instructor of Physics
The North Carolina School of Science and Mathematics

The Project

Several months ago, I decided to publish *A Matter of Faith*, market it primarily to students, parents, alumni and friends of the North Carolina School of Science and Mathematics, and donate the proceeds to the School. I talked with several friends from my graduating class, '85, and our juniors, '86, and sent them copies. When Gina Norman '86 said, "Brian, it's really good. No, I'm not just saying it—it is good. I would tell you it is anyway, but at least now I don't have to lie," the project was born.

We are printing 2000 copies at a cost of under $5000, and selling them for $15 each. All of the proceeds will be donated to the School as an unrestricted donation. We'll be visiting the School on Alumni Day to sell signed copies (and sign copies bought elsewhere). Copies will be available through our website, www.amatteroffaith.org, and through Amazon.com and other web retailers. With luck, a few local bookstores will carry the book, as well as the student store at the School.

After that, sales of the book will depend on you, the reader. If you like it, please tell your friends. Send them an email. Put a link to our website on your site. Publish a review on Amazon. Ask your friend at the local newspaper to review it. Help us however you see fit. If you have marketing ideas, please contact me, the author, at 8 New Forest Ct, Greenville, SC 29615, or at brian@morin.ws. I'm also happy to hear your thoughts—the good, the bad, and the ugly.

To Faith

A Letter from the North Carolina School of Science and Mathematics

Dear NCSSM Alumni, Students, and Friends,

In my thirteen year tenure at NCSSM I am continually honored to serve the finest individuals, and impressed with the myriad of talents of such gifted intellectuals. I have known Alumni to solve incredibly complex math problems, provide medical care to disadvantaged populations in rural North Carolina, create software, and now a novelist. After reading Brian Morin's novel it is apparent not only does he possess an incredible writing skill, developing rich characterizations, but after 20 years, he brought to life vivid experiences as a student at NCSSM. Thank you, Brian, for *Faith* and for your desire to contribute proceeds to future NCSSM students. How very fortunate we are that your poignant thoughts on paper will help to insure the future of a place that meant so much to you.

Warmest Regards,
Therese Taxis
NCSSM Director of Annual Fund & Alumni Programs

A Matter of Faith

A novel, by

Brian Morin

First Edition
First Printing
August, 2005

To Faith

For my three lovely nieces.

Lilian Caroline Morin

Isabella Hope Morin

Julia Camille Morin

To Faith

Author's Note

When I took my first real job out of graduate school in 1994, the late Mike Gilpatrick, one of the more established physicists in the company, very accurately summed up the beginnings of my career at Milliken & Company. He said, "Brian's confidence far outweighs his competence." I'm afraid that, in 2000 when I started writing this novel, the statement also accurately described my writing ability. I finished the first draft two years later, and it was terrible. My wife couldn't even finish it.

We're now ten drafts later, including several major rewrites, one of which dropped the page count from over 600 (manuscript) pages to the current 365. Gone are several long soliloquies, including a ten page oration by John Kolena on the difference between particles and waves. Please let me know if you miss them.

Several years later, while trying to set me up on a blind date with my wife, and after a long monologue on my virtues, my best friend told her, "Brian is a little desperate, but he has a big heart." The writing here, I'm afraid, remains true to that. There are rough places, and places where even the most untrained reader will know what I was trying to say, but will wish I had said it more clearly. However, the heart of the story is true, and hopefully enough to propel you through to the finish. And I must say, there are other sections that, when I read them, I feel that they are so good that I wonder if I truly wrote them, or had a bigger hand guiding my fingers. They are not frequent, but, like one good hole in a lousy round of golf, are enough to keep bringing me back to the keyboard, working to refine my craft.

To Faith

I have received a tremendous amount of help and inspiration in writing the book. Beautiful Lily was sucking her foot at her Baptism when I had the inspiration to build a book around the letters I had written for her, letters that she will not open for years to come. Of course her letters remain private, and I've taken liberal license with the truth in the ones inside this book. Throughout the years, I have found both inspiration and motivation with Lily, Isabella, and Camille sitting in my lap, bringing me a book to read, or dragging me out to see the cows in the back yard yet one more time.

Brian Burkhart was the first to read one of those early drafts all the way through, back when I wasn't showing anyone. Brian gave me the idea to encapsulate the timeline of the story in Caroline's recovery from her coma, and deserves credit for the idea, while I'll take the blame for any deficiencies in its execution. When his wife Julie read the revised version, and told me she loved it, I finally began to believe it might be publishable.

Elizabeth Cates '87 helped me to think through the changes in point of view, which I admit are still sometimes awkward, and to refine the characters into really different people, rather than twelve different versions of myself. Nearing the final drafts, I had much help from several insightful readers from recent NCSSM graduating classes, including Sam Van Oort '04, Grace Goff '04, Austin Luton '03, and Morgan Brown '03.

Tom Camp, who was my most faithful correspondent outside my mother and father during my lonely days at boot camp at Fort Jackson in 1986, has encouraged me from day one, and his love for even the early terrible drafts helped me to continue. Try though he might, he was unable to compel his old high school buddies to publish this commercially, and through my own frustration with the process the idea for this project was born. When I brought the idea of self-publishing and donating the proceeds to the School up to Therese Taxis in the Alumni Office, she responded so enthusiastically that I knew I had to do it. I got a similar response from the other alumni who joined the push-this-baby-out publication team, including Stephen Cole '85, Peter McRae '85, Gina Norman '86, and Mary Jean (Camp) Leonardi '86. You can find a short bio (and recent picture) of each at the end, along with my own. Steve and Gina told me in no uncertain terms what was crap, and how to fix it; Peter did a wonderful job on the cover, and Mary Jean has helped tremendously with the logistics of turning the bytes on my computer into a finished paper version that we can sell.

After a frustrating twelve hour day of standing on concrete floors, I found myself face to face with a young Ruby Tuesday's manager in Vidalia, Georgia. She announced that she was a Christian missionary, and we were her missionary field, and then described her tattoos and piercings. Soon after, Julia was born and the book began to take final form.

Almost 80% of the proceeds will go straight to the North Carolina School of Science and Math as an unrestricted donation. The rest will pay for printing and what minor marketing we do. My hope is that the money will help the School to inspire the young students in the same way it did me. My time there remains one of my fondest memories, and most meaningful periods in my life. I will close with a quote from the end of Chapter 6, which captures my feelings as accurately as my craft will allow.

> After nearly five hundred telescoping days of intense study and intense friendship, seniors at the North Carolina School of Science and Mathematics are ready to graduate. We approach graduation the way a sailor, long at sea, approaches the shore. As it grows closer, we stand on the rails, longing for the new life it offers. We leap off early and sprint through the shallow waters of the days just before, and then dive into it and kiss the first land we touch.
>
> Then, not days after we have gone home, we miss the sea; we miss our School. It has shaped me like no place, no group of people, no singular event has before or since. I love it; I miss it; I am forever grateful for the memories it gave me and the changes it imparted to me.

Chapter 1: Nathan

"I had a papa once, Miss Caroline," he said as he hobbled behind her
into the infirmary. "He didn't leave me."

Caroline's eyes softened as she guided the ten-year-old boy onto the
examining table and laid a light hand on his chest. He dropped first to his
elbows, then to his back, crinkling the paper beneath him. He gripped his
belt buckle and raised his head to look me right in the eye, neck muscles
straining. Caroline went to the sink to wash her hands.

"What happened, then, if he didn't leave you?"

"Some men took him."

She turned back, drying her hands on a paper towel. "What men?"

"Some men," he said, and looked at me again, then out the window.

"Why?"

"I was only four."

She came over to him and looked down, having to stand a half step
away to see him past the nearly ripe protrusion in her belly. His striped
short sleeved shirt was faded, and his blue jeans were brown around the
cuffs. One of the patches on his knees had torn through, showing two
more patches and a trickle of blood beneath it. Caroline laid her hand on
his dirty forearm, and as she leaned over him and smiled his neck relaxed
and his head lowered to the table. A cleaner sweat had dripped from
Caroline's brow moments before, when she passed the basketball and
taught Nathan and the other orphans the secrets of the three-man weave.
Then he and the other boy fell, and Nathan had rolled and cried in more
pain than she'd seen. After he quieted down, she had cleaned up and
pulled her white lab coat on, leaving it unbuttoned in front, her belly
sticking out under it.

"What happened when you were four?"

"Mama said it was my fault; she said I made them come get him."

She waited for him to continue, and the silence filled the room like fifty pounds of goose down. She went back to the sink and washed her hands again, and I saw her lips tighten as she faced away from him. Returning, she reached down to his belt buckle. He turned his head away, but held both hands tight on the buckle.

"I'm going to have to have a look, so we can see what's hurting."

"It doesn't hurt anymore, Miss Caroline." She smiled, and Nathan looked back with a defiant smirk, and I thought he might be flirting. There I stood, a grown man, married less than a year and jealous of a ten-year-old boy with bloody knees.

Caroline waited, then pulled lightly on his hand, the milk-white skin of her fingers contrasted against his dirty, unkempt hands. He didn't respond, but gripped his belt more tightly, squeezing his legs so hard that his knees lifted off the examining table.

She let go and went back to the sink and washed her hands yet another time. This time, her hands fully, thoroughly clean, she reached into the cardboard container and pulled on two latex gloves, popping them tight about her wrist. She turned to Nathan and pushed her lower lip up in deep thought, not squinting, but not quite focusing, either. Nathan remained in his half sit-up position, eyes on Caroline and dare-you-not smirk on his face.

Caroline stared at him for a long time, then pulled the gloves off, took off her white coat and folded it over the back of a chair. She sat down beside him, and leaned forward as far as her belly would let her, and brushed his hair.

"Sit up," she said. He smiled, then sat up and swung his legs over the edge of the table.

"I don't have to look at anything if you don't want me to … but if something's wrong, I might help."

"I'm all better now," he said. "Ready to go." He sat still, back rigid, with an expectant look on his face.

"Maybe there will be children in your future after all," she said, and he blushed cherry Kool-aid. "Why did your mother blame it on you?"

Nathan's smile disappeared, and his face went white. "I hate my mother." I don't believe I'd ever seen him angry before.

"I'm sorry, Nathan."

"She beat me blue, and when I complained she beat me twice as hard."

"So they took you away from her?"

"I ran away, and the last time, they didn't make me go back to her, after I showed them the spots."

"Bruises?"

"All over."

"And your father? He couldn't take you?"

"He's in jail."

"For something you did?"

"Mama said that to make me feel bad. I bet it was something she did."

Caroline lifted her arm slowly to his shoulder and drew him into the reluctant hug of a boy who wants much more, but can't trust anyone to stay in his life. She kissed the top of his head and breathed in his sweaty musk. She drew one hand up to touch the corner of her eye before she let go.

"Miss Caroline?"

"Yes," she said as she stood up.

"You're a pretty good basketball coach…"

"Thanks, Nathan," she said, and smiled.

"…and I don't mind you taking my blood pressure and making me say, 'aaahhh.'"

Caroline smiled.

"But if I ever need a doctor for down there, I'd like to have a man-doctor."

"Okay, Nathan. If you have any troubles, you let me know, and we'll get you a man-doctor."

"Thanks, Miss Caroline."

*   *   *

Caroline was quiet that night at dinner, which was late as usual. I had come home early—early for us at 7pm—and made alfredo sauce with chicken and sautéed onions, and crumbled bacon and Romano cheese. We ate on the back porch with lemonade.

It was Thursday, and Thursdays are nice. We eat, we relax, sometimes we make love, and then we have the weekend.

She finished her meal and slipped from the table to a cushioned lounge chair. I piled the dishes and took them inside, then pulled my chair behind her and held her, letting my arms drift down her sides to hold our baby.

"Hi baby," I said. "Dis you daddy talkin'. I'm glad you learned some basketball today, but I hope you're not upset like your mommy." I nuzzled my chin on Caroline's shoulder.

"I'm not upset."

"Baby, your mommy's lying to me. You don't listen to her, okay?"

"I got a card from Dad today."

"That's right. I forgot. Your birthday is this weekend. How kind of him! When was the last time we heard from him? Christmas?"

"He sent money."

"Right. I'm a professor; you're a doctor—obviously the edge of subsistence."

"We can't take it."

"We'll give it to the orphanage, then. They need it."

"It's not that—we really can't take it."

"What?"

She sat up and leaned forward, then turned to me. "I wish he could just let Kevin go."

Kevin—her ex-husband. "You know those love triangles—someone always gets hurt."

She smiled and I felt her shoulders loosen. "Dad and Kevin. A perfect match!"

I was relieved to see her talking again. "Did you find out anything else about Nathan?"

"He should have stayed with his mom," she said with a sad smile.

"One tough kid."

"His dad pled guilty to first degree sexual abuse. Wal Mart caught him on a random drug test when he worked there, and he told the counselor everything. She hit the record button, and he told her again."

"What did he do?"

"You don't want to know."

"And it got worse after he left his mom?"

"Yes."

4

"Right. So, back to your father. How do you think his golf game is going?"

"He always beats his broker," she said, and we both laughed.

*   *   *

Caroline's father can bring out the piranha in her with a single word, but I knew that when she got up at four the next morning and put on her running clothes, which in her pregnancy had become "walking" clothes, it wasn't her father that had interrupted her dreams. She might be angry with him, but she knew in the sense of Matthew 5:24, he was the one who needed to make things right before the Lord.

Instead, Nathan's troubles had kept her from sleeping, and forced her to find comfort in the solitude of physical exertion, as best she could with a somewhat fragile twenty-five pound weight strapped to her stomach.

She was out for an hour, and when she came in I pretended to be asleep and rolled over groggily as she showered quickly, then joined me in the bed. I never knew when she would talk. I knew she would, eventually. And she knew I would listen, whenever she was ready. She was my troubled princess, and I her safe harbor. Among only a few other things, that is what made our marriage work.

That particular morning, she wasn't ready. She climbed into bed and I spooned her and placed my hand over her stomach and felt the rustlings of the fragile life being formed there. It's as if our daughter knew my touch and was trying to kick an "I love you, Daddy" through the thick muscle of Caroline's uterus. Then Caroline rolled over and placed her head on my chest, and, slowly, patiently, gingerly, we began to make love. Afterwards, we showered together, and she went off to the hospital, while I went to the back porch to work on my novel for a few hours before class.

*   *   *

My classes ended at 3 on Friday, so I headed to the orphanage early. Two blocks off Rosemary St. in Chapel Hill, it shares a dingy block near the border with Carrboro with a weird Mexican-Chinese restaurant and an apartment building. It's a large, three story house that began as a bakery, and grew through a dozen additions over the decades to a fourteen bedroom maze of awkward hallways and low-ceilinged parlors, and had in its previous lives been both a fraternity house and a boarding home for young women. Today, it housed forty-odd boys whose lives were in various states of disrepair, providing some semblance of security for those who either could not, or would not be placed in foster homes. Most of the boys there didn't know what a family really was. After Caroline left hers, she adopted them as her own, even before she adopted me.

From two blocks away, I could hear the ball bouncing, and knew the maestro of that curious rhythm. For me, dribbling a basketball is an up-and-down, ball-in-front-of-me repetitive motion. On rare moments, I'll let the ball drift to my right side, and dribble there, but always with one eye on the ball. Nathan doesn't dribble the ball, but instead seems to massage its trajectory in a maelstrom of orbits, the ball stopping in his hand, then rocketing out in an unpredictable direction. Every time, I am sure he will miss it, but somehow his hand, or his other hand, intercepts it in some unlikely position, where the ball stops and his expert blue eyes take in every action on the court before flipping the ball out again, like some robotic yoyo. As I approached, he was alone with his imagination, dribbling, turning, twisting, driving, and always, at the end, passing, then a quick imaginary high-five before he chased the ball down and brought it to the top of the key for the next round.

This time, though, he put the ball up in a lopsided lay-up that clanked against the rusted backboard and, as the backboard twisted left, rolled forward around the dipping rim and over the front. I believe all Nathan's struggles revolve around trust. The ball, with its roundness, its predictable response to spin and bounce ... he believed in the ball and trusted it, and it gave him a confidence that allowed him to perform miraculous feats. But the rim, the wobbly, rusty, unpredictable hoop of ancient metal perched atop a half-rotted wooden pole, was an evil, untrustworthy specter in his mind, and he could not bring his wonderful globe through its portal. Alone, with no one watching, he would hit barely one of seven lay-ups. In a game, he never shot.

He saw me as I came close, and yelled to me, "I'll get the others, Mr. Josh!" and sprinted into the orphanage.

I changed into shorts, and came out to find a motley crew of five boys,

6

all older than Nathan, and we split quickly into teams of three. Nathan and I filled out one team with another boy, a thirteen year old with stumpy legs and a round pudding-like chin. He was Nathan's antithesis, a boy who could neither dribble nor move, but whose every touch sent the ball sailing through the net. In the hour that we played, I touched the ball only to pass it back to Nathan, or take a couple of fake dribbles and then pass to this other boy. We handily beat the three older boys in three games to 21, with Nathan and I contributing only a couple of buckets each.

Caroline showed up with a dozen pizzas in the back of her car, and the game broke. Nathan and the round boy helped her carry the pizzas in, and within minutes the lunchroom was filled with the gnawing sounds of two dozen underfed teenagers with a seemingly endless supply of pizza. Two hours later, we settled in with the boys to a double feature of *Remember the Titans*, after which we put the younger kids to bed and watched *The Good, the Bad, and the Ugly* with a few of the older boys.

* * *

Most of the boys were asleep when we left, and Miss Baldwin, their middle aged caretaker, had drifted off as well. We cleaned up the popcorn bowls, half-filled cans of soda, and empty pizza boxes, and sent the last few stragglers up to brush their teeth and turn in before locking up and collapsing in Caroline's car for the short drive home.

"Have you ever thought of adopting one of the boys, Josh?" she asked me as we began to undress.

"Yeah. But, I'd want all of them. Or at least a good basketball team's worth."

"I know."

"And once you've got that, why not get a few outfielders to flesh out the crew."

"Right."

"And then we might as well just move into the orphanage with them, which we've almost done, except they don't have a bedroom to spare."

She smiled and touched my arm and pushed me into the shower, and for a moment the water ran brackish. Two quick passes with the soap, and we were both drifting about our bedtime rituals. We came to the bed just as Jay Leno began his monologue, exhausted and ready to be entertained.

"Nathan, right?" I asked.

"Right," she said, and we let Jay distract us with another battery of Condoleeza Rice, Bill Clinton and Michael Jackson.

After a funny round of Jaywalking, I said, "It's fine, if that's what you want to do," and she smiled and touched my hand, then drew it to her belly where our little girl kicked a few more "I love you's" to me as I drifted off to sleep.

*   *   *

Caroline didn't come out to play basketball with us on Monday when she came to the orphanage. She spent the afternoon in the office, with Miss Baldwin and two women from the Department of Social Services, which the boys and I all call "SS" for short.

"Where's Miss Caroline," Nathan asked me.

"In the office," I said, walking away to pick up an errant ball.

"That's boring," he said, and I checked him the ball. After he had missed his layup, one of the older boys asked, "What's she doing in there," and another answered, "The SS is in there with her," then a third said, "They musta found out she was Jewish," and Nathan came back with, "Miss Caroline isn't Jewish. I've been to church with her." I smiled and checked him the ball again.

This time he dribbled right to the basket, and like every time, my defender stepped toward him, leaving me open for his no-look pass, which I took and tossed up for an easy bucket. I felt as if I was the only one who knew he couldn't shoot.

Caroline looked troubled as she left the office, a thick brown folder of papers in her hand. She walked straight to her car, and though it was early, I grabbed my bag and followed her. "See you tomorrow," I said, and they waved, hardly disguising their shaking heads.

We didn't talk on the way home. I sat in my sweat in the passenger seat and tried to dissipate the static electricity of her anger, waiting for the explosion and knowing I was no bomb expert.

At home, we both showered and then met on the back porch for leftovers. Clean, she had cooled down a little, but still hardly touched her food. She didn't speak, but I could tell that the voltages were drifting lower. When she took her perch on the padded lounge chair, I picked up the dishes and took them inside. Returning, I got on my knees and put my ear to her belly.

"Wooooooweee! I know, baby, yo mommy is mad, but I don't think she's ready to talk about it yet." I pretended to listen for a minute, then said, "I know it's tight in there when she's mad. If it gets too bad, you just kick her in the colon, and that'll clear her right out."

Caroline laughed and shook her head. "I don't even know where to start."

"I'll just guess, then." She frowned and flared her nose at me, which I took as permission, so I went on. "Nathan was a boy genius at the age of four, until her mother realized he was smarter than she was, so she stuck a knitting needle in his ear. That made his father horny, so he went at him while his Mama beat them both black and blue."

She shook her head and breathed in fits. "It's not that far off," she said, and her lips pursed and I handed her a napkin from the table to wipe the tears that were gathering in the lower parts of her eyes. She took two more deep breaths, then said, "He's been in seven foster homes in five years. Two of his foster-fathers are in jail for abusing him, and they suspect another. His own father sexually abused him from his second birthday until they took him away."

"Nathan doesn't remember any of it. One of them could come back, do it again tomorrow, and by the next day it would be gone from his memory. DSS can't place him. They don't have any idea how much damage there is, or if it can ever be fixed. The counselor I talked to today felt certain he would be a rapist before he turned twenty. Cut and dried, no way around it. His emotions have been ground to hamburger."

"Good Lord," I said, and meant it. I took her hands and leaned into her and kissed her forehead, and she wrapped her arms around me.

"That's not the worst," she said.

"What?"

"His father gets out of prison in a month," she said.

"I'll kill him."

"You may have to," she said. "He could get custody, if he can prove to DSS that he's well. They said it's even odds.

"But we could adopt him now, before he gets out?"

"I told them I needed a day to think about it, but I don't," she said.

"Me neither," I said.

"It takes two weeks."

"I'll clean out the guest room."

"No, he can have my room. My reading room. I don't need it. It's bigger."

"You sure?"

"Yeah. We'll go this weekend and get a real basketball goal."

"Won't that be something," I said, and smiled, thinking about how his dribbling would improve on a driveway that was paved flat, and imagining him putting up lay-ups that deftly rolled into a solid, shining orange rim.

Chapter 2: Caroline

"Caroline? Silver spoon in her mouth? No—nearly had stainless steel forceps in her eye, though. Bonehead doctor couldn't get the stubborn little thing out, and gouged her at the corner of her eye socket.

"Donna screamed at a drop of blood next to her eye—sent the doctor into a tizzy. 'Course she can see fine, but she's got a scar—looks like a sad, dark tear."

—John Novak, Caroline's Father

Caroline tickled her fingers through my thinning double cowlick and slipped onto my lap with a sorry-to-intrude smile on her face. The creamy silk of her robe rustled as she slipped her arm around my neck and began to read the phrases I had been aching onto the computer screen all morning. I had been trying to rescue my novel, which was in mud up to both knees, while she slept. I looked out our back patio, red brick with cast iron railings, over a long crabgrass lawn to a row of cedars and cypress, through which I could just read a sign in the cow pasture beyond which read, "Not for sale—don't ask."

I pulled my chair back to accommodate her pumpkin-sized belly as she turned toward the laptop screen and scrolled up. "What's Madison up to this morning?" she asked.

"Torture," I answered.

"About time she did something interesting!" I closed my eyes and waited, and when I opened them, she was scrolling down again.

I watched patiently, reading alongside her. "Well, at least you love her," she said when she had finished. Her bashful dimple peeked out, and amid the typhoon of my love for her surfaced my frequent wish to capture its dewy scent on my computer screen.

It was late by my standards, and the sun peered through the tops of the tallest trees. Caroline, my wife of only a year, loved to lie in on Saturdays, to bask in the warm glow of the early morning sunshine on the thin sheet covering her naked body. On this particular morning, I pictured her lying on her side, a pillow between her knees and another supporting her back, her arm resting on her swollen belly, maybe probing with a finger in an effort to touch our unborn daughter, her mind drifting to when she would hold her in her arms without the thick covering of skin and muscle between them.

"Need anything from downtown?" she said as she lumbered off my lap, supporting herself with her arm on my shoulder.

"Inspiration," I said. Then, "Any other birthdays today?"

"Just Nathan," she said. His birthday was on Wednesday, and we were planning on taking him out for pizza to ask him if he'd like to live with us, as our son. One of St. Joan's forty three kids had a birthday almost every week, so Caroline spent most Saturdays wandering through the shops across from the UNC campus in Chapel Hill looking for birthday gifts. Afterwards, she would drive to Ninth Street Bakery in Durham to pick up a cake. "It's worth the drive," she'd say.

"Olive juice," she said, and flatfooted into the house. This was a hangover from a childhood love, one she told me about before we got married, and meant "I love you." "Elephant shoe," meant the same thing.

"Tobacco chew," I said, after she had closed the door. My only addition to this little language meant "back at you."

Those were our last words.

*   *   *

The phone rang later that afternoon. I had moved into the house, and was leaning back in the leather chair in my office, typing some, but mostly staring at the dusty blue walls of my office. I struggled with Madison, and her testy dialogue. I wanted her to be strong willed, stubborn, free thinking, and yet be relenting to the one man she accepted into her life; to be endlessly happy and yet have a deep, hidden sadness. In my inability to choose, poor Madison became the nether-woman, impossible to understand and difficult to like even for the author who created her. Caroline understood my silent adoration for all women, and my need to capture that adoration in one character. That she knew I was doomed to fail did not keep her from loving me more for it.

The voice on the phone was like a message from a distant planet rattled through a thousand miles of tin cans. I caught words only in pieces, my mind refusing to settle on a single syllable, refusing to let even one consonant gain traction past my inner ear. "The hospital," I said, after a pause grew long enough I was sure a question had been asked.

"Yes, can you come to the hospital now?" she asked. Again, I suppose.

"Yeah, I'll … okay. Should I bring anything?" I was reaching.

"No, sir, we just need to discuss a few things with the doctors before they go into surgery."

"I'll be there in ten minutes," I said, and then hung up.

*   *   *

My mind buzzed like a bee in a mason jar. I did not cry, nor get angry. Caroline had been in an accident, I thought, and I was going to talk with the doctors. I forced these facts to take grip in my mind, to become solid. What then? I forced myself to think like a detective. What had happened? What decisions would I have to make? I refused to react. Find out the facts first, make the appropriate decisions, then react later.

Though Caroline worked there, I hadn't been to the UNC hospital in years, not since she was a medical student and we had shared bag lunches on the lawn outside, when she had been dating Kevin and we had just been friends. I loved her then, but felt I had come in too late, that Kevin had gotten his claws in too deep to be extracted cleanly. How right I was.

I stepped into the front room of the hospital, a large open room with a receptionist's desk in front and elevators and hallways leading to important places where lives are begun and ended, and decisions like those I was about to face were made every day. I stepped up to the receptionist.

"Um, the, uh … the emergency room called me—my wife was in an accident."

"I'm sorry sir. What is your wife's name?" She was young and brown, and her eyebrows were too thin and unicolored to be natural.

"Caroline Studeman."

Her face saddened beneath her artificial brows, and her mascara laden lashes dipped twice. "Caroline's in x-ray right now. Dr. Dansen wants to see you. Wait over there and I'll page him." She motioned me toward a small waiting area with couches and a rack of magazines in vinyl covers. As I turned and left, I saw her touch the corner of her eye with her finger.

I pretended to page through a magazine until a man in green scrubs walked toward me and introduced himself.

"I'm Dr. Dansen," he said, extending his hand. I had met Jim Dansen at the hospital Christmas party, and I wondered again why doctors never use their first names.

"Josh Studeman," I said, "Caroline's husband."

He came right to the point.

"Caroline was hit by a car. She's unconscious, but stable, and in testing. She ... took a hit to the head."

"How about the baby?" I asked.

"Everything's okay—heartbeat, motion ... no obvious trauma. We're watching closely and we'll do a c-section at the first sign of trouble." He touched my arm. "You can breathe now—she's going to be okay." I let out my breath, then felt the ground grow steady beneath my feet as I inhaled deeply.

We talked for several more minutes. Caroline had a broken hip, and they wanted to operate, but not right away. She wanted a natural birth, and a pin in the broken hip would give it more strength before she went into labor. She had also hit her head on the pavement. I agreed to the operation, and he told me he wanted to give her another day to come out of her coma, but then would have to do it before the bones set. She would be out of testing in a few hours, and I might see her if I liked. I went back to my magazine. The receptionist with the narrow eyebrows brought some paperwork a few minutes later. When I finished with it, I was on my own.

* * *

Caroline is a woman of action. Were I to have an accident, she would get me the best doctor in the state, then call my mother and our pastor and everyone else important to me. She would insist on observing any tests and surgery. She would minister to my family, bringing tissues and snacks, ginger ale and warm blankets. I can see the hospital room, filled with flowers and cards from the orphanage kids; it would be some show.

I was different. I sat, *Time Magazine* in hand, scared to delve past the receptionist's desk, afraid I might get lost and never get out, or even worse have to ask for help. I paged through the whole magazine, until I knew I should call her family to let them know. But given how they felt about me, I didn't know where to start.

Her whole family had boycotted our wedding, which we had funded ourselves in a small church filled to the back row by lots of my friends and a few of hers.

Her father, John Novak, an oversized partner in a tort law firm, joked he had *Management by Intimidation* sitting in the open on his desk. He was friendly back when Caroline was living in my guest room and I was the "friend" helping her get settled on the East Coast after her divorce. "You're a good friend, Josh," he said, his big hand clamping down on my shoulder. "You need to find a good woman." Of course, under no circumstances was that "good woman" to be his daughter. No way. "Someone who can keep your life straight while you teach and write that great American novel." I am sure he thought I was gay.

Donna, her mother, was very sweet. She was *sure* I was gay. "I love your home," she said. "Beautiful, simple, yet—with—elegance." She meant it was small, plain, old and clean. I don't think she would have been surprised to walk into the bedroom and see black leather whips on the walls and a mirror on the ceiling. She was devastated when she found out Caroline and I were getting married.

There was only one alternative—her sister Hope. She didn't come to our wedding, either, but did spend the day before with Caroline shopping for another new bathing suit. She was the only person to stay with us when we were roommates. I remember thinking how beautiful she was, but how unlike Caroline. Caroline was strong, aggressive, a go-getter, while Hope was, well, like me. She wore glasses, liked a clean house, and thought things through before acting. After she left, Caroline told me, "She likes you. She said you were cute, in a gay, English teacher kind of way."

"Great," I said. "Your whole family thinks I'm gay."

"If it weren't for the first night, I'd wonder myself," she said.

15

*   *   *

The sun was low on the horizon when a nurse came to tell me I could go see Caroline. I followed her down a long hall, grateful I wouldn't have to live through an elevator ride with her. I just wasn't up to speaking. I followed a half step behind her as she rounded a few corners and pushed through swinging doors.

The nurse stopped at a closed door, then opened it to reveal a private room. I closed my eyes, steeling myself against what lay beyond. I fought the inclination to turn and run, to hide in my back yard and pretend it was all okay. I set my shoulders back, stood tall and said a small prayer of submission. Then, opening my eyes, I stepped forward into the room.

Caroline lay in a bed in the middle of the room. Her stomach rose high, a minor Mt. Vesuvius, rising and falling in even breaths, preparing for eruption. A bandage covered her head, and one eye was a deep red, almost purple and sure to turn nasty shades of black and green over the next several days. Caroline was going to love that, I thought. Her eyes were closed, and her cheeks were soft, and just a shade pale. Her lips were—not blue—but a bit bluer than their natural pink. They moved subtly as she breathed in and out. An I.V. dripped fluid into a butterfly needle in her wrist. I moved closer to her, and the nurse closed the door and left.

As I drew near, I could see her legs unnaturally close under her sheets, bandaged together. I did not dare to raise the sheet. Instead, I placed both hands on her stomach, covering her navel, feeling for movement, for life within. As if she knew I needed a sign, I felt our daughter kick, a gentle protrusion in the lower portion of my palm, and I closed my eyes. "Hi baby," I said. "Dis you daddy talking. You and mommy took a hit today, but it looks like you're ready for round two. You gonna come out and be my little girl real soon, and then that car don't stand a chance." Tears fell, dribbling down my cheeks as I dropped to my knees, holding my hands still, waiting for another kick. When it came, I said my prayer of supplication.

"I am small, dear God, and do not know your will. I pray only for your guidance, Lord, and submit myself; I need you more than anything.

Any sacrifice I could make is nothing compared to what you gave for me. Show me the way, Lord, and I will follow.

"But," I added, "if it is not too far outside of your will, please heal my wife and, if not that, then please Lord let this child be born healthy and give me strength to raise her."

I knelt by Caroline's bed, feeling for more kicks. After a few minutes, I rose and took a seat in the chair next to the bed and covered Caroline's hand with my own. She remained motionless, but her skin was warm beneath my hand.

*   *   *

I awoke the next morning as they came to prepare her for her surgery. My lips were dry, and my eyes ached. Caroline's hand was warm and wet in mine; I'm sure I was the one sweating. A nurse came in first and checked her temperature and a bunch of other things, making notes on a clipboard hanging on the end of her bed. A few moments later an orderly came in, and they transitioned Caroline, along with all of her tubes and attachments, to a gurney and wheeled her out. I didn't speak, and hardly moved the whole time they worked. When they left, I picked up my magazine, but couldn't concentrate and went back to sleep, this time in the bed.

*   *   *

I remember the first day I met Caroline, in the summer of 1996. I was new to UNC, and had just driven up to a party I'd been invited to by a friend's wife. Caroline leapt into the air to catch a Frisbee. She turned as she landed, then twisted and took a long lunge, throwing it back with a quick snap in her wrist. When I stopped my vintage convertible, she looked up at me, still in her Frisbee launching position. Her hair was blown, and a bit of sweat stuck a long brown strand to her forehead.

She smiled as she stood up. I'm not used to that, but managed to smile back as I got out of the car and walked toward the house.

Later, as I ate a cheeseburger by the pool, she brought me a glass of fruity stuff from the punch bowl. She wore a blue bathing suit, with a broad black stripe accentuating her shoulders and chest. She jumped in the pool, and her hair stuck to the back of her head as she came out, then bristled in a thousand directions when she toweled it dry. She sat next to me, and I watched the water glistening on her skin, drying slowly, stubborn wet drops clinging to her shoulders as we talked. I noticed her scar then, a small dark ripple on the side of her left eye, like a make-up tear painted on a clown.

We talked first of impersonal things, of school, our education. As the evening sun set and everyone else moved inside, we sat on strapped pool chairs, wrapped in towels, and talked of our families and our childhoods.

Like most of our times together, I just listened. I nodded and my eyes followed her, and when she smiled and looked at me sideways I laughed and fell back and I'm sure I made some comment. For a few fateful hours, I listened and enjoyed the enchanting woman talking with me.

A very thin man with freckled skin and red hair, gone blond in the sun, approached us with a slow, almost stumbling walk. His feet shuffled left and the right as he swayed toward us in the moonlight. Caroline sat up as he approached, her face all dimples and teeth. He sat on the edge of her chair and she leaned forward and slid her arms around his neck and kissed his cheek. He looked at me through a fog, and his look was not friendly. I thought he was a childhood friend she had mentioned.

I offered my hand, "You're lucky to have grown up with Caroline," I said. He shook my hand and smiled. The words percolated slowly from his brain to his mouth.

"You bet, dude. Don't I know it." He looked at Caroline and said, "I'm going back inside to," he paused, the percolation still incomplete. "Continue," he finally said, obviously proud of his complete, grammatically correct sentence.

When he had gone, Caroline said, "You have to excuse Kevin—he's under a lot of pressure right now and is winding down. You'd like him when he's not … like this."

"I understand," I said, relieved it wasn't Peter. A half hour later, we exchanged phone numbers and I left.

* * *

I felt someone wiggling my foot, and slowly, as lucidity returned, realized I was still asleep in Caroline's hospital bed. "Mr. Studeman? Mr. Studeman … your wife is back from surgery now." As my eyes adjusted, I could see an older nurse standing at the end of my bed, not the same one from this morning. Behind her was a gurney with a bag of fluid hanging from a pole like a bicycle flag. I rose up to my elbows, then rolled off the bed and moved to my chair. I didn't speak.

They moved Caroline to the bed. She was in a body splint, with big elastic Velcro straps holding her to it. Her skin was pale, and her hair looked matted down and oily. Wrinkles framed the corners of her sunken eyes, accentuating her scar. As I looked at her, I drew my hand to my mouth and breathed in deeply through my nose. I was sad.

"Could I see the doctor?" I asked when it looked as if the nurses were getting ready to leave.

The older nurse stopped at the door. "He'll be by this evening to check on her."

"Oh."

She turned and left. I took my place by Caroline's side, moving the chair so I could hold her hand. I waited for what seemed like an eternity, just staring in front of me, and occasionally tightening my lips together or gritting my teeth in frustration and sadness. After an hour or so, I turned on the television and watched Oprah.

*   *   *

After Oprah, I went out and found vending machines near the elevators and returned with a bottle of Sprite and two packs of cream cheese crackers. I sat back in my chair and stared at Caroline. The bandage on her head looked much smaller than I would have expected, and given the demeanor of the nurses, it appeared the surgery had been routine. Maybe they had used a strong anesthetic. If not, then why wasn't she waking up? She had always been so strong. What could keep her down like this? I played with my wedding ring, pulling it on and off my finger, as I finished the last of my crackers.

The Sprite had grown warm by the time Dr. Dansen came by.

"Josh. I hope you've found everything you needed. You could go home—Caroline's stable, and the nurses will keep watch."

19

"Why isn't she waking up?"

He frowned, then said, "Clearly the head wound. There's no excess swelling or complications. After a hit on the head, she could go into a sort of mental shock, and it takes a while before she'll want to come out of the coma."

"She doesn't want to come out?" I asked.

"It's not clear. She could come out any time. Sometimes, the body of someone who is in a coma will slow down to help her recover from whatever sickness or injury put her down. Not so with Caroline. Her body's resting normally, with a healthy heartbeat and good respiration. The surgery was routine, and the bones should heal well. We're going to keep her on pain killers so she may be a little fuzzy when she comes out, but it could happen at any time."

"She doesn't want to come out," I said. "I don't understand."

Dr. Dansen paused, watching me as I shook my head slowly back and forth, looking at Caroline's motionless body.

"The nurses know how to reach me if anything changes. Otherwise, I'll come back in the morning. I suggest you get some rest, and get cleaned up. You'll feel better."

"Okay," I said, and he left.

*   *   *

I decided to go home and take a shower and get a change of clothes. I knew he was right—I would feel better after a shave and a shower. I also wanted to pick up some clean clothes in case I needed to stay at the hospital a few more days.

After showering, I packed some clothes, and picked up two paperbacks to read. While I was searching for extra bills or paperwork that needed to be done, I found a lavender envelope open on Caroline's desk. Two drops had dried on the surface, smearing the ink. Underneath the envelope was a card. I picked it up and read it. "Under no circumstances should you open this card." On the inside it read, "You still don't listen. Happy Birthday." It was signed "Dad". Inside was a check for $100, written to "Caroline LeChien", her name from when she was married to Kevin. I clenched my fist, then put the card back where I found it and headed out the door.

*   *   *

Caroline chest rose and fell slowly in her bed. She looked peaceful, as if she were waiting patiently for something, or maybe for someone. While never high maintenance, she would never have let herself look like this. No makeup, dry, cracking lips, no bra, hair like a plate of brown spaghetti on her white porcelain sheets. Her stomach rose above this, though, a mountain of new life. How uncomfortable she must be on her back; she would roll to her side if she were awake.

I dropped to my knees, took her hand and said a small prayer. "Dear Lord," I began, "I don't understand why Caroline's father still uses Kevin's name. Please heal whatever is going on in his heart. I love you, God. I ask this in Jesus' name. Amen."

I swear I heard Caroline sigh as I finished this. I felt sure she had moved. Her hips were twisted at a slightly different angle, or maybe her torso canted differently, not quite the same. I dropped back to my knees, clenching her hand, my vision blurring. "God, Caroline, come out. We can make it okay with your family. I love you so much!" I pulled her hand into my face and kissed her fingers hard.

*   *   *

The next morning I felt as if a clamp had tightened on one side of my neck, and the rest of my body was twisted with smaller aches. Caroline's back would be even sorer when she woke up, I thought. I had two Monday classes—Freshman Comp in the morning, and War in Twentieth Century Literature in the afternoon. The kids would only wait twenty minutes if I didn't show, and I felt sure Caroline would wake up, so I decided to skip. Under the circumstances, the department would certainly forgive me.

I found Caroline's cell phone in her things in the closet. I paged through her address book and found Hope's number. Below it, I saw her parents' number also. I wondered when she had last used either one. I hesitated, and, thinking it might be too early, decided to call later. Too early, or I was scared. I left in search of breakfast.

*   *   *

I read my novel all day. John Irving's *The Water Method Man*. That evening, I couldn't justify having Caroline in a coma without someone in her family knowing, no matter how torn the relationship. I called Hope.

"Hi Caroline," Hope said.

"It's me, Hope. Josh."

"Oh. Hi Josh." She waited for me to say something. "I'm sorry; did you dial a wrong number?"

"No. I, um … need to talk to you."

"Oh. Sure." She waited again, but I had no idea what to say. I could hear Tiffany and Melanie, her two daughters, talking in the background. "What's wrong, Josh?" Pause. "Is it Caroline?"

That was my cue. "Yeah," I said. "She's been in an accident."

"Oh! Is she there? Let me talk to her." Melanie was raising her voice over something. It was a loud, logical argument like a high school debate. I stumbled over what to say next, so just said it.

"She's here."

"Can I speak with her, Josh?"

"No." I swallowed. "I'm sorry, Hope. She's in a coma." We were both silent for a minute, my words hovering in the airwaves between us like a dragonfly, perfectly still, but ready to make an immediate dart. Then Hope hammered me with questions, devouring every detail. Before she finished, she realized I was spent, and told me she was coming. I gave her directions to the hospital.

*   *   *

My mind drifted back to when I'd first met Hope, when she was Matron of Honor at Caroline's first wedding. I wasn't close to the family back then, only to Caroline, and to Kevin. Hope walked down the aisle in a powder blue satin dress, off the shoulders. Her dark hair was piled high on her head, revealing pearl earrings against her slender neck. Her skin was creamy white, except for a birthmark above the left side of her small,

22

catlike mouth. I introduced myself in the receiving line as we left the church. She took my hand in both of hers and I was surprised that, while her touch was warm and gentle, her hands were large and strong, with a texture like 240 grit sandpaper. She looked me in the eye and said, "How nice of you to come." I left feeling like she was genuinely grateful for my presence, and I looked forward to getting to know her later. She was a busy bee at the reception, bringing people to see Caroline and Kevin and introducing family to friends. I saw her speak to the band director twice, and noticed her in a *tête-à-tête* with the photographer for a few minutes before the cake was cut. We didn't speak, but I met her eyes a couple times. Each time, she smiled and left me feeling welcome.

* * *

Hope knocked on the hospital door around nine. I opened the door and she looked at me with clear brown eyes and frowned. I stepped out of the way, and felt her hands slip around my arm as we walked into the room. We approached Caroline's bed.

Caroline hadn't moved. Her chest rose and fell with a slow rhythm, and her eyes looked sunken, with dark edges. I asked if she would like a few minutes alone with Caroline, and then took *The Water Method Man* to find a snack and a lobby with a comfy chair.

* * *

A half hour later, I knocked lightly on the door, then entered. Hope was sitting in the chair, holding Caroline's hand just as I had. She frowned without speaking, and I walked to the foot of the bed.

"How did it happen?" Hope asked.

I shook my head. "I don't know, yet. She was hit by a car, and hit her head on the road." I told her the rest of what I knew. She listened quietly, only asking questions when I talked about Caroline's medical condition, and the surgery. Neither of us wanted to talk, and when the conversation lulled, I offered to take her to our home and get her settled into the guest room. "It's a little bigger than my last house," I said.

She followed me home. After I carried her bags to the guest room, she took my arm again and asked me to show her the rest of the house. "I love the red," she said when we walked into the living room, and "so functional," when we entered the kitchen. When we got to the second guest room, she said, "This room belongs to Caroline."

"Yeah," I said. It had Caroline's antique white canopy bed, dresser, and desk in it, and a picture window overlooking our back yard and the pasture beyond. "She comes here for her private times. Her old books and junk are in the closets."

"It's quiet up here," Hope said. "I bet she comes up here to read."

"All the time," I said.

After showing her the rest of the house, I explained I didn't want Caroline to wake up alone. She said she understood, and I left for the hospital.

*   *   *

Hope didn't spend much time at the hospital over the next few days, but her presence was everywhere. Flowers showed up from her family and from people I'd never heard of, but still no visitors. She kept a small cooler in the corner filled with drinks and sandwiches for me. Several times, she insisted I go home to shower and sleep for a few hours. "Not to be rude, but you look like you could use it," she said.

A full week passed with no visitors, no communication from other parts of Caroline's family, and no change in her condition. As each day passed, I grew angrier at her father, at her mother. I didn't understand how they could so completely reject her out of their lives, and in hopelessness I sank into a depression, questioning how they could blame me for her divorce, and how they could love Kevin so completely as to reject their daughter when she divorced him.

And yet, while I hated them, I knew something they did not, a stiletto Kevin had slipped into Caroline's abdomen, that she discovered two years later and is the reason they divorced. As the "gay" second husband, I couldn't tell them. But if they knew, their feelings for Caroline and Kevin would be reversed. I had to find a way to tell them, but didn't know how. And I was sure they wouldn't believe it, coming from me.

I went home the next Saturday afternoon to get a shower and pick up some books. I was bored, and considering preparing lectures for my graduate student to give, or perhaps working on my book. When I walked in, I didn't see Hope and wandered around looking for her.

I found her in the second guest room, Caroline's reading room. She sat on the bed with a lap-sized box open beside her. She had a letter in her hand.

"I'm sorry," she said, placing the letter back in the box, where there were several others. "I guess I was prying."

"Doesn't bother me," I said. "What is it?"

"Just letters—our Uncle wrote them for Caroline when she was young. She never let me see them."

I sat down beside her, and pulled one out. It said, 'Thirteenth Birthday" on the envelope. The letter inside was printed on blue marble stationery. I began to read it, but felt like I was intruding after only a few paragraphs, and put it down.

"I miss her so much," Hope said. "I was looking for her in here, in the closet. I found her."

She lowered her head, and I picked up another envelope. "First Kiss" was on the cover. I picked up another, then another, looking only at the titles, not at the letters. Several were for her birthdays, but there were others, like "First Drink of Alcohol," "First Date," "Driver's License," and "Wedding Day." Most had been opened, but a few were sealed.

"These don't look like normal letters," I said.

"Uncle Paul gave them to her on her twelfth birthday. Caroline kept them secret—a big secret between the two of them."

"Did he do the same for you?"

"No. I was jealous … but it's hard to stay jealous of Caroline, and Paul … well, I forgot them. I hadn't thought about them in fifteen years."

I picked up another stack and paged through the titles. There was a letter for every event in a young girl's life. When I looked up, I saw the sun filtering through Hope's dark, soft hair. She was watching me.

"How well do you know Caroline?" she asked me.

"Well enough, I guess," I said. I met her eyes, and then glanced down to the letter she held in her hand. She turned it up, so I could see the title on the envelope, and flipped the flap up, revealing the letter inside. The words "First Pregnancy, Unmarried" were written in a tight scrawl. I looked back into her eyes, deep brown growing muddy with tears.

"You don't know, do you?" I asked. She shook her head. "Oh God, help me," I said, and then I told her the story.

* * *

I held her as she cried, sobbing tremors shaking her slender shoulders. She punched my chest. I could feel her tears hot on my chest, and her breathing came in gargantuan heaves. I let her cry, then, when she had calmed, asked if she needed some privacy. With the hugest frown I've ever seen, she nodded yes, and I got up to leave. Halfway up, she grabbed me into a giant hug and whispered "Thanks," into my ear. As I walked down the hall, I could hear her crying again.

I put some chicken and vegetables into the crock pot to make soup, and then went up to shower. Two hours later, Hope came downstairs, showered and clean, but still clearly shaken. We chatted, then I got us both a bowl of soup, and we went out to the back porch to eat.

"I owe you an explanation," she said.

"You don't owe me anything. I didn't know her ... I don't know how it fits with everything else." I said.

"She never graduated from high school, you know."

"I didn't know. How did she get into college?"

"Daddy's lawyers," she said, and then smiled.

"Humph. What else?"

She studied her soup for a moment, stirring and raising a cloud of steam that fogged her glasses. "Have you ever had anyone take a punch for you? Right on the chin, no flinching. One that should have hit you?"

"I'm not much of a fighter."

"I guess not," she said. Then she told me the story of how her courageous younger sister took a punch for her, when there was no one else to take it. We talked for the next six hours. We ate all the soup, and drank a bottle of wine. Eventually, we wandered upstairs, and though I refused to snoop in Caroline's letters, we picked up each one, and Hope told me what was going on in Caroline's life when she would have read them. Each had its own story, and with each I learned more of Caroline's rich history.

26

I went into the hospital and slept in my chair, holding Caroline's hand. I told her what had happened, told her all Hope had told me. I would swear she was smiling, but the room was dark and I know that's impossible. The next day, when Hope brought some sandwiches, I asked her to write some of the stories down. I had begun to have an idea.

Chapter 3: Hope

"Yes, officer, she did get a good look at the guy.

"No, she's not coming to the lineup. And she's not going to testify. She hasn't told me what happened, and I don't think she's going to.

"Look, Tom, you're getting plenty of support from her older sister, and that's enough. That's it—you're getting nothing else. This conversation is over!"

--John Novak, on the phone, the summer after Caroline's thirteenth birthday

The supermarket is always a busy place for me with Melanie and Tiffany, nine and seven, in tow and a very picky husband to shop for. I was in the cereal aisle when the phone rang, a calming "meow" signifying a call from someone in my family, in the middle of mediating a major negotiation which was coming down to either the Strawberry-Blueberry or the Peach-Strawberry flavor of Kellogg's Fruit Harvest. I had to let Tiff and Mel continue without my guidance while I took the call from my cell.

I saw Caroline's name on the phone's display and popped it to my ear.

Josh has never come across as a brain child, but this time, his reluctance to make use of the English language, the one he has spent half a lifetime studying, was near to driving me batty. To top it all off, Tiffany would not give in to her older sister, insisting on the Peach-Strawberry, so I had to cut him off for a second to intervene.

"Just a second, Josh," I said as he was trying to explain for the third time exactly what was wrong with Caroline's hip. I covered the flip-phone against my waist. "Is this something that needs to be argued over?" They looked at me with innocence, knowing they had been caught. "No, of course not. We will get both, but no more until they are both gone. Now mother has a very important phone call about your aunt Caroline, so please stand still and wait for me to finish." Being basically good children, they did as they were told, and stood up against the shelved cereal boxes, watching me silently.

After talking to Josh, it became clear Caroline needed me. I walked straight out of the grocery store and called my husband Edward on the way home. Before I got there, he had started packing bags for the girls so they could stay with his parents across town. I helped the girls finish—Melanie is particularly good with selecting her own clothes and thinking about everything she might need, but Tiffany had forgotten extra socks to sleep in, and the tiny toothbrush she uses to brush her Bobo Bear's teeth before they go to sleep. She hasn't yet got it like her older sister, but she will come along.

Dad drove over in his Lincoln Town Car to pick up the girls. While Edward got the girls' suitcase in the back and got them organized in the back seat, Dad pulled me aside. I don't know what Edward had said to him, but he engaged me directly, as if I were one of his clients. "I want you to take care of things down there, Hope. Whatever it takes, whatever it costs, you get it for her. Nothing but the best. Caroline may not have the best judgment, but she's still my girl, and still your sister. You get her out of this, and we'll take care of everything else afterwards."

It's funny when he talks to me like that. He's like me—when the going gets tough, we take care of the tough details. It's why he's such a great lawyer, and why I'm such a great mother. We both know how to take care of the little things that make everything else run smoothly.

"I've got it, Dad. I'll let you know what I find in the morning."

"That new husband of hers gives you any trouble, you let me know. I know how to deal with his kind—I probably should have done something a long time ago."

"Yes sir. Josh won't be a problem. He's no staff sergeant, but he loves her."

"That may be the problem."

"I'll call in the morning," I said as Edward walked over, the girls sitting patiently in the Town Car. They left, and a few minutes later, Edward carried my suitcase to my car.

"Need anything?" he asked me.

"Just say a prayer for Caroline tonight."

"I will."

He kissed me on the lips, more formal than tender, and I slipped into the driver's seat of my Camry. Not my dad's Town Car, but more practical with two "tween" girls, as Dad will soon find out.

Edward tapped the glass, and I rolled down my window. "Sure you've got this?" he asked. "I can come down this weekend..."

"It'll be over by this weekend," I said. "Besides, Josh is a big softie."

"So I've heard," he said, then he looked at me funny.

"What?" I asked.

He pursed his lips, pausing. "I'm ... worried, that's all."

"I'll make sure Caroline is well taken care of."

"I'm not worried about her," he said.

I looked into his eyes, and saw something I had not seen since high school, a swirling cloudiness of doubt. "You're worried about me," I said.

"I'm afraid he'll do to us what he did to Kevin and Caroline."

I took his hand. "He didn't do anything to Kevin and Caroline—they did it to themselves. He just picked up the pieces. Besides, you have nothing to worry about."

He leaned in and kissed me, this time more warmly, and then held my hand, letting his fingers drag slowly away from mine as I drove off. I drove out of the neighborhood thinking about how much I loved Edward, and how lucky I was to meet him when we were both so young.

*   *   *

Lots of couples meet when they are young, and many people are lucky enough to marry their high school sweetheart. But Edward and I are even luckier. We met, officially, when we were both five years old. Unofficially, we may have shared a crib or picked at each other's diapers long before that.

Caroline had one of her rare saintly moments the day we met, one we've joked about for years. We were visiting Edward's family for a cookout. We pulled into their driveway, and I looked up to see Edward wrestling with his younger brother Peter in the front lawn. Dad pulled in, and we all watched, dumbfounded. Our family did not fight.

Edward had Peter pinned beneath him, but Peter bucked and twisted, tossing Edward forward, then left, but Edward held on. Peter bucked two more times, then stopped, appearing to be resting. I saw him pull his legs up even farther, and then give a mighty lurch which threw Edward forward, and slipped out between his legs, then jumped him from behind. Their father came out, took two steps from the front porch, and yanked Peter up into the air, landing him flatfooted, standing straight. Peter began to cry, but stood rock still, and the tears made mud tracks down his face. Their father said a few things to both of them as we got out of the car, and then we all headed inside.

Peter stood where he was as we walked past, a little soldier, rubbing his eyes with one fist. Caroline turned around when she got to the door, then emerged from the minivan with a damp washcloth. "Your brother's mean," she said, wiping the mud from his cheeks. "We won't play with him." She cleaned his face, then his arms and hands, talking the whole time. He still stood like a little soldier, but a smile glimmered from between his lips.

They played together all day, and wouldn't let Edward or me near them. They built Lego trucks and raced them in the back yard. Afterwards, they dammed the creek with stones, and ran through the sprinkler to get cleaned off.

Edward and I were helping our dads get the grill ready when Caroline and Peter had an argument in the backyard. They have nearly the same birthday—Caroline's was June 3rd, while Peter's was June 2nd.

"Three is bigger," Caroline said, "So I'm older."

"I was born first," said Peter.

"But three's bigger," said Caroline

"There's your dad."

They ran to the porch and Caroline jumped into Dad's arms, and he held her up with both hands. "What's wrong?" he asked.

"Peter says he's older than me," she said, almost sobbing.

He caught her and said, "That's nothing to cry about, is it?"

"Three is bigger than two, so I'm older!" she said. Peter joined us, and nudged in under his father's hand to watch.

"Whoa, hold on a minute. When was Peter born?" Dad said.

"June second." she said. Peter's father smiled.

Dad looked her in the eye. "Nope, you're wrong. Peter's been around a day longer than you, so he's older. You're bigger, but Peter's older."

"I want to be older," she whined and buried her head in his neck and cried. Dad held her and made an exaggerated frown at the rest of us, and in a moment it died down.

Peter reached up and touched her. "It's okay, Caroline. You're bigger, and I'm a day older."

Dad put her down, and Peter took her hand. "We were born in the same place," he said. "Maybe we were already friends."

Then, as they walked away, Caroline said, "I think we've always been friends."

*　　*　　*

The highway blurred by. I drove seventy, sometimes seventy-five miles an hour down I-40 from Asheville to Durham, and passed I don't know how many cars which normally would have passed me going away. I passed a highway patrolman and just waved, knowing where I was going was more important than a little ticket. With eighties music on the radio, I stayed in the left lane, and let the worry press my foot harder on the pedal.

When I get worried, I get more like Caroline. I can feel my brain shutting off and going into auto pilot, reacting instead of thinking.

Really, I'm not giving her enough credit. She can think, and when she does she is quite smart. She is just incapable of both thinking and doing something with her body at the same time. I used to joke with her, tickling her while I pretended to find the toggle switch that turned the power from her brain to her body.

It happened that way on June 3rd, 1981, her twelfth birthday. I caught her after dinner, lying on her bed reading. I pulled my shoes off and laid them gently in the hall, and padded into her room. I could see her shoulders rise and fall with each breath, her whole body focused on the book in front of her. When I was close enough, I slipped a hand up and tickled her underarm with the nails on the end of my pointer and middle fingers, while I faked looking for a switch on her back and yelled, "Quick, flip the brain off and the body on before you die of tickle-a-tion!" She squealed and rolled away from me, knocking her book to the floor and turning bright red. She tried to defend herself, but I am not very ticklish, so it took several agonizing minutes. When she had my hands pinned, I said, "Whew, you're safe now that your body is on. Good thing I was here to help!" She pushed me away, smiling but half angry, and I let her go back to her book.

*   *   *

Caroline began thinking deeply at an early age. While I worried about how I looked and who might have a crush on me, she read books about religion, and spent time pondering how to interpret the phrase, "Do not resist an evil doer," or other such things. She prayed every morning and every night in the shower—her special place with God. She said it was her private baptismal, and when we shared a bathroom I sometimes heard her talking. She paid me no mind and went right on talking to God like I wasn't even there.

It came up one time when she was married to Kevin. Caroline and I eavesdropped from the kitchen while Edward and Kevin watched a UNC football game, and the subject of sex came up. Edward was doing the "we're married so we never have sex" thing—which isn't true by the way—and Kevin said, "I'm dying to do it just one time in the shower with her, and she won't let me. It drives me crazy!" Then they saw us listening, and Edward asked what down it was.

Edward asked me about it as we went to bed. "Why is Caroline so sensitive about having Kevin in the shower with her?"

"It's where she prays," I said. He looked at me, eyebrows frowning in question. "Ever since we were kids, that's where she prayed. Every morning and every night, after workouts, after swim team practice—every time she gets in a shower she strikes up a conversation with God."

"That's a little weird," he said.

"Yeah, but it's Caroline, remember?"

*   *   *

The drive went quickly, and I was able to find the hospital without any trouble. I locked the car, and felt that dirty feeling on my fingers that told me my palms had been sweating.

When I came to Caroline's room, I stopped. I breathed out, then breathed in hard and straightened my shirt and hair before knocking.

A few seconds passed, then Josh opened the door only part way. I took one look at him and the apprehension flowed out of me like sand from a broken hour glass. Every other time I'd seen Josh, he had been clean shaven and neatly, if not very stylishly, dressed. Not so this time. He had three days stubble and his hair was oily and disheveled. His shirt hung loosely, buttoned one button off, the right flap draped outside his jeans. Caroline was in a coma and I would do everything I could for her, but her husband also needed me. I slipped my hand through his arm, and let him lead me toward Caroline.

She, though pale with a blackness around her eyes, was lying peacefully on the bed, silver arm rails up. Her hip was bound in a Velcro brace, and at that moment the size of her pregnant stomach hit me full force. I must have gripped Josh's arm, because he asked if I needed some time alone with her, and then picked up a paperback and left.

After he was gone, I stood there and stared at her. My little sister, pregnant. Her stomach rose up like a little mountain above the rest of her broken body. My God, I thought, the baby had been in the accident with her! I stepped forward and put both of my hands on her stomach and lowered my face to listen, to touch my lips to the taut skin holding my new nephew, or niece. I stopped breathing, and kept touching her, feeling the warmth of her skin on my palms, feeling the new life within. I thought I felt a kick, and I broke into a smile and said, "Hi there little guy! I'm your aunty Hope. You be good while we tend to your mother, till we can get you out of there." I smiled, and a single tear dropped off my face and soaked into the white gown covering Caroline's stomach.

I stepped back and sat down in the chair near her bed, then took her hand in both of mine. "I'm sorry, Caroline. I never stopped loving you. When you come out of this, we'll never let things get this bad again. I'll take care of you, like you did for me when we were kids." I was crying openly, the tears running down my face and bringing salt to my mouth. After a few moments, I stopped crying and sat back in the chair and held her hand, whispering, "It's all going to be okay—you just wait and see," over and over.

*   *   *

Caroline and I loved to play outside together when we were kids. One of our favorite games to play was "explorer". I would take my hiking staff and pretend to be a wise old leader, and Caroline would strap on her plastic sword and act as my lieutenant. We would march out into the woods, her scouting the way and "attacking" any "wild animals" we might run into. One time, when she was eleven, she chased a possum, which she called a "dragon," down toward the creek, and when the possum scrambled across a log, she charged right through the water, leaving both shoes behind in the mud. "Be gone, evil beast!" she yelled, standing barefoot on the bank, waving her sword. She picked up a rock and heaved it at the possum, making it scramble away faster.

She walked back through the water to me and bowed, "The way is safe now, m'lord," she said, and I touched her shoulder with my staff. It's not very good of me, but I never loved her more than when we played like this. She knew that.

*   *   *

Josh came back, and we talked for a few minutes before he offered to take me to their home. I followed him in my Camry into a gated community, and saw him press a button on his visor to open the gates. Their house was a stately red brick house at the end of a cul de sac.

Josh met me as I opened my trunk, and carried my bags to an upstairs bedroom. "I hope this will be okay," he said.

"Perfect, Josh," I said. Then, as he turned, looking disheveled and tired, I said, "I'd be delighted if you would show me the rest of this beautiful house," and slipped my hand through his arm again.

The house was beautiful, though basically undecorated. When we entered one guest room, I could tell Caroline had adopted it. Besides having her childhood bedroom furniture in it, it had a stone rabbit by the door. Those were "wolves" during our adventures, and she battled them bravely. Her writing desk had two bunny bookends holding a few books, her Bible open in the middle. A small alcove beside the desk led to a picture window with a quilted seat below. Both walls of the alcove were

35

lined with bookshelves, and I saw several of her favorites. "I bet she loves to come up here to read," I said. Her place to turn the mind on, and the body off.

* * *

I went to bed that night thinking about the last time Caroline had been pregnant. It was the year after she finished medical school, and she had been married to Kevin for less than a year. She was in residency, and we were in the habit of buzzing each other on the cell phone at all sorts of hours. She called me in the middle of the morning, while the kids were still at school.

"Hi Caroline!" I said. Back then, she had a special ring all her own.

"Hope," she said and then, uncharacteristically, stopped.

"What is it?" I asked.

"I'm sorry," she said. "I haven't slept much—shift started at midnight."

"Oh I'm so sorry," I said with a sarcastic lilt. "The rough life of a doctor."

"It's not that. I've ... I've got—"

"... something on your mind?"

"Yeah."

"What is it, sis?"

"You know how sometimes good things happen—"

"—but with bad timing?"

"Exactly," she said, and exhaled.

"Other than you being born? No, I don't think so—"

"Hope!" she said, and I could hear her smiling.

"Yeesss?" I dragged the word out, teasing her even more.

She paused, and then said, "I'm pregnant."

"Oh my God, Caroline! That is so wonderful. I can't believe it!" I stopped, and then the urge to tease caught me again. "How on earth did it happen? I mean, with your schedules and all."

"We make time." She said. Caroline and Kevin were both residents in the same hospital, and the rule was that spouses could not work the same shift. Since they both worked about eighty hours a week, it left almost no time for them to be together. This was a regular topic of our frequent airwave commiseration sessions.

The impact of their schedules sunk in. "So I see what you mean about the timing, a little inconvenient. Are you thinking of taking time off?"

"I don't know. I'm thinking about everything."

We talked for a few more minutes, then her pager went off and we hung up. She made me promise not to tell anyone, not even Edward. I promised.

A few days later, she called me again. This time, it was after midnight, and I took the call in bed, with Edward stirring beside me.

"Hi Caroline. What's up?" She often called late, so I wasn't immediately worried. Her hours were not the same as mine. Then I heard her crying.

"Kevin and I just had a fight," she said.

"What about?"

"The baby. He wants me to quit my residency. He says it's only for a year, but I don't think he'll let me go back." Her voice had a whispery sound like a sad, sad ghost.

"You can work these things out. The baby will be such a wonderful addition—you can't imagine how it will change your life."

"I feel it already. I dream about him, about being a mother. I'm not even sure I want to be a doctor anymore."

"Maybe there's no problem at all."

"Maybe." She paused. "Kevin, well...we talked about getting an abortion."

"Oh..."

"We didn't really talk about it. He yelled it at me. 'Why don't you just get an abortion, then!'" she mimicked.

"He didn't."

"Yes, he did."

"Where is he now?"

"He left—out drinking, I think."

"Oh Caroline..." We talked for a few more minutes, and then she told me she was tired and we both went back to sleep.

The last phone call about the baby came a week and a half later, just before dinner. I picked up my cell phone as I was setting the table.

"Hi Caroline."

"Hi Hope," her voice sounded weak.

"What's wrong?"

"I've been sick."

I smiled, "I thought that only happened in the mornings."

"It's not that."

"It could be—it can be all the time for some people."

"No, I know it's not that. I've just got a bug or something."

"Oh…well, are you taking care of yourself?"

"Yes…" and she started crying.

"What is it?"

"I had a miscarriage," she said, her voice squeaking. We never talked about that baby again.

*   *   *

I found the letters the next day. I was rooting around in Caroline's reading room, and found them in the top drawer of the night stand on the left side of the bed. She slept on that side as a kid, and I remembered crawling into the right side just to be close to her.

I pulled the box out. It was cherry, with a brass plaque on the top engraved with

"And now faith, hope, and love abide, but the greatest of these is love. To Caroline Lilian Novak, June 3, 1970"

I lifted the brass tab on the front and opened the box. Inside were dozens of letters, each on marbled stationery in several different colors. Seeing them there, some opened, some not yet opened…it took me back to the day she got them, her twelfth birthday.

After I saved her from death-by-tickle-ation, she went right back to reading, this time with her door closed. I went downstairs to watch TV.

When the doorbell rang, I jumped up and ran and opened it, then jumped into our uncle Paul's waiting arms. He swung me around as I held on tight around his neck and felt my body sway out behind me in a wide circle. When he put me down, he put one hand on his back. Dad came up and asked him how he was feeling.

"A little older than a few minutes ago," he said. Then he looked up. Caroline had been watching us from the top of the stairs. When he looked, she took a half leap and planted her behind on the railing, and slid down toward us, accelerating as she got closer. She did a little hip flex at the bottom, and flew into Uncle Paul's arms. He caught her, but staggered backwards until Dad caught them both. He lifted Caroline off the ground and gave her a big squeeze. "How's my birthday girl?" he asked.

"I'm okay," she said. My mother appeared carrying the cherry box, engraved with her name and filled with unopened letters. Uncle Paul took the box from her.

"Let's go somewhere and talk," he said to Caroline, and she followed him into the living room.

*   *   *

After showering and cleaning up, I brought a pillow and a cooler with drinks and sandwiches to Josh. I don't think he appreciated it, but he still wasn't quite right. When I got back to his house, I called my father at the office.

"Dad."

"Yes, Hope." He was very business like at the office. I don't think he ever smiled there.

"Dad, you've got to come here to see Caroline."

"Why—is there something you can't handle?"

"No, Dad. She's well taken care of. She looks peaceful."

"Then what?"

"There's something else—I don't think you'll understand unless you see it."

"I don't have time. Tell me what it is and I'll deal with it from here. She is still my daughter after all."

I knew if Dad saw Caroline, saw her lying there with her huge round stomach and could feel the warmth—he would melt and might even shake Josh's hand and congratulate him. I had images of this whole mess going by the wayside, and Dad finally welcoming Josh into the family. But I also knew Dad, in his office, was all bulldog and business, and would get ticked if I told him Caroline was pregnant. I told him anyway.

"Dad, Caroline is pregnant."

"Dammit! I knew something like this was going to happen!" He paused. "Well, that changes things. How far along is she?"

"Far, Dad. More than seven months. It looks like the basketball in her stomach is about to pop."

"Did the baby do okay in the accident? Is it a boy or a girl?"

What was this? Warmth? Did Dad have a chink in his armor after all?

"The baby is fine, and I haven't asked Josh yet whether it's a boy or a girl."

"Josh has sure messed up now—you may have to take it in when I get finished with him."

I hung up on him and called Mom. She reacted no better.

* * *

The next day, when I brought Josh some new sandwiches and cold drinks, there were flowers in Caroline's room. I checked the cards— Edward had sent some, and so had Dad. One other arrangement had come—from Peter. Edward must have told him, which of course was the right thing to do. I bet Edward had been keeping Peter in touch with her through all the years since high school. Those brothers are pretty close.

Josh looked terrible and, honestly, I didn't want to spend much time with him. As near as I could tell, he read and ate and slept, and that was it. Bathing wasn't on his list. I stayed away, but kept his cooler full of food and comforted him as much as I could. More flowers showed up as the week went on, so I guessed word was getting around.

On Thursday, I got bored. I wandered up to Caroline's reading room and poked around through her stuff, reminiscing. I pulled the letters out again, and this time, flipped through the envelopes. Each one had a title written in tight print on the front. The envelopes were made from marbled stationery, much too feminine for Uncle Paul.

Many of the titles didn't surprise me. "Thirteenth Birthday," "Drivers License," and "First Kiss" were each opened. I was surprised to find "First Time You Make Love," though not surprised to find it opened. After all, she was pregnant. Several letters were about her wedding,

"Engagement," "Day before Wedding Day," and "Wedding Day." Seeing nothing surprising on my first go through, I rooted through the box in search of the letter she would have read first, and found it. "Twelfth Birthday." I held it in my hand, feeling the weight of the thick paper inside, then held it up to the sunlight. I walked to the picture window and looked out into the backyard, and out at the few cows feeding on the grass on the hill beyond. I sat down, and, though I had known where she kept these letters for years and never read them, broke her trust by reading this letter.

* * *

Twelfth Birthday

Dearest Caroline,

I'm in an airport enjoying (?*?) a grilled chicken sandwich and waiting for my flight. Yesterday, I babysat for you and your sister in Hendersonville. You are a few months old, with blond hair that is sure to turn brown, and deep, dark blue eyes that will turn emerald green, like your father's. You are already beautiful.

I had fun putting you to sleep last night. I changed your diaper and put your jammies on, and you started to fight. I rocked back and forth in the rocker with you in my lap, drooling all over me. We played for a while—I blew little puffs of air into your face. You smiled and shut your eyes, and then opened them up and blinked a few times. Then I bounced you around. If you ever have trouble with babies, remember two things: An upside down baby is a happy baby, and if you shake them when they're upside down, the Bad Baby will come out, and there will be nothing left but Good Baby.

I shook you a bit and hung you upside down, then righted you and puffed in your face. Eventually you hugged me, and I started singing. I have a voice like an out of tune lawnmower, but it worked on you. Ten minutes later, there was a huge puddle of drool on my shirt, and those beautiful eyes were hidden behind thin fleshy movie screens playing scenes from *Parent Trap*. Or your own version, which is probably better.

Yesterday, before he went out with your mother, your father asked me to be your Godfather. I'm not sure I can explain what this means to me. I'm not married; I don't have children, and there doesn't look to be either on the horizon. I would love a family, and you've just become it. Hopefully, before you read this, I'll be married and have a child of my own. But maybe you're all I'll get. As you lay sleeping in my arms last night, I decided to take good care of my Goddaughter, starting right now. I'm never going to stop.

Caroline, this box, these letters. In them are a lot of stories—about your father and me growing up, about your mother when she was dating my brother, about some of the difficulties I've had. Of course, none of this would make sense to you now. But now is when I'm writing them. I've put a suggestion on the envelope as to when you should read each one. Read them when you like, but you'll appreciate it if you wait. There will be only one first time to read each letter, like there is only one first time for so many things.

Peppered throughout the stories is some advice. I've told you what to wear on your first date, how to kiss, and how to survive a breakup. I've told you how to handle your money, and how to handle your pride.

You're a baby, now, Caroline, a little girl who can't quite walk and likes to put her foot in her mouth. The challenges you face mostly have to do with your digestive system, at one end or the other. The challenges will grow more complicated, and painful, as you grow older. I can't predict how, but I know this world well enough to know it never leaves anyone alone completely. Eventually, it comes around for you. These letters are my way of being there for you when you would never come to me. Because you've accepted the letters, I am there already.

In addition to the stories and advice, there are a few promises. Promises from me now to you in the future. Promises I will keep, that I will remember. You'll have to wait for the stories, but the promises come down to this:

Anything you want, Caroline. Anything, any time, any how—if it is within my power to give it to you, I will. Don't hesitate to ask, and I'll be busy trying to outguess you so I can give it to you before you ask.

I love you, Caroline. My plane is coming, and besides, I have a few more letters to write.

Love,

Paul

*   *   *

I thought back to our tickling match on her twelfth birthday, and how she slid down the rail with a smile all full of innocence and energy and leapt into our uncle's arms, and how Dad had to catch him to keep him from falling. That was the end of the beginning for Caroline, for just over one year later we were both forced to face adulthood all at once, one sunny fall afternoon.

I brought the rest of the box over to Caroline's picture window and sat where she must have sat one hundred times, collecting her strength so she could go back out and face the world. I rooted around, looking for the next letter, and found another surprising one, "First Pregnancy, Married." I wondered if she read this letter back when she was married to Kevin, before her miscarriage, or if she waited and read it just six months ago, sitting in this window, just as I was. I was surprised at the title, because it implied the presence of another letter, one I was sure would remain unopened. I found the letter for her thirteenth birthday, and read it as the sun warmed the back of my neck.

*   *   *

Thirteenth Birthday

Dearest Caroline

I don't know when I realized you were my favorite niece. It wasn't always true, but now I'm wrapped snugly around your tiny little finger, right where I want to be.

We all got together at the beach this past weekend—"we all" being your family, me, and my cousins and aunt, all packed into a little three-bedroom condo. While we were there, I noticed something about your family.

Your parents love you very much, Caroline. Your mother held you while Hope was out playing and making friends on the beach. She raised you high in the air, then set you down and shook her hair in your face, making you laugh. She smiled and laughed with you. When we got back in, your father held you and Hope in his lap and read to you. He tickled you and made you giggle, then chased you around the floor.

I'm sure your parents don't, in any conscious way, choose favorites. If they did, your father would choose Hope, because they are both the oldest, and he loves girls best. Your mother would choose Hope also, because of the special time they spent together before you were born. I'm a second child, and not as tactful. Your parents would never choose a favorite. But I will.

You are my favorite, Caroline. Even though you're only two years old, you've already figured out whenever you ask me for something, I say yes. You've taken refrigerated Swiss Cake Rolls (the BEST!) out of my hands and eaten them yourself. You've stopped me from watching a football game to have me read a book to you over and over. Don't tell your parents, but you've had a taste of merlot off my little finger. (You puckered your face into a knot, then opened your mouth wide and stuck your tongue out, then puckered it again, trying to swallow away the taste.)

I remember your Christening. You were silent through the ceremony. You babbled a little when they sprinkled the water on your forehead. When the pastor held you above his head for everybody to see, you smiled with your huge, dark blue eyes shining. You wore a long white wrap my mother made for you.

I can't wait until you grow up, Caroline. I loved you as a baby. I love you as a child. But I can't WAIT to get to know who you will be as you grow up.

You and I have a lot in common. You are a daredevil, like me. You do everything your older sister does. Yesterday, you chased her, and she climbed the couch then jumped off the back to get away. You struggled to climb up behind her, but when you reached the top, you jumped and took off after her. The landing must have startled you, because you stopped and almost cried, but shook it off then took up the chase.

Seeing you like that makes me love you. Never give up your courage. Second children don't always win, and they don't have the confidence of first children. But they have courage to try new things, and the persistence to shake it off and keep going. That's something I love about me, and I love about you, too.

I love you.
Paul

*　　*　　*

I sniffed the wetness in my nose as I finished this letter, and blinked my eyes twice. Uncle Paul was right—Caroline had unbelievable courage, and, one day when neither of us was expecting it, her courage saved us.

It had happened few months after her thirteenth birthday, in the fall. Caroline was a scrappy thirteen year old, stout and strong and yet growing beautiful as young girls do. She had all the innocence and curiosity of her childhood, and still, as I said before, was unable to make both her mind and her body work at the same time.

*　　*　　*

Caroline and I set out into the woods the same as we had many times before, not knowing this would be our last time. She strapped her plastic sword on her belt and walked bravely into the driveway as I took my long walking stick from the corner of the garage and followed.

"We're getting too old for this," I told her.

"Come on, Hope—it'll be fun! We'll have another adventure!"

A sunny breeze rustled the leaves above as we crossed the street into the Big Woods. We had a clear path of wilderness, unobstructed by building, house, or road, leading all the way around the neighborhood, past the park and the railroad tracks. It led to a farm where we loved to play and throw sticks at the cows. Well, Caroline did, and I scolded her while secretly egging her on. The cows never turned a head, nor gave up their cud or swishing their tails at the flies zipping around them, attracted by you-know-what.

We crossed the street, me with my stick, Caroline charging ahead. She drew her sword and swished at an imaginary spider web. "Down!" she yelled, and leaped forward.

"Caroline, you're not acting thirteen," I said, following behind her. A few steps ahead, she danced forward, did a spin, and swatted some stray blades of grass out of the trail. "Back, serpents!" she yelled. Her voice

45

was high and lofty, like a little girl's, floating through the wooded vale. Though the coolness of fall was coming and leaves were beginning to turn, we wore shorts. Caroline wore one of Dad's UNC sweatshirts which hung loose about her neck and rumpled where she pushed the sleeves up. Her short brown hair hung down to her neck, and swung left and right as she danced and fought the imaginary devils in our way. I scolded her, and she played up her act, chasing a "wolf," that's a squirrel, down the path and up a tree, her sword whistling as she swung it. Through the loose opening in the sweatshirt, I could see the muscles in her neck and shoulder, tight with her youthful strength.

I marched behind, prodding the ground with my stick and pretending to be the wise general. She was my scout, my foot soldier, my apprentice.

We came to the creek where she had lost her shoes, and she turned and held her sword up, motioning me to stop. She crept forward, slowly moving up the creek toward the railroad tracks, tiptoeing through the underbrush, hiding first behind one tree, then another. Far ahead, she turned and motioned for me to follow. "The dragon," she whispered. I came along, careful not to step on a stick, or into thick mud. She would kill me if I scared off the possum, even though I knew it was long gone.

When we were younger, other neighborhood kids would join us, and sometimes we split into teams and had imaginary crusades, stabbing and shooting each other with imaginary swords, dirks and guns. Most of the other neighborhood kids were boys, now a few years older and interested in other things. Some of them liked me that way, but I wasn't ready. Anyway, Caroline and I were the only ones who still played these games, and I only did because she wanted me to.

She had made her way down the creek bed to the ravine where the train tracks crossed, and stood at the bottom of the large pile of rocks supporting the railroad bridge. We could have crossed the creek on the trail and followed it to the park and the farm, but could also climb the rocks and walk along the tracks. Caroline chose to climb, her feet sure on the rocks beneath her strong legs. I walked behind, and checked my nails, knowing I was sure to break one on the rocks. I hesitated, and thought about taking the long way around and meeting her at the top. She was nearly at the top when I heard the crack of a stick breaking behind me.

I turned and saw a large man half hidden behind a tree. He had a bushy beard and long brown hair waving back over his flannel shirt. He held perfectly still, like a statue, and his blue eyes jabbed into me like spears. For what seemed like minutes, all I could hear was the water gurgling down the creek, and the wind in the leaves above our heads. Neither he nor I moved as Caroline finished her climb, still lost in our game.

The man stepped out from behind the tree, and I felt a lump lodge itself firmly in the shallow of my throat. I swallowed and took one step back. He smiled with one side of his mouth, a grisly smile with yellowing teeth and wet, cracked lips.

"Go to the park, Caroline," I said, my voice as normal as I could hold it. Courage was not my strong suit, but I loved Caroline, and was sure she could get away if she ran. "Go to the park. I'm going around by the trail so I don't hurt my nails."

The man had taken three steps forward, but I didn't think he could see Caroline yet through the trees. I took another step back. My voice shook as I said, "Go now!" in a fierce whisper.

The man walked slowly toward me. There was no sound in the whole forest except the sound of his feet shuffling through the leaves. I took another step back, and held my stick in front of me. He walked low, crouching like he was ready to spring. I took one more step, then yelled "RUN!" and turned to climb the rocks.

I heard the man crashing through the brush behind me as I reached the first rocks and started climbing. I held my stick in one hand and scraped my other hand on the first rock I touched. I yanked it back to look at the small stripe of blood forming in the shallow scrape. He caught me before I had even begun to climb.

He wrapped one arm around me and rolled over underneath me, pulling me off my feet and facing me up above him. I saw the sun break through the trees as they waved goodbye to my last innocent day of summer. I saw Caroline at the top of the hill, holding her sword high, crouched in her attack stance. "Run!" I yelled, but my heart was not in it. I felt the man reach under my shirt and wrestle his hand underneath my bra, his other arm holding me tight about the waist. I shook and kicked, but was no match for his strength. He ripped at the button of my shorts, and his wet lips pressed hard against my neck, his beard rough on my young skin. I could still see Caroline at the top of the hill, sword swinging in slow circles, high in the air.

"On guard!" Caroline yelled from the top of the ravine, and jumped into her attack stance, sword held high. She charged down the hill, leaping from one rock to another, first left and then right. The man rolled me off the rocks, and got on top of me on the ground, facing me and pinning me beneath his weight. His hand went hard into the front of my shorts just as I heard Caroline's feet land beside me. "On guard!" she yelled again, ever chivalrous. I heard a whistle, and then a low thud as she crashed my walking stick into the man's ear. He roared in pain and I felt his weight shift as he grabbed his ear with both hands, blood trickling between his fingers. He still had me pinned.

Caroline threw the stick aside and leapt on him from behind adding her weight to his on top of me, then grabbed his hair with one hand and his beard with the other and twisted, her strong shoulders glistening in the streaming sunlight. She turned his head around away from me, and he fell off of me and onto her.

I am not proud of what I did next.

I don't think I will ever be able to explain the fear that gripped me. Later, Caroline called it my "survival instinct", and joked she didn't have any.

Once I was out from under the man, bra unhooked and shorts hanging half off, I rolled away and tried to run. The man grabbed for my jacket and caught it by the sleeve. With tears rolling down my face I let both arms slip out of the jacket, leaving it and my baby sister in the man's arms.

I could hear Caroline growling and fighting as I scrambled up the hill, no longer caring about my hands or my nails. I looked over my shoulder and could see her pinned underneath him. When I reached the top, I picked up a rock and threw it at them, but it landed short, burying itself in the ferns. The park was only a short run down the railroad tracks. I saw Caroline lean in and bite the man on the neck as I turned and ran toward the park. I ran as fast as my legs would carry me.

When I got to the park I saw Mrs. Rosenfeld, a lady from our church, and I ran straight for her. She walked toward me with a worried look on her face, the wrinkles around her eyes going hollow with fear. I was out of breath as I stopped, and she took my arm in both of her hands. "Be still, dear," she said.

"My sis…" I breathed.

"Where is your sister?" she asked, strain in her voice.

"The ravine," I said, still out of breath.

I turned and looked behind me, and saw nothing but empty railroad tracks, the sun breaking through the trees in laser like beams crossing the path, the forest deceptively still and quiet. For a few more breathless moments, there was nothing but warm sunshine, and I felt a sickness forming at the bottom of my stomach as I thought of my little sister and that man, struggling in God only knows what ways at the bottom of the ravine. Time has warped my memory of the moment, and there is no way for me to know whether Caroline was alone with him for one minute or ten. Whichever, it must have loomed like an ominous decade to Caroline, who was struggling in the grip of that evil man.

Then, as suddenly as it began it ended, and her sword flew up from the ravine. A second later she broke the top of the hill and picked it up on the run. She swung it back and forth as she sprinted down the tracks, taking two ties at a time.

I broke free from Mrs. Rosenfeld and ran toward her, and she fell into me in a desperate hug, her sword tangled in my hair. I felt her shoulder muscles ripple beneath bare skin and I realized her sweatshirt was ripped. She held me mightily, as if she were preventing me from being stolen by the winds of a hurricane.

After a moment I felt her muscles loosen, and she said, "Is he coming?" She lowered her sword out of my hair, and I pulled her into a deep hug.

"He's gone," I said.

"That's good," she said, "because if he was coming, I'd have to kick his butt." We both broke down laughing, and the tension drained and flowed from our bodies in buckets onto the moist soil of the park.

Mrs. Rosenfeld held us until we stopped laughing. As we pulled away and began to look around us, she asked, "Did he get to you, Caroline?"

She waited a second, and then said quietly, "We got away." That's all she ever said about what went on back there. Only, "We got away." Neither my mother, father, nor the police got one more word out of her, and when the police caught the man and charged him with several crimes,

Caroline wouldn't go to a line up to identify him.

I did go to the line up. I had no difficulty picking out the man, for even though they shaved him and he looked down the whole time, he was the only man in the lineup with ice blue eyes and when he looked at me, just once through the one way mirror, my blood froze. I had to testify in court and of course I was scared, but by then I was doing this for Caroline, and my love for her and my anger at the injustice replaced any need for courage. He was put away for a long time.

My father told me how brave I was to go to the police station to identify the man, and to stand up in court to testify to what he had done. Like him, I am quick to show great courage behind the safety of armed men and within the structured environment of the courtroom. He somehow saw Caroline as weak because she couldn't, or wouldn't, testify. He doesn't know bravery, or courage, nor does he know cowardice. Caroline and I both do, and we don't speak of it.

*   *   *

The next few days were relatively quiet, and I took to cleaning Caroline's house, making it ready for when she would return. I continued to bring food and drinks to Josh, and occasionally he came back to the house to shower and shave and change out of his rumpled clothing. After I had cleaned every exposed surface, I went to the garden center at Home Depot and bought bulbs to plant out front. I resolved not to tell her about them, but to let her discover the flowers as they began to bloom.

I talked with Mom and Dad and apologized for hanging up. Yes, they were worried and yes they still loved Caroline, but they weren't ready to visit yet because they didn't want Josh to be part of their family. He had caused Caroline's divorce and lured her into a doomed marriage, which they would not condone. It was all clear to them.

Though I tried to explain, they did not see the devoted, broken man sleeping day and night by Caroline's bed, waiting for her eyes to open. I saw patience and kindness, a man bearing everything for her sake, enduring and hoping for her return. I saw his sleepy eyes and his clothes rumpled from a night or an afternoon of restless tossing on an uncomfortable vinyl hospital chair. I do not know how their relationship started, or why he loved her or she loved him, but I could see his love deeply in his actions, and I believed in hers. I could be sure of one thing— Kevin would never have slept by her side the way Josh did, and in this my parents were mistaken.

*   *   *

On the day Uncle Paul gave Caroline the letters, I went to tickle her in her room, and found her reading. I don't remember exactly what book it was—it might have been *The Diary of a Young Woman* by Anne Frank, or something else. She read novels about young women back then. Two years later, what she was reading probably would have been much the same, but I know one book she would have had with her: the Bible. The transformation didn't happen overnight; it's not like she spent hours poring over obtuse dietary habits from the Old Testament. She continued to read her novels and stories. She was a great lover of F. Scott Fitzgerald. But, when she read, she would start by reading the Bible for a few minutes— usually something in the New Testament—and then read her book, whatever it was. She opened her Bible two or three times a day and read a chapter. I remember talking with her about it before she went off to high school, as she was going through her books deciding which ones to bring. Her Bible had been the first one to be pulled out.

"You're going to be the only one there who carries a Bible to every class," I said.

"I hope not," she said back, and continued going through her books, placing two into an open cardboard box.

"I do too—it would be *terrible* if you didn't make any friends and had to come home homesick," I said, exaggerating the sarcasm in my inflection.

"I'm not coming back, Hope. Not to live. You're leaving next year anyway."

"I'm going to miss you my senior year."

"I know. Me, too. But I can't pass this up."

"I passed it up."

"You didn't apply."

"Exactly."

"Can we talk about something else?" she asked. I could tell she was frustrated.

"Okay." I paused, trying to think of something else to talk about when her leaving sat like a huge white elephant in the center of the room. Okay—talk about something, Hope, but please ignore the white elephant in the center of the room, crowding us into the dusty corners where the vacuum can't quite get. "So, um, what do you get out of it when you read your Bible?"

"Directions."

"Directions for what? How to prepare pork?" I smiled, but she didn't take my joke well.

"Directions for life," she said, and pulled out three more books to take with her.

"How in the world could a bunch of shepherds and farmers thousands of years ago know anything about how you should live your life now?"

"'How' indeed?" she said, then looked up at me expectantly.

"Did the Bible tell you to go away to school?" I asked. "Did it say, 'Get ye up out of ye house and get ye to the North Carolina School of Science and Mathematics?'"

Her eyes dropped and her lips tensed, and then she put the books in her hands down and picked up her Bible, opening it somewhere near the back. "It did," she said, finding her place. "I prayed about whether to go, and asked God to give me direction, and this is what came to me afterwards. From 1 Corinthians 9. 'For it is written in the law of Moses, 'You shall not muzzle an ox while it is treading out the grain. … it was indeed written for our sake, for whoever plows should plow in hope and whoever threshes should thresh in hope of a share of the crop. If we have sown spiritual good among you, is it too much if we reap your material benefits?'"

"What does that have to do with you going away to school?" If I didn't love her so much, I would have gotten mad at her.

She turned the page. "Then I read this. 'Do you not know that in a race the runners all compete, but only one receives the prize? Run in such a way that you may win it. Athletes exercise self control in all things; they do it to receive a perishable wreath, but we an imperishable one. So I do not run aimlessly, nor do I box as though beating the air; but I punish my body and enslave it, so that after proclaiming to others I myself should not be disqualified.'"

"Is it a race, then?" I asked.

"Yes," she said.

"And you think God has given you a reward for running the race—a 'material benefit'."

"It's not that simple," she said.

"Well, what, then?" I asked, growing impatient.

"He's asking more of me. Run a more difficult race—probably with more material rewards. He's sending me there so I'll become something I wouldn't otherwise. I work hard in school." She did, of course—much harder than I did. Her grades were no better, because we both had near perfect grades, but she did work harder. "And now I'm getting something in return—a chance to get the best high school education in the state, and have a chance at a good scholarship in a great college. I really believe God wants me to go, to work harder … and I don't know what for, but I trust Him to let me know when I get there."

I didn't know how to answer her, but one thing is for sure, the girl who spoke with me there was not the same one who entered the ravine with me three years earlier, full of innocence and optimism. At the time, I blamed the Bible for her change. Now I've read some of the book myself, I don't blame it for her change, but rather credit it with preserving what remained of her previous self.

*   *   *

Fourteenth Birthday

Dearest Caroline,

When your father and I were young, a church was built near our house. We played football in the church lawn, and a stained glass window was past one end zone. We figured it was special, imbued with some kind of God-stuff, and breaking it would go hard on us. At the time, I thought grace was something a receiver had when he blew past me. We bounced the ball off of the window a couple of times, but never broke it.

Back then, I hated church and most things associated with it. God and creation made me curious, but I could never resolve the difference between a literal Genesis's "magic wand" theory of creation, and science. I still haven't. A few years after I moved to California, I began reading the Bible. I thought I was the only real Christian on the planet—the only one who knew Jesus, talked with him, and got regular responses. I still hated church and figured most church-people were hypocrites, but figured that was expected because most of them never read the Bible without an organ playing, so how could they know anything?

I don't have many answers. I have a handle on some things, but not all. There are a lot of religious folks who think they know the whole story, beginning, middle and end, Amen. Beware, because ... drum roll ... they don't. You may as well pass on what they say because it isn't worth it, and you're not going to change their minds. But there are others who say, "I don't know much," or, "most of it is a mystery to me", but then admit to a few areas they've studied. You should listen to them, and consider what they say.

There's something I'd like to impress upon you, something to tell you, and something for you to do. Two messages and an action item aren't bad in my world.

Something to impress upon you: Presume there is a God, and He has control over any afterlife. If there's no God, you're out nothing. If there is one, and He controls the afterlife, then there's nothing more important during your time on this planet than to answer this right: What do you need to do/be/believe to get to the next life?

That's it. Pass a history test—unimportant. Get asked out by the cute guy with the shiny blue eyes—unimportant. Figure out how to get to the next life—important. Don't be scared—you've probably got time, and God'll take care of you while you think. Do take the time, though, because nothing you will ever do is as important.

Something about me: I've studied, and come to the conclusion the answer lies in the New Testament of the Christian Bible. That's why I'm giving a copy to you. Decide for yourself; no other way of deciding counts.

Something to do. Read it. It's small, and one of the oldest books in the world. It's got good advice, saucy stories, and a message that, if you believe it, will change your life. The book will make its own arguments— it's impressed a few skeptics in its time.

Love you girl.
Uncle Paul

*   *   *

On Saturday, nine days after the accident, after the house was entirely clean and the garden well stocked to bloom beautifully in the spring, I got bored. I had talked with Edward, and, though I missed him dreadfully, I wasn't ready to leave yet. Dr. Dansen had said Caroline was doing no better and no worse than she had been the day I arrived, and unfortunately, he had no strategies better than waiting and letting her body recover. I was determined not to let her be the more stubborn one.

I went back up to her reading room, to snoop a little and perhaps pull out her letters. I kept hoping I would find childhood love letters, maybe something between her and Peter, or something from the beginning of her relationship with Kevin. I found nothing except the same box of letters from Uncle Paul.

I picked up the box, feeling its wood grain beneath my palms, my fingers brushing the unfinished wood underneath the box. I carried it over to the reading nook, as I had come to call it, and sat with it between the two walls of books, the sunshine warm on my dark hair. I pursed my lips the way I do when I know I am doing something wrong, but am determined to do it anyway. Then I flipped the little brass latch holding the box shut, and opened it.

Inside were the familiar piles of letters, with the few I'd opened pushed to one side. I reached for the other stack. This time, I decided to just read the titles of the envelopes, and not peek inside one as I had done the last few times I had been up here. I saw the same familiar titles, flipping through the envelopes; "First Paycheck," "College Graduation," and "Twenty-First Birthday" were among them. I held the stack in front of me, unsatisfied. The hair on the back of my neck grew warm, and when I reached back to pull it up, I let the letters fall into the box. When I looked back down, hot bundle of hair still in my hand, I noticed one envelope held another under its flap, so they opened together like one letter. I let my hair fall, and picked them up to look at them.

On the outside cover of the first was a title I had seen before. It read

"First Pregnancy—Married." I remembered thinking about it, and thinking there had to be a mate. I opened the flap, and then pulled out the other envelope. My hands were sweating as I held it before me and read the title, "First Pregnancy—Unmarried." Slowly, I turned the letter over in my hand, and played with the flap, flipping it up, and then back closed. This letter had been opened, like most of the others.

I went through the letters again, looking to see if they had all been opened. I found several that hadn't. "Something Really Bad Happens," "Thinking about Suicide," "Your Daughter's Wedding"—none of them had been opened. I turned back to the one about unmarried pregnancy, opened it, and read it.

*   *   *

First Pregnancy—Unmarried

Dearest Caroline,

I like dark chocolate, because it is like life: bittersweet. That's how we want it to be. There are people who are all sweet and sugary like nothing has ever gone wrong, and if it did, they would find some sweet and sugary side and it would all be okay. Those people annoy me. I like people who have faults, who make mistakes, and who admit them; they learn to live life with the cards they have.

When you first start drinking wine, you like the sweet stuff. White zinfandel, or strawberry wine that tastes like strawberry soda with a tiny kick. When your palate refines a little, you like wine to be sweet on the tongue, but a little tart after you've swallowed it. I like a full bodied chardonnay, full and rich in the mouth, a little tart, leaving the corners of your tongue wishing it was still there after it's swallowed. But not sweet.

Life is like that. At first, you want everything to be good. Then, at some point, you realize everything isn't going to be good, so you want most things to be tolerable, and you want everything to be real. Then you realize we're pretty hardy folks, and can tolerate almost everything, and the most important thing is it is all real, and we are in this mess together.

I've got this friend. He's never very clean, never clean shaven, and almost always short of cash. If you ask him how he's doing, he comes clean, "Man, the last week has been the best ever. I got a new job and a date with an awesome girl and the car ran all week." Or, "Bummer. My boss didn't have the balls to ax me, but he busted me down to Private Nothing. My girl didn't like how I handled it, so we're on the skids. But hey, I've still got my friends—this round on you?" He's real, and he's genuine. I'll take that over the guy who replies, "Great! How are you?" when I ask how he's doing. Any day.

So, dearest child, depending on your age, this may or may not be a bittersweet occurrence. I'm very happy for you, if you are. Or I'm here for you, if you're not.

Loving you always,
Uncle Paul

*   *   *

I placed the box on the floor, and then read the letter again, thinking about Caroline and her dark chocolate. She had always loved dark chocolate…or had she? I thought back. One of the reasons she went to Europe after college, she had said, was so she could try the chocolate from each country. "Swiss chocolate is much different from German and Belgian chocolate," she had said. "But all European chocolate is better than our milky American stuff." In college, we had loved to give each other chocolate for gifts, and I could expect some in the mail after Edward and I had had a fight. I had always thought her love for chocolate was like any other girl's, and I shared it. "It's not better than sex," she said to me one Christmas as I opened a box of truffles, "but it lasts longer," and we had both broken down laughing while Mom and Dad turned crimson.

I picked up the box and was about to put the letters back when Josh walked in. He looked terrible—like a street person—only in this case I guess he was a hospital-person. His stubble was three days thick, and a mustard stain adorned his light blue oxford shirt, which was half untucked.

"I'm sorry," I said. I placed the letter back in the box. "I guess I was prying."

"Doesn't bother me," he said, stepping toward me. "What is it?" I told him about the letters, about Uncle Paul and his slightly weird gift. He sifted through them, and I decided to ask him about the letter I had just read.

"How well do you know Caroline?" I said.

"Well enough, I guess," he said. His eyes were green, and unreasonably clear considering how the rest of him looked. I held the letter so he could see the title, then flipped the flap open. There was a long silence between us. I was scared to break it, scared to learn the story of why this letter had been opened, of what terrible thing had happened to my sister. I pictured her in college, alone in her dorm room, scared to call me, scared to tell anyone. I pictured her going alone on a cold winter morning to an abortion clinic, sitting naked on the cold crinkly paper covering the examination bench. I pictured her crying in her room, knowing what she had done. Had I been the sister I wished I was, she wouldn't have been alone then. A tear welled up in my eye.

"You don't know, do you?" he asked. I shook my head no. "Oh God, help me," he said.

He took my hand in both of his, and I covered it. Again, I noticed how clear his green eyes were, like bright emeralds shining from deep muddy waters. My heart galloped, and another tear fell.

"I don't even know where to start," he said. "You don't know anything?"

I shook my head no again, and realized I wasn't making it any easier for him. I blinked my eyes and wiped the tears away with my fingers, then sighed deeply and said, "Go ahead—I'm okay."

"Okay," he said, then paused. He took my hand again, and squeezed. The smoothness of his hands betrayed his soft life. They were nothing like Edward's hands, which were strong but not rough. Josh's hands felt more like a girl's hands, and I wondered about my own.

"Caroline had a baby," he said.

I gasped, "Oh my God." I felt more tears coming, and quickly wiped them away and composed myself.

"Nobody knows."

Josh stopped, and I could see him fighting for words. He looked up at me, and his green eyes were clouded. "I guess I'll just say it then." He paused. "She had the baby in high school, and put it up for adoption. She named her 'Faith.'"

I took a moment to take it all in. My sister had a daughter, who was now probably a teen-ager. I was an aunt, and I had never touched this child, never given her a birthday present, never kissed the top of her head or put a band-aid on a cut that didn't need one. Faith was older than Melanie, my oldest.

I brought my hands up to my face as I thought of Caroline, lying in her hospital bed, maybe on the edge of life, now in her third pregnancy and never having known the joys of motherhood.

*   *   *

I called Uncle Paul that evening, after I sent Josh back to the hospital with extra sandwiches and drinks.

"Hiya Hope! Howya doing'?" he said, and I thought again what a funny thing northern California had done to his North Carolina mountain-redneck accent.

"You keep secrets pretty well, Uncle Paul."

"Like a Venus fly trap. Got something on your mind?"

The answer, of course, was "yes," and he knew this because I was never this direct. I rubbed my nose nervously.

"Yes." I waited, unsure how to start.

"Do you want to tell me about it? We could chit-chat a bit first if you'd like—weather's fine out here."

"No, we don't need to chit chat." I played with the phone cord for a second, then continued, "Caroline's been in an accident."

"Oh, God," he said. "Is she okay?"

"I don't know. She's in a coma, and they say she is steadily getting better. They say it's just her body's way of healing."

"When did it happen?"

I gave him the rest of the details, and when he was satisfied, went on. "I left a couple things out of the story," I said. "She's pregnant."

"Good news. Baby's okay, I assume?"

"Yes, she's due next month."

"That's a blessing."

"Yes. Uncle Paul—this is the third time she's been pregnant. Only Kevin and I know about the second time. I think you know about the first. I want to hear about it."

The line went silent for long enough that I worried about the connection.

"This isn't a story for the telephone, Hope."

"There probably isn't a good way to tell it, I'm guessing."

"Listen, I can't get there for a few days," he said.

"I really can't wait," I said. I hesitated before I said what I said next. I'm really a nice girl, but there is a little bit of my father in me. "If you won't tell me now, I'll tell Dad, and he'll beat it out of you."

"Now Hope, don't do that. He'll have every lawyer in California in my living room, and that's bad. Take an East Coast lawyer, give him a fake tan, expensive suit—no tie—a smoothie in one arm and a handshake slathered with hand cream…don't do that to me. Let me think a minute."

"Think fast," I said, smiling. I do enjoy winning.

"Give me a few minutes, and I'll have someone call you. Okay?"

"Okay. If I don't hear from someone in the next half hour, I'm calling Dad."

"Don't do that—not until you know the story."

"Okay." We hung up.

I took my cell phone up to Caroline's reading room, and sat down in the picture window to think. I couldn't imagine who was going to call—probably the father. Or maybe Caroline had confided in someone, maybe a girlfriend or sorority sister from college, and Paul knew how to get in touch with her.

When the phone rang and I heard the voice on the other end, my heart beat hard once, then stopped dead as if a trucker had applied the air brakes.

"Hi Hope—it's me, Peter," the voice said. I stood up in surprise.

I said nothing. The thought that my brother-in-law knew about my sister's secret pregnancy, and I had been kept in the dark—he'd been my brother-in-law for fourteen years—brought my world to a halt. I paced out of the picture window and into the room.

"Hi Peter. How good to hear from you—how are you doing?" I said, hoping it was a coincidence, or maybe Edward had told him about the accident.

"I'm fine. Listen, I'm packing now—Paul filled me in, and I'll tell you whatever you want when I get there—it'll be about eight hours."

"What do you mean?"

"It's just," he stopped, and the silence hissed in my ears. "It's … this is a long story…and I want to see Caroline. I've explained to JJ and the kids, and they understand. I'll tell you everything when I get there. Call my cell if anything happens." He hung up.

I walked slowly back into the nook and sat down. I leaned back, took off my shoes and stretched my legs as I massaged my temples. Don't think about it, I thought, massaging my temples firmly, trying to use pressure to drive the spinning sensation out of my skull. As far as I knew, other than at my wedding and at hers, Caroline and Peter hadn't seen each other for more than about fifteen minutes since they left high school. Now he's the father of my sister's bastard daughter. I just couldn't think about that.

Chapter 4: Peter

"Just tell me what happened, Hope, why she won't talk with me.

"You can't, or you won't? Fine! You girls are—I just don't get it. Like fire and ice and nothing in between!"

--Peter

Dearest Faith,

I'm not your dad, but I wish I were. I kissed your mother a month after you were conceived. I proposed and asked to raise you as my own. I proposed twice more, and she rejected me all three times. My brother Edward married her sister, so I have been able to keep up a bit. I'm not in love with her like I once was. But there is something that lingers, like putting your homemade banana pudding on the plate you had baked spaghetti on—it flavors everything to come. My love for Caroline is like that, and it's here with me now like the dry, crusty spaghetti sauce that won't quite let go.

I remember the day we met—we were five years old. Edward and I were fighting in the front lawn when Caroline's family drove up. Edward had been grinding my face in the ground for like ten minutes, and I'd just gotten out from under him. I started to pay him back when Dad walked out and yanked me off, then yelled at me. He always did that, and it frustrated me so I started bawling. Dad laid into me, then I stood there crying while Dad went through the pleasantries with Caroline's family, then they headed inside. Caroline got a wet wash cloth from inside and washed my face. She was tender on my raw skin, and I could see the mud dirtying the wash cloth. She said, "Your brother's mean. He can't play with us."

That's how our friendship ended, too. She saw something happening to me she didn't think was fair, and she rescued me.

I'm scared to meet you, Faith. I've buried my love for your mother in a deep, secret place, and I'm afraid if I meet you, it will all come back. She's a different person now, so I can keep it buried. You'll have to be gentle with me, especially if you look like her. That's what I'm afraid of—that you'll look like she did back then.

Terrified to love you,

Peter

*   *   *

It will be difficult to tell my part of Caroline's story without giving some of our history together. She was my first love, and despite everything, she will always keep a special place in my heart.

Caroline and I grew up in Hendersonville, a sleepy little town on a plateau in the mountains of North Carolina, just a dozen miles or so south of Asheville. To this day I joke it was a town of "about five thousand people, and if you'd like I'll name them for you." For me, it was claustrophobic; for Caroline, it was and is her peaceful heaven, her safe harbor.

Caroline and I lived on opposite ends of this sleepy little county, which due to some quirk in the phone system made telephoning a long distance affair too expensive for young wallets. For most of our childhood, we saw each other only at festivals downtown, or when our parents invited one another over for an afternoon cookout.

I was twelve when I was finally allowed to ride my bike as far as downtown. On one of my first visits there, I rode up to Barbara's Bookstore on the corner of Main Street and Sixth Avenue. I kicked down my kickstand, and left my bike, for even in those late days we never worried about someone stealing anything. I walked in and saw Caroline with her sandy brown hair up in a small bow, thumbing through the Young Adult section, looking for a new Judy Blume title. I went over, and we talked for twenty minutes about our love of Judy Blume and *Encyclopedia Brown* books, and as she left I turned to spend my hard earned allowance on two titles she had suggested.

Over the next year, I became a regular at Barbara's, and Barbara herself noticed the budding friendship between Caroline and me as we both cultured our love of reading. Sometimes I would stop in three or four times on a Saturday afternoon, and Barbara would say to me, "She hasn't been here yet, but I wouldn't be surprised to see her later," or, "Caroline was here a little while ago, and said to tell you she was going down to the Justus Family Pharmacy for a soda and would be back in a bit." Sometimes I would wait, and sometimes I would walk down Main Street and get a soda with her. Our friendship was slow and sleepy and grew without the stress that comes with worrying what others think—we went to different school systems and so didn't share many common friends. We could and did talk about anything we wanted, knowing we enjoyed each other's company.

There came one Saturday when I was thirteen at the end of the school year and I found her at the bookstore looking maybe a little more pretty than she normally did, but also maybe not. We talked for a few minutes and then went down to the arcade in front of the movie theater to play a game of Burger Time. Though I practiced constantly on the machine in the diner across from my junior high school, I still only beat her occasionally, and it was great to be competitive and also so close to someone who was soft and smiled beautifully whether she won or lost. She had one dimple that shined pure and bright, and another that was more bashful.

As we left the arcade, she said, "I was thinking about going roller skating tonight, but Susan is sick and can't make it."

"Really," I said. I could not skate, but on the one or two occasions I'd been, I had noticed they had couples skating, and it was an occasion to hold a girl's hand.

She paused, then slipped her hand up to hold my elbow and said, "Would you like to go with me?"

I waited for her to say, "...you know, just as friends and all," but it never came. I had never been on a date before, nor had I ever even thought about asking a girl out, or what I might do if I did go on a date. I liked Caroline so much that the whole concept of us meeting outside of our casual Saturday afternoons scared me to death. I walked in stunned silence.

"They have a Burger Time machine there," she said. Now she was talking my language, and I relaxed knowing if I couldn't skate and we ran out of things to talk about or a million of her friends showed up who might hate me, we could always retreat to the familiarity of our friendly competition.

"Okay," I said. "What time?"

"I usually go around seven," she said, and that was it. We went back to our normal banter as we walked to the store where her mom was shopping, and I got my bike and went home.

Our date was special only in its exquisite normalcy. She beat me four out of seven games of Burger Time and we split a Coke Icee, and learned after the couples skate that I could make it around the rink much more gracefully with her hand supporting me. We both saw friends from our schools who liked us and were surprised and happy to see us with someone else, on what appeared to be a date, having a normal and happy time. When we waited outside for our parents to show up, her mom showed up first and took a picture of us. She gave me a copy a few weeks later as she picked us up from another date, and I still have it, stuffed in under my telephone list in the top drawer of my desk at work. I don't pull it out, but occasionally will come across it while looking for something else and it will take me back to a time when it seemed nothing could possibly go wrong because of the girl who was standing next to me, holding my hand and smiling with deep blue eyes and one bashful dimple peeking out like the sun from behind a drifting summer cloud. Our love was pure and uninhibited back then, and neither of us would have predicted all the things that came after.

*   *   *

First Date

Dearest Caroline,

This morning, while I was lying awake in bed, you wandered down to find me. You had a book and, not knowing I was awake, hit me with it while batting those dark blue eyes and pouting your lower lip. You said, "Book." "Book" translates to, "Let's go sit on the couch and read this book at least ten times, but let's read the pages in the order I choose, not the order in the book." I understood and sat you in my lap and read the book to you, reading the pages in the order you gave them to me. You are two years old.

Caroline, you will never be this little girl again. You've started down a new road. As a little girl, you've skinned your knees and your elbows. As a teenager, you will skin your heart. As an adult, you will skin your soul. Don't rush down this path, Caroline. Take every step slowly, and enjoy each wonderful moment, for this is a one way path.

I have to admit something to you. When I was a teenager, I was strong, but very clumsy. I was smart, but had no common sense. A wiz at geometry, I couldn't think of anything to say to a girl. I was like every other teenage boy.

My first date was on Friday night, two days after my sixteenth birthday. I'd been planning the date for two weeks. I'd saved money from mowing lawns, and was going to take poor Whitney to dinner. Whitney had fair skin and white blond hair. She had elf-like features and a smile that made me feel like I shared some sinister secret with her. Her smile would make me jealous for years when she flashed it at other boys. Whitney didn't really like me, but she did take more pity on me than on most boys. She went out with me because she hoped I wouldn't be awkward and clumsy my whole life. She also went out with me because I helped her with her geometry homework. I would have done that anyway. She smiled at me when I helped her.

Mom took me for my drivers test on my birthday. I passed the written test, but was nervous and failed parallel parking. I couldn't tell Whitney. I hid from her the next day at school. Mom brought me to take the test again, and I failed again! Now I was truly terrified of seeing Whitney. I made Mom promise to take me first thing Friday morning before school started. I practiced parallel parking all night with Dad—I parked the car a hundred times. I couldn't sleep that night; I was parallel parking in my dreams.

Friday morning I was a basket of nerves. I completely ignored my presents at breakfast, focusing entirely on the test. I had the same examiner I had had the first day. "You're back again?" he asked. "Yes, and I practiced parallel parking all night. I have a date tonight and…" I told him the whole story. He told me to calm down, and coached me through every step. "Turn more," "Stop. Now pull out and try it again." I passed.

I went straight to school. I knew every spot Whitney hung out at, and I found her between classes. We talked, and she asked to see my license. "Weird picture!" she said. "Did you make that face on purpose, or did somebody barf?" She was smiling, so I was happy. She looked closer, "PAUL—you're wearing the same clothes you wore to the test?! Go change!" I skipped classes, went home and changed.

Please be kinder to the young gentleman who is taking you out than Whitney was to me.

Love, as always,

Paul

PS—Beneath the harsh treatment, Whitney was gentle and I know she cared for me—and her geometry grade.

*   *   *

I remember the occasion of our first kiss, when Caroline and I were both thirteen. It was late summer, after we had been to the movies and roller skating and playing putt-putt several times already. Her father did some work for my dad's company, and they had grown close over the years. They invited us over for a family cookout. Edward and Hope had not really noticed each other yet, and thought Caroline and I were "cute." They were much too mature for putt putt, roller skating and video games.

I stepped onto the back porch and saw again how Caroline could take the simplest outfit and, in an irresistible but honorable way, use it to pierce my heart with desire. At that age, I didn't desire anything about her body—I wouldn't have known what to do. Rather, I desired to posses, to own, to encapsulate her beauty and make it belong to me. This desire inspired me to any length of sacrifice to attract her attention to me. It created an emptiness that was absurd because I already had every bit of her attention.

The outfit on this occasion was a misty green shorts jumper over a simple white t-shirt, with her hair held back with two matching yellow plastic flower barrettes. It was not and is not logical, yet the effect she had over me was real and uncontrollable. After talking for a few minutes and introducing me to her uncle, she led me downstairs to "show me a new

67

book she was reading."

The steps led down to her basement, where there was a pool table and a couch and love seat with a TV set, and a wet bar off to the side. The wood panel gave the room a warm, homey fun atmosphere. Caroline went to a bookshelf and pulled out a thick paperback, and then took my hand and led me to the love seat. She turned on the TV with the volume low, and she read to me some sections she had marked in the book.

I don't remember any of the words we said, but everything else—the touch of her fingertips on my arm, the smell of her hair, the sound of her low giggle—it has all embedded itself into my permanent memory and I can in an instant draw it all back and relive those special moments. We touched hands as she read, and at the end of one section she laughed and leaned into me, her head brushing on my chest so I could tilt my head ever so slightly and smell the fragrance of her hair, breathing in her essence and holding it in my lungs before slowly letting it float away.

She was reading a romance novel called *The Pearl Necklace*, and had flagged some of the more racy scenes. After Hope called me and I drove down, I found the book on her bookshelf in her reading room, and the passage that led to our first kiss had the corner of the page folded down, now turning brown and brittle with age. It read, "…Evelyn wrestled from his grasp, and slapped him hard on the cheek. With both of his large hands, he grabbed her shoulders and pulled her toward him, falling to the floor as she continued to struggle. They landed, and Brock wrapped her with his arms, squeezing her against his sweaty chest. For long moments he held her, her body pressed hard against his as she strained against him. As suddenly as it began, it stopped, and she sobbed against his chest. She cried for her loss, for her hatred, and for the love of the man who held her. He released her with one arm, and brushed her hair away from her face, pulling her gently against him. She gazed up into his blue eyes, and her fury subsided. Her eyes melted closed as his lips approached. They kissed, gently and long, and her body went fluid as their tongues met between open mouths…"

Caroline stopped reading, and whispered, "I don't understand. I've seen people kiss…but never with their tongues! It seems gross!" It seemed gross to me, too, but as I looked into Caroline's eyes and saw the brown wrinkle of her scar at the corner, I didn't care. Whatever it was that men and women did together, I wanted to do it with Caroline, and didn't really care if it was gross.

We looked at each other for a long moment and I watched her face change from exasperation with the passage to a warm smile, and then, as she reached her hand up to touch my chin and pull it near, her whole face relaxed and drew toward me and our lips touched in our first kiss. We kissed for a long moment, our lips touching but not really moving, and I slid my arms around her and felt her warmth press against me. Then it happened—inexplicably, her lips parted and her tongue brushed lightly against my lips, and without thinking my mouth opened also and her tongue slipped warm and wet into my mouth as I explored hers with mine.

We did this for only a minute before we heard a man's voice on the stairs, "Where's my niece?" We pulled away, though not quickly. Caroline's hand lingered on my chest before she used it to wipe her mouth. A spot of drool had run down her neck and formed a wet spot on the corner of her shirt about the size of a half dollar. She turned forward, and I wiped the drool off her neck as we turned toward the TV.

There were footsteps on the stairs. They stopped, the door opened and was filled with Paul's muscular frame. A smile came to his face as his eyes locked with Caroline's.

Paul swept into the room, "You're a woman now. Don't I get a hug?" He lifted her up into his grasp. She wrapped both arms and both legs around him and squeezed, burying her head into the muscles on his shoulder. He whispered, "Gonna open another letter tonight?" She punched him, then squeezed him tighter.

Out of breath, he put her down. "Peter." Paul smirked, and shook my hand. "Saw her kissing some other guy, can't remember who—" Caroline punched his shoulder hard. He faked pain, and then winked, "Clean up, then come up for dinner." He handed his handkerchief to me. "Carry one of these when you kiss a girl—she'll think you're a gentleman." He winked again and headed upstairs.

*   *   *

First Kiss

Dearest Caroline,

I don't know about your mother's first kiss, but I do know about your father's. It was at a high school football game, when we were in junior high.

It was a little cold, and like always, John wouldn't sit with me. In the middle of the game, he picked up his blanket and headed to the concession stand, then came back with Nancy Provost, the smartest person in his class. She said something, and he laughed a little too loud, throwing his head back. They sat a few rows from the top and covered themselves with the blanket. They were quiet and didn't cheer even for the touchdown. By the end of the third quarter, Nancy had her head on his shoulder, then later they left, blanket draped over Nancy's shoulders. When they didn't come back, I left to look, and found them beneath the bleachers, lip-locked under the blanket.

Nancy was smart and a little uppity...but she was NOT pretty. She had straight black hair and jet black eyes that held you like a teacher who's been hit in the head with a spit ball. Stern, with tight little lips. She and John "went together" for a week, then broke up and started competing, which lasted until they both graduated with perfect GPAs. She won Valedictorian by a faculty vote. John was Salutatorian, and gave a shorter speech. He'll never forgive her, but I'm pretty sure that was his first kiss.

Caroline, I promise to hug you long and hard, and often enough that you never feel like a stranger in a man's arms. I promise to teach you just how hard to squeeze, and to make you feel like nothing in the world can hurt you, like no matter what you do, you can always come back and be accepted for who you are, faults and mistakes and all.

Hugging I can teach you, but kissing I can't, so here's some advice. Some people kiss ... I mean they push their lips against some part of your body, and that's it. Maybe they open their mouths and use their tongues, but that's all there is to it. If a boy kisses you and it feels like that, then stop and go play Scrabble or something.

Kissing is like playing music. Anybody can put the instrument in their lips and hit the right notes at the right tempo...but that's not music. Music comes from the soul. It starts deep in the center of your person and flows out through the entire body all at once. If a boy kisses you and it feels like music, then close your eyes and let his person touch you, and don't you dare be the one to stop…as long as it's just kissing.

Here's how to kiss back. Close your eyes, and in your mind, hear your favorite slow love song. Let it flow through your body, slowly warming your whole person. Now hum, and make the sound in your throat flow with the rhythm and emotion of the song. Let your neck float back and forth with the waves of the music, and hum like you've never hummed before. Now open your mouth, and let your throat go softer, and play music with your lips and tongue and your fingertips on the man in your arms.

Caroline, you've started down the road toward womanhood. Don't rush. Kissing is great, and when you find someone you care about, you should kiss him as a way of singing a love song with no words, that only you two can share. But before you rush to exploring the rest of each other's body, make sure the love song is there. Make sure it's strong and full and is going to last before you sing it with your whole body. Temper your curiosity and savor your youth, and when you take the next step, make sure it is with the right man. If it's not, then call me, and I'll give you another lesson on hugs.

Love,

Paul

* * *

We dated through the summer, meeting downtown to sit on the sidewalk and share a coke, going to movies and loaning each other books then talking for hours outside the bookstore about what we had read. We had a slow, lazy, peaceful summer, and I saw her nearly every day. Yes, we kissed, and in retrospect I guess we kissed a lot. But we also raced our bikes down the side roads leading between schools, then laid down to rest on the warm grass and looked up at the sky to see what stories we could find in the clouds. She, like I, could always find the shapes and faces of people both great and small in the fluffy white contours. On some afternoons, we would find whole novels being played out across the summer sky.

Sometimes, while we lay on our backs looking at the clouds and talking, I would look at her and try to see the clouds reflected in her dark blue eyes. The blue sky gave them a shine warm and pure as the Caribbean ocean. She would smile and pretend I wasn't looking at her, and then point up to divert my attention. When I didn't look away, she would touch my chin with one hand and point with the other, making me look. When I saw what she was pointing at, her face would dart up and plant a friendly, smiling love kiss on my cheek, and then we would go back to talking about Joan of Arc in her armor, or whatever else we had seen in the puffy whiteness above.

School came, and things didn't change very much. We saw each other on Saturdays at the book store, and sometimes went to a football game on Friday night. We never talked on the phone. By some chance of fate, or as I thought, some demonic plan by the executives of the telephone company, we lived in the same county and yet still paid long distance rates to call each other. That was back when money was hard to come by for a fourteen year old, and long distance calls were expensive. Perhaps because of that, I never really asked her out on a date. It would go something like this.

"What are you doing next weekend?" I'd ask.

"Not much, probably hang out at the book store."

"Me too. Were you thinking about going to the football game Friday night?"

"Maybe."

"I'm probably going to go," I'd say.

"Yeah, me too. I'll probably see you there." For us, "probably" meant we would be there if there was any possible way we could get it past our parents. We didn't stand each other up much, and there was always a reason, and usually the apology and forgiveness session afterwards made missing her worth while. Her kisses and gentle touches made forgiveness a very easy thing for me to accept.

We broke up in the fall. Years later, after a high school dance, she told me what happened to her in the ravine, and I felt terrible about how I handled myself that autumn. All I knew back then was she didn't come to the bookstore one Saturday. I rode around all day, hoping to see her. I went past the schools, where we would talk about high school, and what it would be like and how old and mature we would be when we got there. I rode past the drug store, and went inside and asked at the bookstore, but no, Barbara hadn't seen her either, but told me she was sure to come by. When I stopped by for the last time around five, Barbara offered to call Caroline's mom, but I said don't bother, she probably went up to Asheville to go shopping. I rode around on Sunday, too, but downtown stores weren't open much in small towns in the South, and Hendersonville was no exception. I was lonely, but not sad—she had become a permanent fixture in my life and I liked it. Besides, after missing me for a whole weekend, she would need a lot of forgiveness.

I played junior high football, and though I was small, I started on both offensive and defensive lines. We played her school Thursday night, and she had talked for weeks about how excited she was to see me play, and to introduce me to her friends. Despite numerous trips to Barbara's after practice, Thursday came without me seeing or hearing from Caroline. I put on my pads that afternoon in nervous excitement. The air was warm, and I went with some of the other players up to the wrestling room to meditate in its quiet heat. I loved the smell of the mats back then, and I still do. They have the smell of energy, of sweat, of victory and defeat and bodies slamming against each other and falling hard against the stiff foam. Those mats represent the ultimate struggle for control for me, and that essence of competition drew me back, to lay on my back and sweat and meditate and study my playbook. Blocking was not hard for me, but blocking schemes sometimes were, and so I studied, propped up against the corner of the wrestling room, and mentally went through each combination of offensive formation against our opponents defensive formation, walking my body through each successive play, picturing successful blocks and the perfect throws and runs made by the real heroes of the game. I was a foot soldier, the supporting cast, and loved those heroes as if they were already professional athletes making millions of dollars on Sundays.

My meditation and study carried me up to game time, when a chill bit into the air and I heard the familiar sound of pads snapping into place in the locker room below. I lifted myself and went to make my final preparations.

I drank ice water until it sloshed cold in my belly, and then lined up with big Paul McKerney, who I hated but who was the only person who challenged me in a hit. We fired off, snapping each other's shoulders in quick pops, first right and then left. We hit helmets in hard jolts that left my neck tense but limber. I was not the biggest or the strongest lineman, but I was the most fearless, and the most agile. When I saw a running back's feet or hips turn one way or another, I would slip my head to that side of my blocker and use his response to propel me onto those feet, which I would wrap in both arms and roll. So Paul and I limbered each other up before every game, and for a short time we were nearly friends, until after the game when he would go back to making fun of the acne on my face, or the stupid way I defended the things I believed. Paul was popular and I was not, and off the field there was no easy way around it.

I knew Caroline would be sitting on the visitors' stands, and knew she would wait for me after the game. I was so intent on playing my best game ever that I didn't look up during our warm up, or during the game. I channeled my nervousness at playing in front of a girl I thought I loved into a passion for excellence. It turned out I needed it.

The boy blocking me was tall and lean, and he used a hard first pop and good arm work to prevent me from getting to their running back, who was fast and strong. They scored an easy touchdown on the first drive, and as our kick defense team came on the field, the coach called me to the side.

"Their back is killing us, Bennett."

"Yes sir," I said, not quite believing it.

"He gets past you, and he's got seven yards every time."

"I won't let him past me, Coach," I said.

"Yes you will unless I do something." I nodded. "I want you to go out there for McKerney. He's getting eaten up at middle linebacker and if it doesn't stop they'll score three more times. You step up and hit your blocker in the hole, then tackle number forty four. Forty four doesn't get past you, you understand?"

"Yes sir!" I barked.

"Get out there and make something happen!"

I lined up at middle linebacker. I didn't know where to stand, or how to line up in a two point stance, but I knew how to hit a blocker and get off him, and I made tackles. The other linebackers taught me the details soon enough, and the players on the other side stopped smirking as their running game stalled. I tackled number forty four sixteen times that night. Some were at the line of scrimmage, and once I caught him for a loss on a pitch I anticipated. He was a good back, though, and took my game directly to me, eyeing me like an angry bull. He answered my sixteen tackles with one hundred and sixty three yards and two more touchdowns. We lost 21 – 14 and I went into the locker room nervous, and not very anxious to face Caroline and her friends.

Fifteen minutes later the coach let us go and I walked back out to the field to look for Caroline. My shoulders and neck were sore, and my arms were changing color under the grass stains and blood smeared from a cut on my elbow. My hair was matted down, but I knew I looked masculine in my pads, and wanted Caroline to see me before I showered. Besides, I wanted to make sure I caught her before she left.

There weren't many people on the field as I walked out; in dejection I saw the opposing stands nearly empty, only a few mothers and fathers waiting to congratulate their sons on their victory. Caroline was not there.

My heart jumped for a second as my parents waved me over to a small group of people, including my dad, and Edward and Hope. I looked around for Caroline, but couldn't find her. She had to be there somewhere.

My dad whacked me on the shoulders as I walked up. "You gonna play middle linebacker, you're gonna have to miss fewer tackles. That back ran all over you today. What happened to McKerney—he sick?" Dad loved me, but was uncomfortable showing it in public. This was his way of drawing attention to my battlefield promotion.

His arm lingered on my shoulder as I said, "I made sixteen tackles. Best on the team."

"Should have been twenty, then you might have won," he said, and gave my neck a squeeze. I joined the group, and they all circled round to congratulate me. After everyone told me what a great game I'd had and I started to go, Hope approached me, and I noticed she had to let go of Edward's hand to come toward me. She handed me a note. "It's from Caroline," she said. "She explained everything inside." She smiled a sad sisterly smile and she squeezed my elbow and gave me a quick hug and a peck on the cheek, never minding the dirt and grass stains covering me. I turned and left and she rejoined hands with Edward.

*   *   *

75

Dear Peter,

I'm sorry I couldn't come to the game tonight and see you play. I'm sure you did great and I'm really sad I had to miss it.

Something happened this week that has had me thinking about a lot of things, including you and me. I'm sorry, but now isn't the right time for me to get involved with someone seriously. This summer was great, but this fall, your feelings for me have been growing more quickly than mine have for you, and the only way to make it equal again is to not see you for a while.

You can have all of our old hang outs, Peter, and I'll miss them. Just don't look for me to be there when you go for a new book or a coke or to play Burger Time. I wish I could be there but all I can handle right now would be to be just friends, and that's not what you want. Maybe we can be friends someday, and I'm sure if we can, we will be great friends.

Thank you for a wonderful summer, and tell Edward I said he is still mean and he still cannot play with us.

Love,
Caroline

*   *   *

I read the letter once quickly in the hall, and then folded it and put it in my locker as I went back in to shower. That night, I pulled the letter out and read it, and re-read it trying to figure out what had happened, what had changed to make her so scared of getting so serious. None of it made sense and that night is when I first began to hate the world for its unfairness. That night in my room, with the lights off and music playing, I cried a violent cry, soaking my pillow with tears and saliva, beating my mattress and asking "why?" to the great unknown. I cried and then masturbated and finally made it to sleep, and when I awoke the next morning my world had changed.

*   *   *

In December, Edward got his driver's license, and he and Hope began to date in earnest. I hadn't seen Caroline after the football game, and though Hope was over often, the families never got together again. Caroline had exited my life, and it was emptier without her.

Hope must have sensed my sadness, and went to great lengths to be sweet, and was the first girl to give me a Christmas present. It was a sweater. "It matches your blue eyes," she said. "All the women will be falling all over you when you wear it." My silence and the downward look in my eyes betrayed my thoughts. Hope came over to me and held the sweater softly against my chest, looked up in my eyes and said, "A girl would be a fool not to love you in this sweater, Peter," and then kissed my cheek. Edward never got jealous, which left me feeling that he knew Caroline's feelings better than I did.

I found comfort in books and athletics, and set the precedent as the hardest working person in the school. I made straight A's, as I would continue to all through high school, and was, as I put it, "… one of the best athletes with the least natural talent in the whole state." I wouldn't see Caroline for another year, and when I did, it would throw us back together again in a way I had never dreamt.

*   *   *

Fifteenth Birthday,

Dearest Caroline,

I learned to love sunsets on the west coast of Maui. Something about the sun setting over the ocean is so gorgeous and peaceful—reds and blues and oranges and purples running together in a maelstrom of colors. On the East Coast, you don't believe in sunsets like that. Paintings seem contrived compared to what you're used to. I was at a conference in Maui. In the evening, when the sun was setting, I had some time to myself. I took care to choose where I was going be as the sun drifted over the horizon.

Sunsets represent everything special and beautiful to me. A myriad of colors spread on a canvas sky, ever changing and yet still, peaceful. They are the beautiful side of a storm. They are where the known meets the vast unknown, the horizon, the place where learning happens. They change. They are science manifesting itself in beautiful simplicity. Like rainbows or waterfalls, they are water in its most fascinating glory. Like everything loveable, they are temporary.

That's the thing—the loveable thing is temporary, but the love persists. In 1 Corinthians, the Bible says, "And now faith, hope, and love abide, these three; and the greatest of these is love." Faith and hope can be fulfilled. There can be complete faith, and complete hope, but love can always grow to be more than it is.

You don't love someone or something because they're everything you ever wanted. Instead, love comes after you have studied the intimate details, after you understand what it takes from and gives to the world. Sunsets are pretty, but many pretty things are not worth loving. I love sunsets.

Life began in the sunset, gaseous clouds of water and small molecules rearranging themselves into amino acids, the building blocks of life. The sunset recycles, capturing evaporating water from the salty sea, cleansing it and condensing it into clouds that rain down as pure drinkable water, quenching our thirst and giving life. Those oranges and purples are life being created; they are cleansing; they are renewal.

The sunset is the gateway to the heavens. Beyond it are night and the stars, the unknown, the frontier. The sunset is protective—the same bits of water that reflect yellow and orange also reflect uv, protecting us from the sun's damaging rays.

The sunset is light of the most perfect sort. Everything beautiful during the day, and difficult to see at night, is more beautiful at sunset. If your future husband is smart, he will propose to you at sunset, because you will be more beautiful, and that will give him courage. He also stands a better chance of success because you are going to be a sucker for sunsets just like your uncle. If I meet him and like him, I'll tell him.

I'm sure by now you have had crushes on boys. Some boys are good dancers, some are nice looking, some are funny, some are smart, and some have all the right friends. Some boys have charm, charisma. I encourage you to appreciate all those things in boys, and later, in men. But none of them are love.

It is possible, you see, to find someone who is none of those things, but who has somehow gotten close to you, to your heart, to your soul…gotten so close he knows you and all the great things you do, and all the blemishes, too. If you are lucky enough to find this someone, and courageous enough to open up to him, and clever enough to get him, too, to lower his guard…then you might love. He might be funny, or he might be clever, or smart, or charming. But he may not be. He has to see you in those few moments when you are truly loveable, and those moments have to touch his soul. And you have to see him at those few moments when he is loveable, and those moments have to touch you, as well. Once love begins, this person will be no more funny or good looking or charming than he was before…but he will be the one you love, and that is the difference. It is quite okay to love someone for no better reason than for the intimacy you share. Love is the only justification for itself. The rest is window dressing.

Love,

Paul

* * *

When Paul called me to tell me about Caroline's accident, I knew what we had feared all along was beginning to happen. Caroline had asked us to keep her pregnancy, and the subsequent birth of her daughter Faith, a secret, especially from her family and the others involved. I had never told my wife JJ, had never told Hope or my brother Edward. It was her secret. I had promised her I would keep it, and I had.

As I drove south on I-77 through West Virginia, her secret was being levered out of me. You will understand when I am finished with my story it is impossible to love Caroline as I loved her, and not have that love last forever. I had not spoken a word to her in eleven years, and even that was a tense hello and a hug at Hope and Edward's wedding. But I love her today as I did on the day I most loved her. Driving south, my heart ached with betrayal. It made my swallows dry and caught in the back of my throat. Every breath was forced, determined, and I paused between each one, as if I were deciding whether to make the next. Maybe I could not be what she wanted, what she would love. But I had been successful in not being something she would despise.

As I pulled into the driveway, I steeled myself with my story, and prepared to use the words as weapons against Hope's good but misguided intentions.

A warm drizzle cleaned my windshield and made a soft patter on the roof of my Explorer. I hustled to Caroline and Josh's front door, feeling the drops tender on my skin. I rang the bell quickly and waited, still getting wet as the wind blew the drops under the awning. Looking up anxiously, I noticed a note taped to the front door with my name on it. I picked it up and read Hope's loopy, feminine script. "Caroline not well— come to the hospital," was all it said.

*   *   *

Caroline and I saw each other in the winter of our sophomore year in high school. We were both in Junior Achievement clubs, and went to the state Junior Achievement convention in Raleigh together. Initially, it was awkward, and I remember the nervousness I felt in the hollow part of my chest as I walked up to ask her to dance on the first night, and how it lodged itself there, growing like a bubble nearing its popping point as she hesitated, but then finally said yes and smiled. I took her hand and remembered its softness and we danced, tender and slow but not too close. We danced two dances and when the second one was over she hugged me and said thank you and turned directly around and walked away. Though I hated it, I understood the signal.

Later we each had met someone else, and the next day the four of us went to lunch. Caroline and I each introduced the other as "an old friend of the family" and we hugged. It felt good to have Caroline close again, and I knew having her near me helped to cover up my awkwardness with the new girl. Her name was Lynn.

My best friend, Freddy, had a bad step father. I don't know all the details of what a bad step father is, but I know Freddy showed up late one night at the house and said his step father had pulled a .38 on him. He had run away and walked the two miles to my house. My dad called and asked for his mom to return the call, and then drove Freddy home when his mother called.

I wasn't surprised when Freddy came dancing into homeroom one day and asked if I wanted to go away to school. Of course, it wasn't possible, because Mom and Dad had only saved enough money to send me to a state college, so there was no way I could go away to a private high school. Then Freddy told me it was a free boarding school for gifted and talented students in North Carolina, called the North Carolina School of Science and Math. The name made my heart tingle—I was very good at both science and math, and going away sounded exciting. Freddy and I went to an informational session after school and I took the application home for Mom and Dad to look at.

"I was afraid this was going to happen," my mother told me. "Edward decided not to go last year, but I thought you might decide differently." Two weeks later we had the application filled out, and Mom drove me to Asheville for a half day of testing. I wasn't worried—I did well on standardized tests, and knew I was among the best in math and science.

I saw Caroline at the tests. Her hair had grown a little since the winter. As soon as she saw me walk into the testing room, her face went wide with happiness and she jumped up from her friends to give me a hug. When she let go, I noticed she was sitting with Phil, the guy she had met at the Junior Achievement convention. I didn't even mind, and we talked for a few minutes before the testing began.

We left the testing to find our mothers talking, and the four of us went to lunch together. Caroline smiled as we compared notes on the test questions, and I noticed her beautiful straight teeth and thought about the braces that had just come off my own teeth. Her blue eyes had flecks of yellow in the middle which morphed their colors to match what she was wearing. She wore green and her eyes were green as a grove of cypress.

* * *

Sixteenth Birthday

Dear Caroline,

High school was a time I remember being completely stressed out about things that really didn't matter, but mattered quite a bit to me. I've been to a couple high school reunions since then. You should see how people change. Some people peak in high school, while others bloom a little later. I have no idea when you are going to bloom...I just want you to look deeper at your friends than the normal high school student looks, and see the potential within them.

John Roman: John wrestled the 98 pound weight class until his senior year. Everybody liked him, but he never had a single date. He was a little bitty guy we carried around, and patted his head like he was ten years old. He was the manager for every athletic team except wrestling, and he didn't have a real muscle on his body. At our ten year reunion, John had just started his own law practice, and was about 6'3", 210 lbs, and looked like Lou Ferrigno. He grabbed my hand in this huge body-builder handshake and said in a deep voice, "Hi Paul, I'm John Roman, do you remember me?" I said yes, but it was ten minutes before I put it together. He also had a very beautiful wife.

Mary Ann Browning: Mary Ann and I learned how to ride bikes together. We played kick-the-can with the older kids, and she always got picked before me. She was the nicest, smartest, and in a sanitary, antiseptic way, prettiest girl in my class—but I never, ever thought of her as a girl. That changed. My class did "Grease" for our senior class play. Mary Ann (our valedictorian), played the lead, Sandra D. For the first half, she was the Miss Nice-Nice I'd always known. In Act III she came on stage in a black leather halter covering two fleshy bumps I'd never noticed, a tight leather miniskirt and her first real set of panty-hose. Her legs were something! That day, Mary Ann became a woman. She didn't come to our ten year reunion, but sent her newest album—she's the lead singer for a group called "Public Librarian" that plays the bar scene in the Midwest. On the side, she's a lawyer, and I'd still pick her for my team before I picked me.

Tom Danielson: Tom was the son of a lawyer, and the best-looking guy in my grade, and one of only a few that were smarter than me. Before high school, he had already gone steady with every good-looking girl in our tiny school. In high school the rest of us looked down a grade because we couldn't compete for our freshman women. Tom dated the most beautiful, smartest, most popular girl in the sophomore class. He married that sophomore, and now manages a restaurant in our home town. We'd all pictured him as running for governor one day, but having a lousy family with two ex-wives and a mistress. Tom and Lisa have a beautiful teen-age girl and a young boy, and they are still among the most popular people in Hendersonville.

I could go on, but you get the picture. People will change. Who they will be is already inside of them, even in high school. There is more to life than funny, and more to a person's value than whether his blue jeans are the right color and texture. Be friendly to everyone, and try not to assume what they appear to be is what they are. You'll be happier for it. Believe it or not, people will respect you for it.

Love you lots, girl. Have a great time in high school!

Paul

PS: Paul Novak: I was a sloppily-dressed, zit faced athlete with braces and a knack for getting good grades. The seat next to me was only popular during test time, because they knew I didn't mind flashing the right answer to an occasional tough question. Now I'm a quiet, unmarried computer scientist working in Silicon Valley. I have friends, several patents, and I still exercise. I haven't changed much. I had girlfriends in high school, but I couldn't keep them, and that's still the problem.

*   *   *

Caroline ceased to be magical to me on the day before we left for the School. She had been admitted at the end of the summer while her parents were vacationing in Europe. My parents volunteered to bring her to School.

My eyes had grown misty when I told my football coach I wouldn't be coming back next year. He stood up from his desk and went over to the magnetic board where he had next year's line up, and pulled down the magnets with my name on them—first string defense, and second string offense. "You're making the right decision, kid," he told me, and I went out to tell my teammates.

We drove over to pick Caroline up the night before we were to go and she answered the door with a "Hello Mrs. Bennett" and a polite smile for me. I carried her bags, and could feel the newly formed muscles in my arms flexing under the weight. She sat up front with Mom, and I admired the line of her jaw and the soft place behind her ear and wondered what this new school would have in store for me.

*   *   *

Caroline was staying in our guest room. I stopped by as we went to bed, and she and I stayed up late talking. At some point, I asked her the awkward question.

"Me? No, Peter. Look at me. I'm too smart and I wear glasses. Boys want dumb girls with big chests." She pulled her arms and neck back and flexed her chest and her bosoms, stretched thin, were two barely noticeable lumps beneath her pajamas. "At a geek school, I might have a chance," she said, and we laughed. What dumb people she must have in her school, I thought. The skin of her arms and her legs glimmered, and I wanted to both cuddle her soft pajama-clad youth and explore her womanhood.

Before I got up to leave, I leaned over and kissed her, and to my surprise, she didn't pull away. I lingered and she pulled me in and her arms went around my back and I could feel her small breasts hard against my chest, new and high and firm, as we slid slowly back on the couch. In a moment I was lost in a tumultuous reverie and time dilated into oblivion as our bodies intertwined and moved in musical harmony.

Then it happened.

She pulled away and wiped her mouth and smiled politely. "Well, that was a surprise," she said, and rolled away. I lay in stunned astonishment as she sat up and buttoned her pajamas. "Listen," she said, "No promises, okay?"

My heart opened up a fissure like the Grand Canyon and two years of my imaginary relationship with her fell to the bottom like so many dead fish. For two years, I had loved…something. My memory of her, my imagination of what she had become, of the love I knew—I knew!—that she still carried for me. I realized for the first time what had just happened, which was our most passionate moment together and at the time my most passionate moment ever, had nothing to do with what was going on in her heart.

Of course I didn't understand her true story, how scared she was to love me, how she needed to know in the depth of her soul that I wasn't and could never be like the man in the ravine, and how a night of talking and kissing and caressing was not proof enough.

As it was, I sat up and buttoned my shirt in silence. She sat still, watching me collect myself, and didn't rise as I stood to go. I walked over to her and pushed back her disheveled hair and touched her cheek and neck and felt the softness of her flannel pajamas. Her hands remained in her lap.

There are a few moments in every man's life when he has the opportunity to say a few words, to communicate with a crispness and insert into an emptiness a brick that will hold up a wall for all eternity. This was one of those moments for me, and I regret what I did with all my essence, with every joule of my being.

I grinned a sad grin, and nodded, and turned and went to bed.

Chapter 5: Conception

If a man lies with a woman and has an emission of semen, both of them shall bathe in water, and be unclean until the evening.
--Leviticus 15:18

The short drive across town seemed longer than the haul from Columbus. I watched the night scenes go by and tapped my foot nervously when I stopped at a red light. When I got to the hospital, I found Hope and Josh in a lobby on the second floor. Josh was asleep, and Hope rested against him. She opened her eyes and rose when she saw me coming, and a warm smile bloomed on her face.

"Peter, it is so good to see you," she said as she took my hands and leaned in to kiss my cheek. I smiled and looked into her brown eyes and waited. She didn't seem nervous, and that calmed me a little. Then I remembered Hope had the nerves of a M.A.S.H. unit nurse, and got scared again. She pulled me to a bench and we sat down.

"It's her blood pressure," she said. "It had been normal all week, and the baby's heartbeat strong, but then this afternoon her blood pressure dropped and they lost the baby's heartbeat for a little while. That's when I left the note." She reached up and brushed her hair out of her eyes, and I noticed she had the frizzes, like she'd been running her fingers through it too much. Hope did not have nervous twitches, and her hair was normally perfect. I listened intently, waiting to hear what bothered her.

"They put her on medication and had her stabilized before we got here." She smiled and nodded slowly. "The baby, too. She's in for a CAT scan, head and abdomen. If everything isn't okay, they're going to do a c-section tonight."

"Oh boy," I said, and rubbed my eyes hard, feeling the sleep grind in the corners. "Josh can sleep through this?" I asked.

"Leave him alone—he's been a champ."

"I just hope he's ready for fatherhood," I said, and she dropped it.

A few minutes later, Hope leaned in and whispered to Josh that we were going for tea, and he growled and adjusted his neck on the arm of the chair, and we left.

She stood and slipped her arm in mine as she had so many times before, and we walked slowly toward the elevators.

"You are simply amazing Peter Bennett," she said. I smiled, and she went on, "I don't know what you're going to tell me, but it is simply amazing you have been able to keep it a secret all this time."

"I'd like to keep it secret forever," I said.

"Don't be silly. You can either tell me, or my father," she said, and paused and squeezed my bicep. I pressed the button for the elevator.

"Caroline doesn't want you to know," I said. The elevator came, and a young man was inside. We rode down with him in silence.

We found the cafeteria and Hope got a cup of hot tea while I found a large bottle of Pepsi. As we sat down I took a drink and felt the bubbly caffeine rejuvenate the back of my throat. Hope sipped her tea before she spoke.

"Peter, you are my brother-in-law and I love you like a brother." She took another sip of tea. "I love Caroline, too, Peter. You have to trust that. I love her and need to be strong for her right now. And I'm going to. You can either tell me nicely or I torture it out of you, with the aid of my father if I need to." The look in her eyes was calm, but very, very firm.

I told her the story. She sat quietly and listened, and the beauty and anguish of those times, of our last two years of high school, came back to me. The secret was like the water in the creeks that Caroline and I dammed up as children. We would let the dam fill up, flowing to the edges of the creek bed, and then, just before it overflowed, we would create a small leak in the middle, and then watch as clay and sand and rocks were peeled away from this spot until a catastrophic failure occurred and all the water flowed out. My secret was like that water, and letting it out carried us deep into the night.

Hope and I went to Caroline's house, and I settled in to bed in Caroline's childhood bed. As I lay down, I felt the mattress sag under my weight, and thought about the other times I'd been in this bed. I thought about the time we sat here and read her junior high yearbook—she didn't want me to read what people wrote, but I managed to sneak a peak at a few. Her friends didn't like her, thought she was a geek, and not very nice. I remember before that, I don't know how old we were, as she introduced me to a new Fisher Price family she had made up. The Jehusifrounts, who had twelve children. She held each piece up and told me his name, where he (or she) fit in the family, and a little story about each one. They had a stable keep, whose name was George, "… but they call him 'Smelly,'" she said.

I never kissed her on this bed, never laid prone with her, there or anywhere else, until the night before we left for School. And yet, she remains one of the great loves of my life.

Josh came back the next day, and walked in on Hope and me talking upstairs, the box of letters in our hands.

"You guys talking about Faith?" he asked.

I felt a little like I'd been caught with my hand in the cookie jar. "Yeah," I said.

He stepped over to the bed, where I'd been sleeping, opened the bottom drawer of the night stand, and pulled out a hard bound book. He handed it to me. "It's her diary," he said. "It'll help you understand." Then he left to go shower, and headed back to the hospital.

* * *

Caroline and I arrived the next day at the North Carolina School of Science and Mathematics in the early afternoon. The sun was shining, and there was a group of students out on the lawn throwing a Frisbee. We were told Caroline would be in Reynolds dorm, and asked directions. I had no sooner opened the trunk before two strong looking seniors were helping to hoist Caroline's luggage. They carried it up to a table, where a plump senior girl looked for Caroline's name on a list. When we had carried everything up to her room, she turned to my parents and said, "Thank you so much for the ride, Mr. and Mrs. Bennett," and gave my mother a quick sisterly hug, complete with shoulder tapping. She turned to me and said, "I'll see you tonight at the cafeteria." We left to find my own dormitory.

I went through the same ritual at the opposite side of campus in front of Wyche dormitory, and then went for an ice cream with my parents. Mom cried, and my father, who almost never touches me, shook my hand and squeezed my shoulder in something that was very nearly a hug. I promised to write and call, and they left.

At that moment, I had firmly in my possession the brightest future in the state of North Carolina, and I knew it. The campus was an old nursing school which hadn't been used for decades. My own dormitory, Wyche Hall, was old, with finicky plumbing and an energetic and vibrant insect population. Across the street was the husk of a building that had yet to be rebuilt, the 1908 building, which was fenced off and "condemned."

Three cars had pulled in at awkward angles in front of my dorm, and a woman in the passenger seat of another tried to wave down the man unloading from the back as her husband angled through the narrow space between them. As I looked over the crowd of new students and their families, I knew the statistics. Two hundred and fourteen new juniors, and one hundred and ninety seven returning seniors. I saw in others the same feelings I was feeling—nervousness, apprehension, maybe a little fear, but also a feeling of just wanting to get on with it. My nervousness about Caroline took a back seat as I thought about the new life I was starting. I have always loved all things new, all beginnings. And this, this was one of the greatest beginnings of my life.

As I turned to go, I noticed a large navy blue sedan pull up in front of the dormitory, and heard the senior behind the registration table call my name as the occupants signed up.

"Peter," said the senior drone. "This is your new roommate, Alexander Rice."

"Hi Alex," I said as I took his outstretched hand. He wore a white linen jacket, light blue shirt, and a yellow and navy striped tie. I felt a little out of place in my jeans and golf shirt, but then realized he was the one who was out of place.

He gripped my hand and I saw his lips tighten. "That's Alexander," he said crisply, with an accent that wasn't quite British, but definitely spoke of money.

"Can I carry something?" I said, motioning to the rear of the car, where a small, well dressed Italian man was pulling luggage out onto a cart.

"No need, Vincent will get it," he said. "Which room is ours?" After I told him, he called the number back to Vincent and we walked down the hall. My hands were empty, but he carried a brown leather briefcase in his left hand.

*   *   *

We had a bunch of orientation stuff, and the next night, Saturday, there was a school dance held in the parking lot outside the cafeteria. Outdoor dances since have been banned, but back then, we had great fun with them.

Alexander and I grew to be great friends over the year, and even after high school, but those first days it was touch and go. Later, he applied to college with me at Ohio State, because he said he wanted to apply to at least one "pedestrian" school, and "you don't get more pedestrian than Ohio State." I wanted to walk on to their football program. But he ended up going to Yale, and we parted as friends. He did visit several times, and we did some very pedestrian things and had some great pedestrian fun.

When Vincent brought all his clothes down and they wouldn't fit in his closet, I gave him space in mine. They hung very neatly, color coded and still in their dry cleaner bags. I had never worn dry cleaned clothes.

The next morning, Vincent showed up with a Wall Street Journal under his arm and handed it to Alexander. He took us to breakfast at a place with cloth napkins and the tenderest waffles ever cut with a fork. Alexander read "the Journal," as he called it, and told me, "You can read it when I'm finished. It really is fascinating." Later, I heard Alexander on the hall phone changing the address on his Journal subscription and calling the local dry cleaners to see who would pick up and deliver. He left his clothes in the lobby every Tuesday and Thursday for the rest of our time at the School.

Alexander got ready for the dance more quickly than I did. "You learn to tie a tie expeditiously when you do it every day," he said with a chuckle. He wore a brown v-neck vest over a yellow shirt with a brown tie with yellow anchors all over it. His wool slacks were creased, and his wing tips polished. I wore my best blue jeans and a mock turtle neck shirt that showed off my physique.

Caroline walked in to the dance a few minutes after we did, and had with her one of the most amazing women I have ever met. "Peter, this is my roommate, Julia." Julia was short, maybe 5'2" and very petite. Her hair fell in kinky curls all about her shoulders, and beautiful freckles covered her face. One ear had a single, large gold cross dangling gently against her neck, and the other had what looked like a school of silver fish swimming from her lobe to the top of her ear. She wore a sky blue satin shirt split at the shoulders and draped loosely about her arms, and some black tight pants that turned to a dark blur when she danced. Later, I would learn the rest. "I have my navel and my nipples pierced, too, and seven tattoos, each one depicting a Jesus in a different way." She dubbed herself a "modern day missionary" and told me I "would be one of her projects this year." I wondered how such an annoying personality could come in such a wonderfully sexy package.

Alexander stepped forward and took Caroline's hand, "You must be Catherine—Peter has told me so much about you!" Caroline didn't say anything, but a minute later, I heard Julia pull Alexander close and whisper in his ear "it's Caroline."

Alexander and I refused to dance fast with them, so they left in search of other quarry. "Do you think they will return?" Alexander asked.

"Not if we won't dance with them," I said.

"Then we'll have to learn to dance," he said, and two songs later we found them and danced for most of the night.

They started playing slow songs as our curfew drew near, and Caroline stepped in to hold me close for the first one. She wore a soft black turtleneck sweater that both hid and accentuated her curves, and I felt the muscles on the small of her back moving underneath it in rhythm with the music. After the first slow dance, she pulled away and said, "I promised one to someone else," and left to search the crowd. I walked to the edge of the dance to watch.

They call people like me "wall flowers" and it comes with a certain stigma, but that is where I would rather be. I loved watching the dance— not the bodies dancing with each other—but rather the slow and timid dance of two souls sharing their intimacy, growing close, then scared and pulling away, then comforting and close again. Over the next two years I would watch couples form, pull away and form again. I learned how some girls charged into love like a knight into a joust, while others tested it first with their toes and then, only when everything was safe and sure, slipped into it like a young girl skinny dipping on a warm summer night.

As I watched, I saw Caroline enter the dance floor with a tall good looking blond fellow. She didn't dance close, like she did with me, but rather they talked and she laughed and I could tell she was looking at his eyes in a way she hadn't looked at mine in two years, and I saw on her face the natural, care free beauty of a young girl falling in love. I was happy for her and loved her for her capacity to care and to give, and was more than a little jealous of Curt, the blond fellow who I now recognized as a senior who lived on my hall. At the end of the dance, Caroline hugged him tightly around the neck, but didn't kiss him, and then she came over to me, where we were joined by Alexander and Julia, hand in hand.

I put my arm on Caroline's shoulders and hers slipped around my waist, and Alexander and I walked two of the most beautiful junior women at the geekiest high school in the country back to their dormitory. We stopped on our way at the mail room, but Caroline was the only one to get a letter. I got a soft hug from Caroline, and then satin Julia slipped quickly in and out of my arms. She broke by saying to me, "If you won't join us for church, then at least come afterwards so I can tell you about my tattoos."

"Do I get to see the piercings?" I asked.

She laughed and threw her head back, and I inspected the soft satin on top of her breasts for untoward lumps, but didn't find any. "Not this time," she said, and then kissed Alexander on the cheek.

Alexander was quiet as we walked back across campus in the cool night air. Other students were crossing this way and that, and a game of Frisbee was going on outside the front steps of Wyche. When we got back into our room, he said, "I'm going to like it here, Peter."

"Me, too," I said. "Me, too."

*   *   *

Dearest Caroline,

You had me stumped. How could I predict you would grow up and leave home when you're barely breaking out of girlhood? You're not old enough to face what you have to face…and that's the best time to do it. No use waiting until you're comfortable—by then it's too late.

I left for college at about the same age as everyone else. There was nothing special about me, but I wanted to be noticed, to be different. I made sure I was the first person on the dance floor, sat at the table with the most people in the cafeteria, played all the intramural sports. I ended up known-of by everybody, but known by very few. That's not the way to do it. I eventually made some friends, though. The hard way.

Melynda was very cute. She was dating one of the guys in my dorm, and I saw her frequently in the lobby. Occasionally, I'd see her in the cafeteria and eat with her. When she and this guy broke up, I flirted hard.

Dexter, one of the few people who would let me hang out with him, asked her out. She said yes, though she wasn't really interested in him. She liked his company, though, so they went out for ice cream and to movies.

A week later we had a mixer with Melynda's dorm. Melynda and I were the last two on the dance floor—I guess we just didn't get tired quickly. We danced all sorts of dances—twist, shag…then they played a slow song, and we ended up in each other's arms and really liked it. We stayed there the rest of the night. I walked her back to her dorm and said goodnight like a gentleman should, on her doorstep.

Three days later, Melynda got a letter from Dexter, signed in blood. He was angry and depressed. The next month was a cacophony of letters passed back and forth between Melynda and Dexter. I tried to help Melynda let Dexter understand she cared for him, but was coming to love me. She was the sweetest girl.

I finally went upstairs to talk with Dexter. He made it clear I was not welcome, but didn't shut the door, either. I started talking. I told him everything, from my messed up childhood to Melynda, my second love. After I'd opened up completely, with no reply from Dexter, I stopped and left. A few days later, he came to talk to me, and we talked almost all night. We ended the talk with our only hug.

This was twenty years ago. Dexter and I are still friends, and I still see Melynda, who's happily married, with children. I couldn't tell you the names of the other people I called friends back then. The struggling to get attention, to be out in front of the crowd—didn't make me any friends.

Opening up did which is the only route to true friendship.

Have a great time!

Love,

Uncle Paul

*   *   *

North Carolina in the fall is a wonderful place, with warm sunshine and the fierce whisper of wind blowing through the trees overhead. Alexander and Julia became quickly inseparable, and loved to study on a picnic table on the green across from Wyche. The first time I joined them, I walked timidly up to them carrying my books. Alexander had his briefcase open in front of him, and was reading the technology section of his Journal. Julia, looking much more wholesome but just as sexy, cradled a history book in her arms. She wore a Duke sweatshirt and shorts, her pink legs covered with goose bumps from the cold. "Mind if I join you?" I asked. Alexander nodded, and then went back to his Journal.

"You can join us, Peter, but first, you have to memorize a Bible verse."

"I what?" I asked.

"You can't sit here unless you memorize a Bible verse—one of my choosing."

I was stunned, but I liked her, so I decided to go along and said, "Okay, if it's a short one."

"It's whatever I choose," she said. "If you don't like it, you can leave." She looked at me, her eyes boring into my own, defying me to argue with her.

"I do it, too," Alexander said, turning the page and smoothing it flat.

I sat down. "Shoot," I said.

"I don't think you're ready for anything advanced, so we'll start simple."

"Do I have to live with the insults, too?" I asked.

"If you want to stay here you do," she said. How did she know she had me so entranced?

"Okay." I shook my head.

"John 3:16, she said. 'For God so loved the world that he gave his only Son, so that everyone who believes in him may not perish but may have eternal life.'"

I repeated the verse, word for word. At least I had been gifted with a good memory, so this wouldn't be difficult. I wondered what else she had in store.

"Good," she said. "Don't forget it."

"I won't," I said.

Later, Caroline joined us, and after an hour or so we got hungry and went to the cafeteria for dinner. We had quickly adopted the student body slang for the place, "craperteria." Admittedly, it was full of food, and not bad by my undiscerning tastes, but that's because I didn't mind over-boiled vegetables and miscellaneous meat patties with names like "Chuck Wagon." And there was always the good old stand by—peanut butter and jelly sandwiches. I had at least one with every meal.

I filled my tray with food, made my PBJ sandwich, and then found the table in back where the other three had already settled.

As I approached, Julia said, "Say it," to me, and again gave me the defiant eyes. I set my tray down and pulled out my chair, but as I went to sit down, Julia stood up and said, "You can't sit with me unless you say it."

Caroline looked on with amusement—she clearly enjoyed my pain and didn't care what it was about.

Julia remained standing, and Alexander spoke up. "Christienne has decided Peter and I will learn the Bible one verse at a time," he said, the edge of frustration in his voice.

Caroline smiled, "Oh really?" she asked in mock question.

"What was your verse?" I asked Alexander.

"'Be perfect, therefore, as your heavenly father is perfect,'" he said. "Matthew 5:48."

I hesitated for a moment, but honestly didn't mind having the stage in front of these two very cute women, and so I said my verse. When I finished, Julia nodded and turned to her dinner, and Caroline smiled at me. Then I heard a single loud clap, pause, and then another clap from behind me. I turned to see the blond figure of Curt standing behind me. He gave his head a shake, but not enough of one to knock the smirk off, as he said, "Well done, Peter. Well done." He continued the slow, sarcastic clapping.

Julia looked livid. "You, too," she said. "If you're going to sit with us, you have to memorize a verse also." Her eyes narrowed to slits. "And I've got the perfect verse for you."

"No thanks," Curt said. "I'm not playing." He looked at Caroline. "See you later tonight," and flashed a winning smile before turning away to go back to his senior friends.

I sat down to eat. "Whatever," I said. Then I looked at Alexander. "Hey, what did you call her, anyway?"

He looked up and grinned. "Her name," he said. "Julia Christienne. It's a beautiful name."

I widened my eyes in surprise, and then looked at Julia. "It is a beautiful name. Nice initials, too."

"You call me 'Julia'," she said, the hint of a smile peeking out from behind her annoyance. "Only Alexander gets to call me that."

"That's her ticket for admission to sit with me," he said. "I memorize Bible verses, she allows me to use her given name." He grinned, lips closed, but obviously proud of his small victory.

* * *

Later, after Caroline had gone off with Curt, Alexander excused himself to go to the bathroom. Julia turned to me after he had gone. "I'll show you three of them," she said. She twisted her slim shoulder out the top of her sweatshirt, pulling the neck down near her elbow. Her shoulder was thin but muscular, and covered with freckles. On it was a scene showing the side of a mountain with a cave, and a large rock sitting halfway in front of the cave with a large piece of cloth draped over it. The detail was amazing, and I could see drops of blood on the cloth. "Jesus said, 'I am the resurrection and the life. He who believes in me shall live even if he dies.'"

"My goodness," I said, reveling in the detail of this tattoo. I reached my finger out to touch it, but she twisted away.

"Look, but don't touch," she said, and I caught a twinkle of mischief in her eye. She turned 180 degrees, her shoulder slipping back under the cover of her Duke sweatshirt. She lifted it slightly off the front of her hip, and lowered the elastic of her shorts. I could see the dark blue strap of her

Jockey underwear. In the small wedge of skin she was exposing was another tattoo, this one a gate, half open along a fence. "'I am the gate; if anyone enters through me, he shall be saved and find pasture.'" I leaned in to look closer, but as I did, the wedge of skin disappeared and she stepped back away from me, untucking her shirt.

I saw on her stomach a lamb, caught in a narrow valley, and a shepherd crawling down to him. The fur of the lamb was dotted with Julia's freckles, and it appeared that the shepherd would have to crawl past her miniscule belly button to rescue his quarry.

"What is He this time?" I asked.

"'I am the good shepherd; the good shepherd lays down his life for his sheep," she said. She smiled at my curiosity.

"Did he?" I asked.

"He did, even for the lost sheep, and those who've run away. But after he gave his life, he was resurrected," she said.

*   *   *

Two weeks later, I found myself alone on a Friday night. Caroline, Curt, Alexander and Julia had all disappeared, as couples do, and so I gathered my physics books and hopped the fence surrounding the old 1908 building. I wandered around through broken glass and rubble, and found a stairway leading upstairs. I had seen a balcony on the second floor I wanted to check out. It turned out to be close enough to a street lamp to be able to read, and I dragged in an old office chair and settled in to study. I enjoyed the solitude and the private view it gave me of everything happening on this side of campus, and definitely needed the time to study. I was already getting behind.

Most of the night was quiet, and I read both my physics and history assignments without looking up much. As curfew approached, more and more couples began to wander the grounds, and a Frisbee game struck up in front of Wyche. There was a group of students on a picnic table below me playing cards, enjoying the benefits of the same street lamp I was using. A small crowd collected at each of the four visible dorm entrances.

I saw Caroline emerge from the shadows of the woods behind Wyche Hall, with Curt by her side. She took his hand in both of hers and rested her head against his shoulder. He kissed the top of her head.

They walked slowly back to her dorm. They stopped outside where several other couples were saying good-bye. Caroline turned and snaked her bare arms around his neck. She leaned against him on her tiptoes and kissed him sweetly. Still kissing, I saw Caroline smile, then giggle lightly and pull away, placing her cheek on his chest. They talked for a few minutes, but the words were lost in the distance between us and I frowned, thinking back to the time when I had enjoyed Caroline's attentions.

*   *   *

I went back to my dorm, planning to settle in early and read my novel for a while before I went to sleep. Alexander was asleep when I got in, so I undressed quietly and put on my pajamas. I heard some noises in the hall as I found my toothbrush and toothpaste, and opened the door to step out.

I saw a crowd gathered about halfway down the hall, and several boys stepped out of their rooms as I did, curious about the noise. Curt was at the other end of the hall, in the center of the crowd, and received pats on the back, high fives, slaps, and butt-taps from the other students. "Was this a one night thing, or are you going to claim her?"

"I'm going back to that well," Curt replied, "over and over and over!"

"How far did you get?" "Did you pop her cherry?" "Is her body what it looks like?"

A boy across the hall asked his roommate, "Who is the most recent victim of Curt's ego?"

"Somebody said it was Caroline, but I don't believe it."

I couldn't speak. My face tightened slowly, my lips clenched and I balled my fingers into tight fists as I watched Curt parade down the hall. Anger burned white hot at the base of my shoulders, and spread into my arms and through the rest of my body. I tensed with anticipation.

The boys continued their jibes and slaps. "You getting another tomorrow, or hanging with her for a while?" "I'm following and watching!" "I want my turn!" "Get in line, Buddy!"

Three boys lined up beside me, waiting their turn to congratulate the returning victor. Two smiled and raised their hands to high-five Curt, one on each side in a triple-jumping, high-five masterpiece. Curt leaped up to slap their hands. I launched forward, and caught Curt in mid-air with both hands hard on his chest. His feet came forward and he landed flat on his back. The hall went quiet and everybody turned to look. I was smaller than Curt by far, but felt sure I could do some more damage before I went down.

Curt hit the ground hard, and lay flat for a split second before pulling his legs back and preparing to spring up at me. I placed my right foot between Curt's thighs and shoved him back to the ground, "Don't even think about it asshole, or you'll wish you never had a dick."

Curt leaned back down on his arms, his face relaxing, "You're right, Pete. I deserved that." Curt reached up to shake my hand. I gave him my best nasty look, then went back to my room.

*   *   *

Ten o'clock the next morning, the day was bright and sunny and promising. Campus was quiet on Saturday mornings, after Friday evenings abundant with adolescence. I lay in bed, not sleeping, not yet awake. Alexander had long since gone, and I figured him to be reciting at least his second Bible verse of the day.

I first heard the footsteps clomp – clomping through the dorm lobby. Then came the shrill sound of a scream, yelling my name. "PETER BENNETT!!" Her voice was clear, breaking the quiet on the hall. I lay motionless, hoping it would go away.

"PETER BENNETT!!! Get up right now!" There was more silence, and I rolled away, facing the wall. Then I heard a door open.

"Peter Bennett, get up right now, or I'm coming down the hall to get you!" Her voice was softer now.

A boy's voice said, "Do you want me to knock on his door, Caroline?"

"Thanks, Mike, but I'd prefer if you'd knock on his head."

"I'll get him." There was a knock, not a gentle one, on my door. Time passed. The knock came again, this time even more firmly. I got up and cracked the door open. Mike, the youngest boy in our class, was there. He said, "Caroline is at the end of the hall. She wants to talk to you."

I looked down the hall, and waved. Caroline stood at the end, one hand on her waist, her hip cocked to one side. Her hair was back in a pony

99

tail, held by a soft blue cotton tie. Like the rarest of all women, she was most beautiful in her anger.

I was wearing nothing but boxers. "Just a minute, Caroline," I said. "Let me put on some clothes."

"You'd better put on some armor!"

I came out a minute later in blue jeans and a t-shirt, carrying shoes and socks and wearing a ball cap. I headed down the hall.

Caroline's voice was low, her grin completely gone. "Just who do you think you are, Peter Bennett?!" she said. "Can't you find someone else to pick fights with?"

"I didn't pick the fight," I said. "I just stopped him from doing what he was doing."

When I got to her, I said, "Can I put my socks and shoes on before we fight?"

"Too late!" Caroline said, but then broke into a grin. She took my arm and leaned her shoulder into it as we walked to the lobby and sat down.

"I could really like him, Pete. Don't mess things up." She sat close.

"You wouldn't if you saw what happened."

"Stop changing the subject," her voice was stern. "I might really like Curt, and I want you out of it. We're still friends, Pete, but I want the chance for things to work out. If you get in the way, you can't be my friend." She grabbed my arm, pulling me around so we were looking directly at each other. Her face was serious, "Do you understand?"

"I understand, Caroline. I understand he's tall, popular, good looking, and you like that. I understand him, too, and I don't like it." Her face went slack, listening. "I was here before he showed up, and I'll be here when he's gone."

She listened, and I could tell she was thinking about what I said. I softened, then, wanting for her what she wanted. I put my arm around her. "I won't mess things up, Caroline. But I'm not putting up with any bull, either."

She put both arms around me in a hug. "Thanks," she whispered. We broke and Caroline got up to leave. "I can't wait to hear what your Bible verse is after Julia hears about last night."

I smiled and walked back down the hall to my room.

*   *   *

First Boyfriend

Dearest Caroline,

If your first kiss was like mine, then it was a quick, embarrassing peck during a game of spin the bottle. For me, it was spin the snorkel, played in a swimming pool during a class party. We ducked under water to kiss. I don't really count those. My first real kiss was a snake-tongue, slobbery mess, and I don't think either one of us knew why we were supposed to enjoy it. We knew we were supposed to, though, and we sure wanted to do it with each other and nobody else. Well, maybe not nobody else...

Even at two years old, Caroline, you are beautiful. I know you will be plagued with boys for the next fifteen years or so, until you finally decide one is good enough to settle down with. Or you give up and make house for yourself, in which case you will be plagued for another fifteen years at least. Here is the best advice I know to give you. Read this letter now, but re-read it again every time you screw up.

What to Look for in a Boy:

This is so mind-bogglingly simple, I am amazed at how often people get it wrong. But they do. Look for these things:

Character
Integrity
Balance
Responsibility
Generosity
Wisdom.

I promise you, if you find a man with those things, you will be happy, even if he is a fat impotent taxi cab driver. Without them, the most virile stock broker will be a disappointment.

What Not to Look for in a Boy:

This is a little tougher, because some are deceptive. But if you see any of these, RUN:

Love at first sight (if it works, it should be renamed "luck at first sight".)

Driving ambition (…if it's driven by self. If driven by generosity, then move it up to the first list, but be careful.)

Recklessness

Spontaneity (a little is okay, a lot will find your child's college education under the hood of a Porsche)

Uncontrollable sexual passion (The first word is the key. But if they can't control it with you, then you can almost bet they won't be able to control it when you're not around. And be careful of another thing—a boy who will cheat with you, will also cheat on you. This also goes for lying and stealing.)

Violence

Debt, or any high material demands. (If you can find him, choose a boy whose first priority is on the spiritual, next on the personal (not his, but yours), and last on the material. You'll be better disposed in a small house with a smile and few worries, than in a large house, but lonely and full of stress. Don't forget this.)

What is Nice to Have, but Doesn't Matter:

These are the problem characteristics because, if you find a guy who has them, you might be tempted to overlook some of his weaknesses from the first list. Pass over those boys…it's only going to be trouble.

Wealth

Health

Good looks

Athleticism

Exceptional intelligence

Social grace

Popularity

Caroline, the love of the moment will score well on this last score card, but you will be lucky if he becomes the love of your life, and often he will have to grow into it. Use the first scorecard for the love of your life. Let these last guys take you to dinner and make you smile occasionally, but don't make a habit of it, because, like alcohol, drugs, and other highly pleasurable sensations, it can become addictive.

I love you dearly.

Love,

Uncle Paul

PS: I left off maybe the most important one. Even if you choose a man who is perfect in every other way, if you and he are not at the same place spiritually, it will be difficult, and it carries with it a special burden. In 1 Corinthians 7:12-14, the Bible says, "To the rest I say—I and not the Lord—that if any believer has a wife who is an unbeliever, and she consents to live with him, he should not divorce her. And if any woman has a husband who is an unbeliever, and he consents to live with her, she should not divorce him. For the unbelieving husband is made holy through his wife, and the unbelieving wife is made holy through her husband." Many couples mature at different rates, and there is no helping that, but there is a special burden in yoking yourself to someone who does not mature at all, and you should be sure it is one you are willing to bear.

*   *   *

I ate dinner with Alexander and Julia, and she did give me a verse. "If we say that we have no sin, we deceive ourselves, and the truth is not in us." 1 John 1:7. She must have felt it was important, because the next day, she gave me the next two consecutive verses. "If we confess our sins, he who is faithful and just will forgive us our sins and cleanse us from all unrighteousness." And, "If we say that we have not sinned, we make him a liar, and his word is not in us." She liked Curt no more than I did, but she took the high road, and she was encouraging me to do the same. I wonder sometimes, if I had been different that fall, might things have worked out differently? It's a question I've never answered, but is one of my favorites to chew on, especially around holidays when I see Hope and I'm reminded of her sister and all she was to me.

I loved that fall. I spent hundreds of hours with Alexander, Julia and Caroline—all during the day, of course. In the evenings, Alexander and Julia would find a space to spend time alone, and Caroline would disappear with Curt. The two relationships couldn't have been any more different. Curt hardly spoke to Caroline, except to disappear with her, or drag her along to cheer for him in one of his soccer or basketball games. I was her friend, her companion, and often her confidante. Curt fulfilled other needs, and, in my eyes at least, preyed on her insecurities.

Julia and Alexander, on the other hand, made it clear the target of their relationship was marriage, and this period was a pleasant, enjoyable testing period. "I get to kiss her only once each day, as we say goodnight," Alexander told me. "It is the sweetest thing I can imagine, like a beacon carrying me through each day." It sounded so corny, and yet I was insanely jealous of him.

One Friday night, when Alexander was away for a debate tournament, Julia found me typing away at a computer terminal. The computer lab was empty except for me. She came up behind me and started massaging my shoulders. "What was your verse from lunch?" she asked.

"'But I am not ashamed, for I know the one in whom I have put my trust, and I am sure that he is able to guard until that day what I have entrusted to him.' 2 Timothy 1:11," I said.

"That has earned you a backrub," she said, and began kneading the tight spot at the base of my neck. I leaned forward and touched my forehead to the computer screen as she worked her fingers, then palms and then elbows in small circles in a slow rhythm across my back. Each body part took me to a new level of relaxation, and when she used her fingers to tickle behind my ears as a signal she was finished, I let out a deep sigh.

I sat up slowly, and leaned back. To my surprise, rather than coming around to my side to talk to me, her arms slipped around my neck in a warm, gentle hug, and I felt her face smooth next to my cheek. Her cross dangled cold against my neck.

"Mmmmmm," she said in a low, husky voice. "I'm glad I found you."

"Me too," I said, and with one hand, I tickled the dewy fur covering her soft, freckled arm. I leaned my neck into her head, and we stayed there for longer than we should have.

"Have you ever wanted to be really, really bad?" she asked me, her voice flowing wetly across my cheek.

"I do—I mean, I have," I said, then smiled and breathed a quick laugh through my nose. "Busted," I said.

She pulled away. "Me too. Your verse for today, and mine, is James 1:12, 'Blessed is anyone who endures temptation. Such a one has stood the test and will receive the crown of life that the Lord has promised to those who love him.'" She stood, and when I turned around the flush in her face created amazing, sensual images in my mind. Unfortunately, her partner in those images was Alexander, as it should be. I stood also.

She turned around, and I admired the curls of her hair. She did something in her front, and then when she turned around again, she held a small crucifix in her hand between her breasts, held by a loop of chain that disappeared inside her shirt. I reached forward and took the crucifix in my hands studying the detail of the man on the cross. As I held it, I felt the gentle pulling on the ends of the chain from her breasts. I let go, and it slipped back between the buttons of her shirt and disappeared.

She took my hand and pulled. "Walk me back to my dorm," she said, and I did. We didn't talk, and when I turned to go, she slipped her arms around my neck and I felt her slender body against mine as she whispered into my ear, "Thank you," and kissed me gently on the neck.

I can remember that kiss today, and when times are bad and I stop believing in the potential for man to sustain goodness within him, I close my eyes and can feel her lips, warm and wet, nibble a bit of flesh at the tip of my neck, just behind my ear.

* * *

Fall grew chillier and took on some of the milder features of winter, and I grew restless. Caroline and Julia both loved me, and took to introducing me to a steady stream of cute, nice girls, most of whom would have passed my meager list of girlfriend criteria without trying. I made several good friends, but, as we began to say, "They didn't take."

Sports at the School of Science and Math were a little haphazard. We had no football team, and though we had a basketball team, we had no gym, and so played a schedule with no home games. Daniel, a friend in the next dorm, lobbied hard to start a wrestling team, and managed to get the School to chip in for a mat. We cleaned up a storage room in the basement of Wyche and cut the mat into a hodgepodge of pieces to cover the floor and a few feet up each of the columns scattered throughout the room. Eleven of us showed up on the first day for practice, and three quit the first week. Four weeks later, eight of us showed up for our first match. We were self-coached, and three of the eight, including Alexander, had never wrestled before.

Alexander, though not large, was the third largest person on the team, and because our heavyweight rarely showed up for practice, he and I sparred with each other frequently. That fall and winter we began a practice of taking out our frustrations on each other on the mat, which we continued for the next two years, and occasionally when he visited in college. Alexander, a deliberate and pondering wrestler, would have a rather poor wrestling career on the varsity team at Yale. I wrestled completely differently, helter-skelter by wit and luck, and usually relying on adrenaline in the third period to bridge out of a pin, or grind my opponent into one.

Our styles showed up in the first match, against Wilmington Country Day. Our "heavyweight," who could qualify for the 185 pound weight class, chose to wrestle up against their true heavyweight, a slow tub of Crisco whom he beat easily. That left me the choice of wrestling up to 185, or sticking at my normal class, 167 lbs. I found out my opponent at 167 was ranked number 1 in the state private school league, and planned to wrestle up to 185, also, when Alexander came up to me and said, "My opponent won the State Tournament last year. Though I welcome the challenge, Daniel advises me to wrestle at 185."

"Dan should tell you to take your lumps—the guy will outweigh you by 30 lbs."

Dan walked up behind us. "You can take the guy at 167, Peter. He's a one move wonder—likes to bear hug you and squeeze the life out of you." I'd seen his biceps and shoulders, and had no doubt he could do just that.

"I'd rather pass," I said. "Let him squeeze the life out of Alexander."

Dan took my arm and pulled me aside. "Look, we can win this match if just one of the two of you wins. Alexander will get caught in this guy's hug and get creamed, but he has a chance against the redneck at 185. Your chances are about even either way."

"Okay," I said, and Alexander and I stepped together onto the mat to walk through a few moves and warm up.

Mr. Number-One-Ranked had baby smooth skin stretched tightly over an ironclad jaw, and his bones rang thick with meaty muscles I felt sure could squeeze every ounce of gumption out of me. We stepped onto the mat, and the referee blew the whistle. I danced and played hand games for the first minute, trying hard to stay out of his grasp, and then we were both whistled for a stalling warning. I managed to grab a leg in a takedown attempt without getting caught, but he slipped away before I got control, and we finished the first round on our feet.

I started the next round on top, and by using both arms and one leg managed to get one of his arms out from under him, and forced his cheek to the mat. Then came the fun part, as I placed my forehead into the base of his shoulder, and drove it with all my weight into the mat. After a minute of this, I was flagged for stalling, and he got a point and we went back to the center of the mat. He escaped, and I scored a quick takedown before the buzzer sounded to end the period tied. I had managed to stay out of his arms for two periods, but I was exhausted, and he looked amused.

I kneeled and took my position in the center of the mat, and I felt his arm slip around my waist and grip my elbow, both strong and firm but barely touching me. When the whistle blew, I jumped out for an escape, but he caught my ankle and stopped me. I flexed my whole body like a desperate fish and managed to lift up against him, using one leg to stand, and the other held firmly against my bottom. This could only last a second, and so I did another fish-flip desperation move, and turned to face him as we both fell out of bounds. I got a point for an escape, and we went back to the center.

He did get me into his arms as the clock ticked down, and I could feel the world drift away as his muscles flexed against the efforts of my diaphragm. He nearly killed me, but didn't get behind me, and I won the match three to two.

I lay flat on my back breathing heavily as Alexander wrestled his opponent, a furry redneck with a pot belly, but still thirty pounds heavier than poor Alexander, who looked a little uncomfortable without his briefcase and jacket. On his fourth attempt at a single leg takedown, Alexander was able to bring Sasquatch to his belly. He put all his weight on the center of his back, and began to walk his leg around and then, at the end of the first period, executed a near perfect half nelson, pinning the confused redneck just as the clock ticked its last ticks.

We won the match, one of four team wins that year. I finished dead even at .500, and Alexander a little better at .588. Our practice-less heavyweight won nearly all his matches and went on to lose a bitterly fought semi-final match at the State Tournament.

*   *   *

I agonized daily over my love for both Caroline and Julia, and awoke some nights gnashing my teeth. Dealing with it was easy, though, as I was falling behind in several classes, and finding out quickly that the level of competition for good grades was like nothing I had experienced in tiny Hendersonville. I turned to my schoolwork to escape from these contradictions of the heart—I wasn't mature enough to try to deal with them, so I left them behind. I still studied each afternoon with both of them, but in the evenings, rather than find my own woman to love, I found my balcony in the 1908 building and watched the romances unfold in the cool nights below me.

One night, early in the year, I had gotten up to use the bathroom at some untoward hour, and as I opened the door, saw a figure slip into the kitchen at the end of the hall. I padded slowly down the hall and found Mike hiding behind the kitchen door.

"Oh, hi Peter," he said, looking somewhat relieved.

"What are you doing up?" I asked.

"I don't like the alarms on this door," he said. "Come here. See this chip—that's a DSP logic chip which accepts a signal ..." He went on to explain the entire circuitry. "... and the problem is this detector, which can be fooled by just covering the sensor in aluminum foil. Now a much better method would be to—"

"Wait. Mike, did you say the sensor could be fooled by covering it with aluminum foil?"

"Of course. It just needs to detect an eddy current of sufficient magnitude to—"

"Show me."

"—give a logical one which it sends on to the DSP chip—"

"Show me."

"I can't."

"Why?"

"I don't have any aluminum foil."

"We're in the kitchen, Mike. Let's find some."

We found some in the cabinet under the sink, and Mike took a two inch square piece, folded it in half "... to make sure we get enough eddy current ..." and slipped it in next to the detector. He then opened the door casually, and we looked out on the night air, which had been forbidden by this electronic watchdog from curfew until five thirty each morning.

"Mike, this is great," I said.

"I know. I'm going to recommend a double redundant magnetic circuit relying on—"

"Let me know if they implement anything."

"—the frequency response of a ferrite—"

"Let me know if they put anything in, okay?"

"Sure, Peter."

I spoke with him a week later on the porch of our dorm.

"Anything change with our little secret?" I asked.

"No. They really liked my new design, and are setting up a review at Interlogic, the manufacturers who happen to be here in the Triangle—"

"But they're not going to use it?"

"No, they said it was too expensive, and besides it's just to keep high school students from getting into too much trouble."

I smiled inwardly, and decided to let him tell me about all sorts of locks, both electrical and mechanical. He even taught me how to pick a few.

*   *   *

Caroline and Julia introduced me to girls from their dormitory, from their classes, from Caroline's swim team, and from Julia's Bible study. Most of the introductions were casual—a conversation at a dance, someone joining us to study, or sitting with us at the craperteria. Every now and then, when I was particularly lonely or one of these girls was particularly desperate, a real date would evolve. Dates were limited to going to the movies at nearby North Gate Mall, or getting a sundae at the ice cream shop on 9th Avenue, as none of the students at NCSSM are allowed access to cars on campus.

One Friday night, after working hard all week and finishing my last mid term after lunch, I stopped to throw Frisbee with the crowd outside Wyche. After a half hour, I walked, sweaty and hot, down the hall to my room, then collapsed onto my bed with a new science fiction novel I'd been saving. Julia had invited a friend from her American Literature class to go to a movie with us, and I'd forgotten.

I get angry when I think back to this night. It was the first night I'd met Kevin, Caroline's first husband, and my feelings have not changed since that night.

We were to get pizza at the mall at seven, then see an eight o'clock movie. At five till seven, Alexander opened the door to find me leaning against a wad of dirty clothes, heavily entranced in a paperback with the picture of an interplanetary cruiser on the front. The book was *Ender's Game* by Orson Scott Card, and it remains one of my favorites to this day.

"Ready to go?" he asked. I didn't look up, or make any sign of recognition. He pulled the book down and said again, "Ready to go?"

I shook my head. "I'm staying here—you guys go without me."

He surprised me by saying okay, and turned to leave. I went back to my novel. A second later his foot slammed into my hand painfully and sent the novel flying across the room. Alexander marched over, picked up the book, and turned to leave. He stopped at the door and said, "You can get this from Lindsey at the pizza place in a half hour. Get cleaned up, and hurry." He paused before shutting the door, "I'll save you a slice."

My hand smarted, pulsing embarrassment flowing through my cartilage, but it did knock me back into reality. I wish I could explain what my mind did back then. I studied, nonstop, for seven days. Morning, noon and night is a poor cliché, but wholly accurate. And after the test, when all the knowledge jammed in my head came rushing out, my mind went into hibernation, and an escape like Ender's Game was exactly what I needed. However, dates back then were rare enough for me that I couldn't skip them for a science fiction novel, and that reality came back to me through the pain in my reddened knuckles.

I hurried, and made it to the pizza place just before eight o'clock. They were all there, jabbering and laughing and the aroma seduced my appetite out of its wrestling-induced hibernation. Two empty pizza tins sat in the center of the table, crusts scattered on greasy paper plates. One slice was wrapped in napkins in front of Lindsey. Then I noticed there were no empty chairs, and sitting in the seat next to Lindsey, my date, was a tall, thin boy with ruddy blond hair. My paperback was nowhere to be seen.

I met Caroline's eyes, and she gave me a sad, sorrowful look. I got the drift, and said, "Lindsey, I guess I goofed. Can you forgive me?"

Lindsey looked up, anger red and hot on her face. Before she said anything, Curt said, "Peter, bud! You got to learn how to treat a lady. What kind of boy are you? You forgot a date 'cause you're reading science fiction trash? Clean up, man, or get out! Isn't that right, Dog?"

"I hear ya," said the ruddy blond boy.

"Nice, Curt," I said. "Thanks for the tip. Now if you don't mind, I'm in the middle of apologizing, and I'm about to ask for another chance. Could you mind your own business?"

"Another chance? Dog here's replaced you, dude," said Curt, then he knocked fists with the blond boy.

"Replaced?" I turned to the blond boy, "I don't have a bone to pick with you, Kevin, but it's time for you to leave." The blond boy looked from Peter to Lindsey, who nodded, then stood up.

"See you, dudes," he said. Then, to Lindsey, "Another time?" She smiled and he walked away.

"Don't worry, Dog, we'll find you another bitch," Curt yelled at him as he walked away. Kevin raised his hand and half turned his head, then turned the corner.

"I could never date him," said Caroline.

"Why's that?" asked Alexander.

"The nickname. He's 'Dog', so his girlfriend's always going to be 'Bitch'. I couldn't do it."

"Me neither," said Julia.

I looked at Curt. "Stay out of this, okay?" he said.

There was a moment of silence. I turned to Lindsey with a soft look on my face. As I began to speak, Curt mumbled, "Sure, whatever. Just don't look around here for your book."

I wrenched back in Curt's direction, "What did you do with my book?"

Alexander spoke up, "I surrendered it to Lindsey, who let Curt see it for a minute, after which he threw it into a trash receptacle."

I took three quick steps toward Curt, and drew my hand back in anger, remembering the night in the dorm. Curt rose slightly in his chair, his eyes widening. I saw Caroline's lips tense as her eyes narrowed, and I stopped just before I reached Curt. I looked at Caroline, her face relaxed, and we locked eyes. I dropped my hands, slumped my shoulders, and turned to Lindsey, "Sorry, Lindsey." Then I turned to Curt, "Curt, you're an asshole."

I sat down in the empty seat between Lindsey and Caroline, reached across the table and took the pizza slice in one hand, and found Lindsey's hand with the other and held it. We were quiet while I finished the pizza. We left when I was done.

Caroline had remained silent during the whole confrontation.

Lindsey left to go to the bathroom a few minutes after the movie started.

I sat in silence as the movie continued. During the quiet scenes, I heard the low patter of rain on the ceiling, far above. After Lindsey's absence was painfully long, I leaned over to Alexander, "I pissed her off, huh?"

Alexander spoke softly, "I nearly had an altercation with Curt before you arrived."

"How about Caroline and Julia?"

"They both remained silent, though I believe Lindsey was not unhappy when Curt put your novel in the trash receptacle, and called his friend to take your place."

"I better go find her."

Alexander put out a restraining hand, "Give her another moment. If needed, I'll send Julia." I nodded and sat low in my seat, feeling miserable.

Several minutes later, Alexander leaned over and whispered to Julia, and she left.

Julia was gone for even longer than Lindsey. I kept looking straight ahead, wondering if I had blown another chance at having a real girlfriend. Most of the others had been polite, but not interested. Lindsey, at least, might have been interested if I hadn't been such a jerk.

Almost halfway through the movie, Julia came back. She looked past Alexander to me, "I found her—she'll be back in a minute. You'd better be nice."

I sucked in a huge breath and let it out slowly, my eyes jerking around the room looking for Lindsey's fluffy brown hair.

Eventually, she appeared, carrying her pocketbook and a small bag.

She sat down next to me, and I felt rain wet on the back of her hand as she took mine in hers. Her head drifted onto my shoulder, and she picked up the small bag with her free hand and placed it in my lap. Inside the bag was a copy of my book. "It was a little gross in the dumpster, so I bought a new one. Promise not to read it until after curfew, okay?"

With one hand on the book, the other holding Lindsey's, I kissed her on the side of the head and said, "I promise." I didn't see her tears so much as smell them, then touched her cheek lightly with the side of my finger and wiped one away.

*　　*　　*

I can't pinpoint the day, or even the week, that Faith was conceived, though I know now it was sometime between Thanksgiving and Christmas break. From my perch on the balcony of the 1908 building, I saw Caroline and Curt on walks either toward or away from the woods behind Wyche. I know many couples sought rare private moments walking hand in hand, or leaning up against a tree, kissing and speaking sweet nothings. I also know, by rumor only, a few sought more passionate moments at the nearby Carolina-Duke motel, though from the look of the place, the ambiance would be anything but conducive.

After Thanksgiving, after Lindsey and I had been on a few dates but not yet kissed, she and Julia decided to visit Julia's family for a weekend. That left Alexander and me without distractions, and the thought of actual company lured me away from my nocturnal study.

The evening started innocuously, first at the arcade, and then with a bucket of buttered popcorn at an action movie. Had Julia been along, she would have let us enjoy neither the action movie nor the popcorn, so we felt absurdly naughty already. Little did we know what the night had in store.

*　　*　　*

We got back to campus too late to order a pizza, but still very hungry.

"Think the craperteria is still open?" I asked. All juniors were required to work either in the cafeteria or on the grounds, and some

113

worked late. Alexander worked in the cafeteria, mostly cleaning dishes and the kitchen after meals.

"They close at nine thirty," Alexander said. "But I have heard it is possible to make a surreptitious entry through an elevator in the rear of the kitchen."

I was startled. My stomach had a pale ache I knew would be an angry growl as I tried to go to sleep. "I'd love a sandwich," I said. "Do you know how to get in?"

The elevator went to the Math Department on the third floor, and the Biology and Chemistry Departments on the second floor. Since those places were not illegal after hours, the elevator was left working, though the door to the cafeteria was locked on the ground floor. Alexander led the way to Bryan Hall and up the stairs to the Biology Department. We turned down the hall toward the elevator. The hall reached a tee; to the left was the elevator, and to the right, a small alcove leading to a teacher's office. As we approached, I heard rustling of cloth in the alcove on the right. At the corner, I turned and looked.

Two students had carried a chair from the lounge and were kissing passionately. I caught a glimpse of a shirtless, bra-less shoulder. Alexander said, "Let's depart."

My stomach whined, and I grabbed Alexander's arm and turned toward the elevator and said, "Wait—they don't even know we're here."

A voice rose out of the alcove, cocky and sure, "We know you're there, Peter Bennett, we just don't care." It was Curt's voice. Caroline giggled, "Hi Pete. Be good and don't look."

"I won't," I said. Alexander tugged at my shirt sleeve. I pushed the button for the elevator, and seconds later, we were inside and headed down. The doors didn't open at the bottom. I studied the elevator door, puzzled, and then saw the keyhole was a lock with three pins, one Mike had taught me about. We went back up. When we were out of earshot of the affectionate couple, I said, "Wait here," and took off in a jog.

I returned carrying a wire coat hanger and two paper clips. "Come on," I said and tugged Alexander down the hall. We approached the tee where Caroline and Curt engaged in their Nubian frolic, and I said, "Hi Caroline—we're back. Don't mind us—we'll be gone in sec."

Curt's whisper strained over the back of the chair, "Now is not the time!"

Caroline rose slowly until we could see her over the back of the chair, first just her head, then her shoulders and then even more. Her skin, smooth and virginal, sloped gently down to her breasts, which were barely hidden below the chair back. One hand reached down and moved in a slow rhythm, "Hi Pete," she said, "what are you guys doing here? Not spying, I hope." Curt moaned softly.

I locked eyes with her. I wished she would move up a few more inches; wished I were Curt, but also wished nothing like this was happening. It was out of cadence with how I thought of Caroline, and yet irresistibly desirable, I felt an overpowering need to get away and not a small urge to vomit. "No," I said, "Just breaking into the cafeteria to steal some sandwiches."

"I won't tell if you don't," she said. Her hand continued to move. She lifted herself up, giving both Alexander and me a full view of her petite, proud, bosoms. She smiled at us, her one dimple and her mussed hair enchantingly erotic.

Alexander pulled himself away first. He tugged me toward the elevator. When we reached the bottom, I fed the coat hanger through a small hole in the elevator door, bending it as I fed it in, and using a paperclip to engage the pins. I struggled to concentrate as I thought of the sounds above us.

Finally, I angled the coat hanger correctly, and the doors opened. The coat hanger stuck in the open door, but I could see through to the cafeteria. We made two PBJs each, and then headed back up. As we passed by, I said, "See ya Caroline. Don't miss curfew." There was no reply, and the earlier noises had abated. The elevator doors shut, leaving the coat hanger dangling inside.

* * *

First Time You Make Love

"Pretty women endure this abuse all the time. They are pursued, but not really; they are wanted, but only superficially. They learn to offer their bodies but never, ever their souls. Most men, you see, marry for safety;

they choose a woman who will make them feel like a man but never really challenge them to be one."

John Eldridge, *Wild at Heart*

Dearest Caroline,

Today, as I write, you are four years old. It's late here, so I'm sure you are sleeping soundly and safely in your bed, surrounded by your family. Your father is asleep several yards away from you, ready to protect you from any danger. As you read this you have stepped into a new and wonderful, and yet potentially dangerous part of your life. You have gone somewhere your father may not be able to protect you.

Keep reading, Caroline. There isn't a moralistic lesson in here. I haven't lived the life that would allow me to preach to you. You have not done anything evil. What you have done is just what you were made to do. I have for you a very important lesson, and then a question.

The lesson is very simple; three words. You are precious. You are a wonderful, beautiful, special and tender woman, and you deserve to be treasured above anything else in a man's life, save the Lord. That's the whole message. Any man who doesn't have that engraved in the core of his being doesn't deserve you. If your new lover doesn't, then get rid of him, and wait for one who does.

My history of lovemaking is not a good one. It's filled with my pursuit of wild desires, of me attaching my ego to success in a sexual arena. I wanted a woman who, by being at my side, would make me a man. Ironically, the women who could challenge me to be a man wouldn't have me because I was no man worth having. I was a boy, searching vainly for my manhood between the legs of strange women.

Several years ago, I fell for a woman who wanted to save her virginity until she was married. I loved her, yet felt she invalidated me by disallowing me to penetrate her most vulnerable parts. I wanted to possess her, to own her, to score her. She insisted, instead, that I treasure her. We broke up after only a few months, but her insistence remained with me. I decided to learn how to treasure a woman. I quit dating, and began to search for my manhood. I found it, not in the arms of a woman, but on the tops of glaciated mountains, in the gym, in the pages of great novels, and, believe it or not, in conference rooms when I stood to defend what I believed in.

I'd like to say the transformation was complete, that I found my lost confidence and never again searched for it in unsavory places. It was not, and is not. I struggle daily, hourly, almost minutely.

Caroline, you are a precious, special woman. You are not a little girl to be protected, shielded or limited, but a woman. You deserve to be desired, to be treasured, to be held above. Don't settle for a man who won't sacrifice for you. That is the true test. The man who desires you powerfully, but will sacrifice his reward, deserves to get it. The one who wants it and will not sacrifice it cannot be trusted to handle it.

Only you can be the judge of your man, and only you the protector of your heart. So now the question: is this man, your new lover, a man who can handle a treasure like you, and still be a man? If he doesn't hold up, if he is still a boy, then throw the fish back into the pond and wait for a man to take your bait. Find yourself a man, Caroline, make him prove to you he is one, and then keep him. Don't condemn yourself if you stub your toe a couple times along the way. Many of us have and God forgave us before we did it.

I love you more than you can know. I treasure your precious soul, and all you are.

Love,
Uncle Paul

Chapter 6: Birth

Winter in the Carolinas has none of the glamour of snowy northern winters. February is a rainy month, and that year was no exception. Cold rain fell, collecting in the low areas and seeping into the dirt to form brown mud on the soles of shoes and in the entryways to the dorms and classrooms. Our socks and the cuffs of our jeans collected this mud, each day adding a new layer to the strata. Only at the end of February does the sun begin to shine, peeking shyly through ever-present gray clouds, growing stronger with each day.

At four a.m. on a Wednesday morning, Caroline rolled from sleeping on her left side to her right. She slept uneasily, one arm holding her stomach, the other under her pillow. The wrinkles in her pillow had made creases in her cheek, visible on her face, which, even in sleep, was tense. She slept in one of Curt's flannel shirts and flannel boxers. A fuzzy, abused teddy bear lay on the bed behind her, where she had been holding it before she rolled over.

Caroline pulled in to a fetal position, drawing her legs up to her abdomen, holding her stomach now with both hands. One eye opened and she moaned softly, first drawing close then laying back, stretching onto her back and grimacing with obvious discomfort. She swung her legs over the edge of the bed and quietly sat up. Slowly, uneasy in the early morning semi-consciousness, she stood and walked to the door. She watched Julia, sleeping soundly in satin pajamas, as she creaked the door open and slipped into the hall.

Her bare feet padded softly on the cold tile as she walked down the hall, her arms holding Curt's flannel shirt tightly. She opened the door to the bathroom, entered a stall and sat down. She acted to relieve the discomfort in her lower abdomen, but was overcome by the discomfort, and lowered her head into her arms, where it remained through several forceful spasms. When she felt better, she reached for the toilet paper. She was disappointed; the toilet paper came up with no redness on it. Her eyes wrinkled in aggravation. When she stood and pulled up her flannel boxers, she was disorientated and had to lean on the door.

She left the stall slowly, and walked to the sink where she looked in the mirror. Her hair was a mess, falling in tangles about her shoulders. She squinted as she ran the water, washing her hands and splashing her face. One hand held tightly to the sink for balance. She went for paper towels and before she got there, a wave of nausea hit her and she turned into a stall, dropping to her knees and throwing up violently, emptying her abdomen from the other end in wrenching spasms.

The spasms came and went as her dinner flowed from her mouth into the waiting pool of water. Her wrenching grew empty, and then later subsided. She arose feeling better. She again washed her hands and face in the sink, this time standing straight. She dried herself then returned to the sink and looked hard at her reflection in the mirror.

She was sixteen years old. Her hair was messy, her face pillow-wrinkled. She was wearing the shirt of a boy she was sure didn't love her for anything she wanted to give, but rather for what she could do for him. Her body, while lovely and strong, was nowhere near full development. A tear rolled from the corner of her eye, seeming to drop straight from her scar. She was pregnant.

*   *   *

Winter at the School was a time for diligence and persistence. Noses were held tightly to slowly spinning grindstones; knowledge was forced through capillary walls as if under the pressure of a deep sea. Studying and grades were all important and all other activities rode second saddle. Dances, in particular, were sparsely attended in the winter as students spent their time studying, alone with their boyfriend or girlfriend, or in small groups of friends at the movies or in the dorm lounges.

There was a dance the Friday after Caroline discovered her pregnancy. This one was held in the wide hallway outside the cafeteria. I went to the dance out of boredom, my 1908 balcony having grown cold and lonely. Lindsey and Curt had both signed out to their homes, though Curt lived in Raleigh and signing out was an excuse to go get his car. Alexander and Julia were at the movies, and Caroline was unaccounted for. I watched the bodies go left and right, sometimes with the music, sometimes following a beat of their own. In the winter, the dances were for students like me, with nowhere else to go.

Caroline walked in at the far end. She turned left and right, standing on tip-toes, until finally she met my eyes. She walked directly toward me, through the dance floor populated by slowly swaying couples.

Her hands were cold and hard as she took mine and pulled me backwards onto the dance floor. She wore blue jeans and a NCSSM sweatshirt with a unicorn on the chest. She wore no makeup, and her eyes were red and swollen. She pulled her body close to mine, both arms holding my shoulders tightly, her face a nascent torpedo in my chest. I held her and we swayed slowly. I smelled the fragrance of her hair and got lost in the closeness, the desperation of her grip. The dance went on and on.

When the music ended, she squeezed me hard, kissed my chest and said "Thank you" into my shirt. I kissed the top of her head, "Anytime." As she pulled away, she took my hand and pulled me. "Do you have time?" she asked. "I need to talk."

"Yeah," I said quietly. I felt the cool sweat of her hand, strong but soft, in mine. We walked to the stairs and dropped hands, then climbed one floor and turned down the Math hallway. She pulled me into the alcove across from the elevator where Alexander and I had seen her with Curt. A chair was there, empty except for a teddy bear leaning awkwardly against the arm rest.

"I came here to think but got tired of crying alone." She climbed over the back of the chair, taking my hand and pulling me with her. She pushed me down, and then sat on my lap sideways, like a little girl. She picked up her teddy bear and curled almost into a fetal position. Her arm around me, she leaned her face against my chest and held the teddy bear tightly. I remained silent.

"This is where it happened." She said quietly.

"What?" I asked.

"Be quiet and I'll tell you," she said.

I tensed my lips and spoke very slowly. "If Curt did anything to you, I will kill him." The words were soft but determined.

"I did it to myself, Peter. Just be quiet for a minute."

I brushed her hair gently away from her face, waiting for her to continue.

"I'm pregnant," she said.

The words hung in the air like the cloud of chalk after cleaning chalkboard erasers, leaving the same dry taste in both of our mouths. Our breathing was deep and loud, each breath bringing new dryness to coat our lips and tongues and the backs of our throats. I slipped my hand behind her neck and pulled her head into my chest. I kissed the top of her head.

"Did it happen the night we saw you?" I could still see Caroline's shirtless shoulders rising up above the chair. That image, which first caused such jealousy, now scared me.

"Not that night, but it could have been any night afterwards."

"When is it due?"

"I don't know." Her voice was soft, and muffled through my sweatshirt. "It happened in December, maybe January. So, maybe August or September."

"How do you feel?"

"I'm sick some mornings. I get dizzy. I cry sometimes. Like now."

I brushed a tear off her cheek and felt the smoothness and warm wetness of her skin. "Do you love Curt?"

"No." Her answer came without hesitation.

"Who else knows?"

"Just you, Curt and Uncle Paul. I have a doctor's appointment next week. Uncle Paul set it up."

"What are you going to do?"

"I don't know!" she said, her voice high and squeaky. She started crying hard, the sobs shaking her shoulders. She held me, sobbing, then dropped her teddy bear and hit me on the chest, making a hollow, echoing thump. "Why me?" she whined in her crying and hit my chest again. I just held her, and tried not to let her hurt me.

I held her close until the crying subsided, stroking her hair and kissing the top of her head. I knew the night before we came to this school I had made a mistake with my silence. As I held her, I felt it was my fault she was pregnant, that by not speaking the night after we kissed, I had let her go down this path that could lead nowhere other than where she was. I vowed never to let that happen again, not to Caroline or to anyone else. When I spoke, it was deliberately.

"You know I love you, Caroline."

"I know you do, Pete. I love you, too." We sat in silence for a moment. "Do you remember the morning after Curt and I first hooked up? You were right. You were here before he showed up, and you're here after he's gone."

I loosened my arms and pulled slightly away, then lifted her chin so she looked me in the eyes. I saw sadness in her eyes, yet I also saw every happy moment we shared, every bike ride, every kiss, every time I looked deep into those sea blue eyes to see the clouds reflecting in them. My words were as smooth and sweet as banana pudding. "Caroline, I want to be here forever. Will you marry me?"

She looked at me hard, the tears flowing again, then frowned and broke into a crazy one-dimpled crying smile and said, "No." She paused to see how I reacted, and then added, "But thank you," and her lips came up to mine. She kissed me, first tenderly, sweetly, like our kisses had been two years before. I kissed back, and slowly her mouth opened and her tongue found mine. I let my hand drift around her shoulders, and both of her arms slipped around my neck. We kissed, not passionately, but lovingly.

Eventually, I turned my head, still kissing, and looked at my watch. I pulled away, "Ten minutes till curfew." She snuggled my neck, and I said, "That's the best proposal rejection I've ever had."

"How many girls have you proposed to, Peter?" she asked, laughing.

"Just you." I held her in silence. "Lindsey's going to be mad about this."

"I hope it was worth it."

"Depends on how it works out."

"You were supposed to say, 'Boy howdy, was that ever worth it!'"

"Boy howdy, was that ever worth it!" I said. I looked into her eyes. "I'd raise it as my own, you know. If you'd let me."

"I know you would, Peter. I'm not ready yet, okay?"

"Okay," I said. "We'd better get back. I'm around if you need me, Caroline. I won't tell. I don't know what I'll tell Lindsey."

"Don't tell her the truth yet, okay?"

"Okay."

Slowly, we disentangled ourselves from each other and stood up. I dragged the chair back out into the lounge, and then walked Caroline to her dorm in silence. I hugged her good-bye, but as I leaned down to kiss her, she turned away and said, "Not here," and squeezed my hand.

*　　*　　*

I stepped outside and breathed a deep bite of cold winter air and stepped the first few steps toward Wyche Hall. I was going to be alone tonight, and I looked forward to it. I wanted to lie in my bed and pray to my God and whisper to him all the things I had experienced in the last two hours. I wasn't sure if my God was the same God Julia talked about and Alexander studied. I only knew that I felt—, that I knew I was—, created, and for me to be created, then there must be a Creator. The rest I would have to learn with time, and I felt sure I would.

Julia had given me a verse one time, Romans 1:19-20, "For what can be known about God is plain to them, because God has shown it to them. Ever since the creation of the world his eternal power and divine nature, invisible though they are, have been understood and seen through the things he has made." There is no contradiction between the Bible and science—only human misinterpretation of the two bodies of evidence.

It was that way with Caroline, also. I knew in my heart and in my soul that my relationship with her had purpose—I knew I had been led to her to fulfill some need, to enact some change, to do something larger than the both of us. I liked my relationship with Lindsey—I liked talking with her, being with her, kissing her, and knowing she was there even when she was away—but there was no purpose to our relationship.

With these thoughts running through my mind, I walked the short, bitter cold walk across campus and mounted the steps of Wyche. I said a few short words to Chris, my RA, so he would know I wasn't drunk, and then walked down the hall to my room, intent on a half hour of meditation and eight hours of blissful sleep.

I opened my door and stepped into the room, half lit by moonlight. I shut the door, and as I reached for the light, a voice said, "Don't turn on the light, Peter." The voice was Curt's. "Have a seat on your bed." My eyes adjusted, and I saw him leaning against the wall on Alexander's bed, feet splayed in front of him. Even in the dimly lit room, I saw his hand raised up, pointing a pistol at his own temple.

"Lock the door, and have a seat. I want to talk." I turned the lock in the door, and took three steps to my bed, then sat on the edge.

Curt lowered the gun to his lap. "Don't get any bright ideas, kid." I leaned back against the wall. Curt reached between his legs and picked up a bottle in a brown paper bag. He took a long drink from the bottle then screwed the cap on one-handed and tossed it to me. "Have a drink, kid. It'll do you some good."

The bottle sloshed when I caught it, and I felt it's warmth in my hands. *Wild Turkey. What the hell.* I unscrewed it slowly, and then took a long drink. It was hot on my throat and in my stomach and burned where moments before the outside air had frozen.

"I saw you dance with my girl tonight, Peter." Curt was calm, and his bitter calmness made me believe he just might kill himself, right there on Alexander's dry cleaned sheets and comforter. For a second, I had an image of a blood splattered carcass growing cold on Alexander's bed, and I smiled. Then I saw Curt, drunk with a gun in his hand, and realized this wasn't the right time to smile. I remembered Curt knew about Caroline.

"Yeah. Look Curt, she's a good friend. This isn't easy…"

"Cut the crap, huh?" Curt barked. He paused before he spoke again. "You know the funny part, Peter, the part that kills me?"

I opened the bottle again and sighed. "No," I said, and took another drink.

"I never loved her, Pete. I'm the father of some peanut-sized kid, who I'm gonna pay to kill, and there's no way I'd spend the rest of my life with Caroline."

I waited to see if more came, but it didn't. I spoke softly, "I proposed to Caroline tonight. I'll raise your kid if she lets me, Curt. We won't tell anyone. Nobody'll know but us three."

"I said cut the crap!" yelled Curt, and he raised the gun to his temple and it shook with his rage. He sat there and I watched the gun shake and the blood pour through the veins on his forehead and I knew in an instant he could turn his brains into a casserole. I was terrified and I only watched. This was another moment, one in which I could choose to step in and change the course of events, and thinking of how I felt about Curt, and what he had done, I chose to pass. In a moment, I saw the blood stop surging through his temples, and the gun lowered just an inch. He crinkled the empty bag in his lap with his free hand. "Take another swig, and then toss me the bottle." I did. Curt opened the bottle and took a long drink, and the gun, still pointed just above his right ear, stopped shaking.

When he finished, he dried his mouth on his wrist and closed the bottle. He threw it back to me. Then he said, "I know you'd do it. You're a better person than me, kid. That's why I'm such scum. I'm eighteen, and I ain't gonna marry some girl I don't love. I never loved her. I just *wanted* her. Hell, Pete, there were days when I didn't even *like* her. Days when I avoided her so I didn't have to see her. She was just a prize, a trophy." Curt sniffed lightly, and it was obvious he was crying.

"Hey Curt," I said. I had changed my mind about stepping in, about saying something that could change the course of events.

"What, kid?"

"Don't kill yourself over this."

Curt's hand, holding the gun to his temple this whole time, fell a few inches, and then dropped into his lap. "No, kid, I don't think I will. But I gotta change. I gotta find someone I can love like you love her. Then I gotta be good to her. That's what I gotta do." He reached into his lap and found a second paper bag, with another bottle of Wild Turkey in it. He opened it and turned it up. "I was counting on you tonight, kid." He twisted the cap onto the bottle, then off again, opening the bottle.

Curt leaned his head back and took another swig of whiskey. He swallowed, and then leaned forward, lowering the bottle from his face. "Peter, you won't understand this. Right now, after all that's happened, after all that's gone wrong. I love Caroline now, Pete. Now it's too late. I love her.

"Take care of her, Pete. She never deserved me, or this. I wish I'd known her like you did—I might have loved her. She was never like that to me."

"Only because you never looked, Curt. She's always been like that.

You just didn't notice."

"I know. I gotta go. You want the bottle?" Curt got up to leave.

"No. But I want the bullets."

* * *

Curt left, and I was motionless in my bed. I heard a pat pat on the window as a gentle rain began and watched it pour down the window in wide sheets. The bullets were warm where I had been holding them, and their metallic smell was sweet to my nostrils. My mind was too numb to meditate, to numb to pray, and for an hour I watched the rain and played with the bullets, turning them over and over between my fingers.

At one a.m., I rose from my bed slowly, sitting up. I grabbed my blue jean jacket, and put the bullets in my pocket. I opened the door silently and looked out into the dark hall, lit at both ends by small emergency lights. I walked to the rear of the building, and ducked into the kitchen for some foil. The sign above the door said, "Emergency Exit Only, Alarm Will Sound." I placed the foil, and then opened the door and walked down the stairs of the fire escape.

Out in the night, the rain fell on my head and shoulders. My hair quickly soaked and water ran cold down my scalp. I walked away from the School, toward Walltown and the donut shop on the other side.

I passed through Walltown unmolested. I tossed the bullets into the trash dumpster behind the donut shop and went in. Inside were two employees, one a young white woman and the other an elderly black man. A couple talked quietly in a booth and two drunken college kids shared coffee in another booth. I sat at the bar and ordered two glazed donuts and a glass of milk. The white woman went back into the kitchen.

Serving me, the black man said, "You from the School of Science and Math?"

"That's right."

"I'm betting you ain't supposed to be out this time of night."

"I just need something to eat."

"I'm guessing you especially ain't supposed to be out this time of night after you been drinking. I'm guessing you ain't supposed to be drinking at all."

"Right. But I wasn't supposed to get much sleep tonight, either, so here I am."

"Something keeping you up besides the rain? Where'd you get the drink?" The white woman came back, bringing coffee to the couple in the booth.

I judged him to be an honest man. "I came back to my room, and my best friend's boyfriend had a gun to his head and a bottle of liquor in his lap. We got drunk and I talked him out of killing himself."

The black man said, "Some nights you aren't supposed to sleep much, are you?"

"Some nights," I said.

"Why'd he want to kill his self?" the black man asked.

"She's pregnant with his baby."

"You don't have to tell me anymore if you don't want to."

"I don't. I hope you can keep this secret."

"I can do that. You sit and eat all the donuts you want. There's more in back. When you get ready to go, you bring some back to your friend, but don't tell her how you got them, okay?"

"Okay."

* * *

First Time You Are Dumped

Dearest Caroline,

I know how tough this is, because it has happened to me many times. As I write this, I am thirty-two years old. Over the last sixteen years, I've dated something like a hundred women—only a few more than casually. Of those few, the dumper to dumpee ratio is pretty even. With all that, I still don't know how to do either one well. I know it hurts. I know something is ripped away, and afterwards, I have to rebuild.

You might be interested to know about your parents' love lives before they were married. They met, as I've told you, and dated several times. Both of them are right-here, right-now kind of people, and when they went to different colleges, they got "distracted". Then, when they came home, they were the best of friends, and sometimes more. Both your father and your mother had very serious relationships with other people after they met. When those relationships ended, they turned to each other for comfort, for healing, for friendship. They found a simple, reliable strength in their love for each other, the love that warmed them through many cold winters and colder summers.

A simple observation: sometimes great boyfriends don't make the best husbands. Sometimes really great husbands and fathers don't make very good boyfriends.

I heard a story on a radio talk show on the way to work today—you might get a jolt out of it right now. Today's topic was, "Forgive and Forget". A young woman called in, probably in her early twenties, and said, "There's someone I've had a very hard time forgiving, but finally did." The host asked her to tell what she had to forgive. "I had this boyfriend in high school. He was popular, the football player type. At the time, I was taking a stand for virginity, and his friends joked the only way he was going to get me into bed was to propose to me. They made a bet he wouldn't do it, and even bought a ring for me. We'd been dating a few months—I was completely enamored with him—he took me out for a nice dinner, and after the main course, proposed in a very romantic way. I said yes, and a few weeks later, gave him my virginity. Two days later, he told me the whole story, and ripped my heart out."

Some men are scum. Sometimes you don't find out until you know them better. Your heart is a precious thing, Caroline, to be guarded and defended. Make sure whoever you trust with your heart cherishes it as much as you do, as I do. When it gets ripped out and stomped flat, say a prayer, call your mother, share some ice cream with an old friend, take a jog, and then find a good thick book, and read with big belly laughs until your stomach aches. (*Catch-22* will make you laugh; *Les Miserables* will make you believe in the power of love and the goodness of a strong man.) Then go buy yourself something you've always wanted—I tended towards electronic toys, or new pens. When everyone else is tired of hearing you, and they will, come spend a weekend with me, and I'll take you canoeing on a lake at dawn and show you a part of life you can forget if you don't remember to look for it. Take care, Caroline. We all love you.

Love,
Paul

*   *   *

Caroline and I talked a lot over the next week. She told me about Curt, everything she loved about him. She told me about a dinner he had cooked for her during her dorm's intervisitation—a romantic dinner, complete with his grandmother's spaghetti sauce he'd been cooking all day. He even snuck in a real bottle of Merlot. She laughed when she talked about him, and how he made her the darling of the Senior Class as soon as they were together. To hear her tell it, I nearly began to like him.

She told me about her pregnancy, and how she found out last Wednesday morning, when she woke up sick and her period was four weeks late. We talked about abortion, and that's what she'd planned, but she had promised not to have it until Paul had a chance to spend a weekend with her. He had set up a doctor's appointment for her, and promised to take care of whatever she wanted. We talked about the other options, too, about giving it up for adoption, about raising it herself. We didn't talk about the last option, about me marrying her, and us raising the baby, but we both knew it was there. Halfway through the week, she got a hand written letter from her uncle with a check inside, and we went shopping for a new bathing suit.

*   *   *

Dearest Caroline,

Fifteen years ago, I spent a week on Maui at a conference. At the end of each day, I found somewhere to sit, relax and enjoy the sunset. The colors cascaded left and right, up and down in a maelstrom of bright colored ink. It was like a sunset you see in a painting, then say, "That guy had some imagination, because there's never been a sunset like this." Then there it was, every night. Most sunsets are a hint, a diluted watercolor, of the wonderful sunsets I found on Maui—but the splendor lives on in my head.

Last night, while resting on the Ingraham glacier, I found competition for those sunsets in the most amazing sunrise I've ever seen. I didn't take a picture, because a picture wouldn't do. It was five fifteen in the morning. I'd been climbing since two thirty, and we took a break to stuff some cold, frozen pizza down our throats. It was COLD. Sitting on a glacier is never warm, and I was covered up with a big thick parka over my Gore-tex over my fleece over my long johns over my cold damp skin. Inside my fleece my second water bottle was melting—or freezing me, one.

The glacier ran up the side of the mountain above me like a frozen blue river, glowing in light of the moon. About a thousand yards up, it turned straight uphill in a jumbled pile of ice chunks the size of office buildings, all laying on top of each other. This daiquiri blender's dream had carved a shallow valley out between two peaks, which rose to either side. A full moon shone like a single bright eye between the peaks. Below me the glacier spread out flat. To my right was Disappointment Cleaver, a huge outcropping of rock marking the edge of where the glacier had chiseled its nest.

We climbed through a storm yesterday into the clear sunshine of the afternoon. On the ground and in life I remind myself: above every storm is sunshine if you climb high enough. The glacier continued below me in a smooth sheet of ice, blue ice turning to the dull lavender of morning. It ran smoothly, imperceptibly, into the cloud which was the storm I had climbed through. The mountain was a great jagged pile of rock and ice sticking out of the smooth blue cotton glacier cloud field. In the distance, I saw the tip of Mt Washington and Mt Baker sticking out of the cloud, two more piles of rock jutting up like great God-made pyramids. The most beautiful part, the part that brought tears to my eyes, was that the very edge of the cloud was turning yellow and orange with morning.

We didn't make it to the top today, so I've still got a mountain to climb. You've got a mountain to climb, too, girl, an emotional mountain. I'm not going to take you out here to do it. I'm taking you to Maui, to watch sunsets with me. Our plane leaves on Friday at one; we'll be there just after dinner. We're coming back on the red-eye on Monday night—I cleared it with the School. We have good rooms sharing a deck, facing west so we can watch our sunsets. There is a check in here to buy a new bathing suit. We'll watch the sunsets and talk about life and yes, even climb a mountain (volcano). I'll see you Friday. Try to get ahead in your classes—NO HOMEWORK after we arrive.

I love you. We'll get you through this.
Uncle Paul

*   *   *

Caroline asked me to go with her to the doctor's office, and so we got a cab early the next Tuesday morning, and left. The doctor's office smelled...well, like a doctor's office—sterile, vaguely like freshener spray and cleaner, with a residue of unidentified but potent chemicals underneath. She signed in, and I sat down and picked up a Time magazine. They called her in quickly, and I passed the time thinking, worrying, and loving.

Caroline came out an hour later, and we stepped outside and right into a cab a nurse had called. I held her hand, and it was cold and sweaty. I let her into my side of the cab, and then sat with her, my arm around her shoulders.

She buried her head in my chest for a minute, and then looked up. "It went okay," she said. "I'm healthy, normal and very pregnant," she said, and then started to cry. The cab ride was short, so I didn't say anything else until we got there, just held her as she cried softly into my chest.

It was a school day, so when we got to school, she cleaned up and we both went to class.

Emotions come strangely in high school. They are much more powerful—maybe because they are new, or maybe because children have much more capacity for strong emotions than do adults. Maybe, as adults, we learn over the years it is safer and easier not to have strong feelings, that it makes us vulnerable, and so we suppress them and build our suburban nests around people we care about, but can live without, and people we care deeply about who can't live without us.

I don't know the reason, but I know my love for Caroline cut through my heart like the Colorado River, carving the Grand Canyon in one week. It was all-consuming in a good, generous, almost sacrificial way. I wanted to do anything, to give anything, to make any personal sacrifice if it could make her life a little bit better. I wanted to bear her load. I did the little things—I met her after class and carried her books. I took her to lunch, and to dinner. When she needed to talk, I listened. When she needed to be distracted, I entertained her. And when she needed to be alone, I left.

She left the next Friday with her uncle for a long weekend in Hawaii. He wanted to get her away, to help her make a decision. "I'm going," she told me, "because I love my uncle. But I've already made up my mind." She sighed. "I can't have this baby."

I sent a letter with her to Hawaii. "Don't open it until you get there." I said. She kissed me good-bye on the lips, a friendly, loving kiss, and said, right in front of her uncle, "I love you Peter." I said "I love you, too," and she got in the car. I knew she wouldn't open the letter until she got there, because that's exactly who she was.

*　　*　　*

Dear Caroline,

It was warm enough to play ultimate Frisbee today, and I was out there for two hours. Now I'm tired. Exercise helps me think more clearly. I may go out for the track team—it will help my grades.

Every now and then I know my actions will have a major effect on either my life or someone else's. It happened when I interviewed to get in here. Another time was when we read the book in the basement and kissed. I've had two more this week, and this letter is a third one.

A guy can tell, you know, when he kisses a girl who's been crying. All girls' mouths taste sweet just under the tongue; I don't know why. There really isn't any taste on the tops of their tongues, unless they've just eaten something, and that can be gross. On the bottom, they taste sweet. If a girl has been crying, then there is a salty flavor at the back of her mouth, on the sides of her tongue where they attach. The other night, when we kissed, your mouth tasted salty back there.

I love kissing you, Caroline. With other girls, sometimes I can't wait to get my hands going and see what I can touch. It's a contest, like a race, to see how far I can get. It's not that way with you. When my lips touch yours, every kiss we've ever had is there, and we're together again in the movie theater or Mom & Dad's basement. This weekend, when we kissed, I was in all of those places.

When you told me what happened, I couldn't let you go through it alone. When I proposed, it was a real proposal, with a real rejection, even if I didn't have a ring. I would do it, and that's what's important. There was a lot more to it, though. I have to make sure you understand that after you read this letter. I proposed to you out of love. I proposed to you because, if you're going to have this baby, then there is no way I can let you go through that without me being there by your side for every day of it. I want to enjoy all the love and sorrow and happiness and pain and everything else that comes with it. I proposed to you because, Caroline, I love you and I can't think of any better future than the one we could have together, fighting our way through college and raising your child and struggling together through everything life throws at us.

Now for the end. Caroline, my proposal was real. If you will have this baby, then please, please let me be by your side as you raise it. I want to share that with you. I beg you, Caroline. My world will never be complete if you do this alone.

I know, in the bottom of my heart, even as you struggle to decide, that you will not have this baby, that you will have an abortion. That is not the end of my world, and as your closest, most reliable friend, I will be there for you in any way you need. I know if you don't have the baby, you will never consent to marry me. You're much too independent. Please understand that is what I love about you. I love your fight, your spunkiness, your spirit and your energy. You display, like no one else I've met, the spirit and energy of a woman. I love that spirit, Caroline, and I will never try to tame it.

Here's a promise from me, and I want one from you in return. If we're both unmarried in ten years, I promise I will propose to you. I will hunt you down with a "Diamond as Big as the Ritz," and propose to you in a way you could never refuse. I want you to promise me, if you don't marry anyone else in the next ten years, to say yes. March 4th, 1998, will be our wedding day, on which we take our vows to each other.

If you kissed me now, you would taste a bit of saltiness at the sides of my tongue, in back where it attaches. Have a wonderful time in Hawaii. I'm around if you need me.

Love,
Peter

* * *

Caroline read my letter after dinner that night, in her hotel room. She had just had a long talk with her uncle. He told her about a girl he'd dated before he got married, one he fell in love with, strongly enough to change his ways. Evidently he'd spent several years as a California playboy type. But Brooke was different, and he wanted to give that up for her. But as she got to know him and understand who he had been, she grew distant and scared.

"She left him, not because of who he was when they were dating, but because of the things he did before they dated," Caroline told me. "She loved who he was, deeply and passionately, but couldn't believe he changed." This scared Caroline, to think she could be doing things now that would prevent someone who truly loved her from staying with her. "I'll never have a clean slate again," she said, "and that scared me." After she read my letter, she opened up a blank diary Hope had given her for her twelfth birthday, and began to write.

* * *

My Letter to My Future Husband
March 5th, 1988

Dear Future Husband,

I had dinner with my Uncle Paul—I'll tell you about him in a bit. We talked about the expectations a woman has of the man she will marry. If you're reading this, then you pass—but I may not—and I have to do something to make sure you, whoever you are, know what you're getting into. I hope this helps.

After dinner, I read a letter from someone I love very dearly. In it, he proposed to me. He wants to marry me, to raise a family with me. Though he is dearer to me than love itself, I can't marry him. He knows that, and loves me still. I fully expect when you read this, Peter will still be a very special friend.

Why am I writing this? It's not to throw in your face that I got proposed to in high school. High school boys do crazy things sometimes. It's because I have a secret, one you may not know. I want to tell you before you marry me, but don't think I'll be able to once I know you. I'll be too scared. So I'm telling you now, when I don't know you. There may be other secrets in the future to tell, both good and bad (this one is both *wonderful* and *terrible!*), and I want a place to keep them. I hope you love me enough to understand. One thing is for sure, reading this will either make you love me more, or it will make you leave. Either way, I'll be glad I showed it to you.

Looking at this open, empty diary, I tried to decide who to address it to. "Dear Diary" is so cliché! Anne Frank used a name in her diary. I almost called you Blake because I like the way it sounds. Don't you? Solid, it's the sound a tailgate makes when you shut it hard: "Blake!" Or when a softball hits a tin roof, "Blake!" Solid, dependable, trustworthy, someone who takes up a lot of space and doesn't get shoved around, and who is always there for me, my support, my structure, my love.

I won't give you a real name, because I want you to think your name has always been my favorite. So you get a fake name. You are Mr. Future Husband Man, or F.H. Man for short. Maybe I'll call you "Manny." I hope you like your new moniker, FH, because you're stuck with it until I find out who you really are.

Where should I start? I'm in Hawaii with my uncle, Paul, because I need to get away, to make some decisions. He brought me here to Hawaii (to Hawaii!) to give me time to think about this secret of mine. Only I'm going to be snorkeling and swimming and sunbathing and reading and eating—not much thinking! I'll do that when I get back.

I know you don't need to share ALL secrets in a relationship. We'll both need to have some. The deep dark depth of my soul is not a pretty place, and you don't want a full tour of duty there. I'll go to the parts of your soul you need me to, gladly, but you don't have to share everything, and I certainly won't share everything with you in here. Example: I will not rant over every boy that touches me, how and where. We'll pretend it never happened, any other details I will keep to myself. Please keep yours, also.

I'm sorry to have reprimanded you, FH. By now you're probably already a little tempered to my pushings and shovings. Stick around. I've got some good stories I want to tell you, including my secret, and future secrets even I don't know about yet. Stick around. That's my advice to you as long as we are married. Stick around. I'll do the same. As long as that is true, we'll have the power to work everything else out. I will work and work and work until it does work out. Just stick around.

At least stick around long enough to read the rest of this sappy story of my life.

I'm sure I love you, though it feels funny to say so when I don't even know what color hair you have.

Caroline.

*　　*　　*

March 6th, 1988

Dear Manny,

It's the next morning, around five a.m. That makes it eleven on the East Coast, so I've slept long enough. No sign of sunrise yet, so I'm out on the balcony, waiting and watching. I've got plenty to tell, so I'll see it before I'm done.

My conversation with Uncle Paul last night made me realize who I am now is part of who I will be when you fall in love with me, and I want to preserve some of it for you, good and bad. I daydreamed about you last night, about the day I give this to you, about finding someone I love so much, who makes me feel so secure I can tell you my big secret. It made me so happy to believe it could happen to me. That you're reading this makes you a dream come true.

My English teacher told me it is best to show what you want the reader to know, rather than tell it. I'm not the type to drip melodramatic nonsense anyway, so I'll just tell you some stories. You figure out what they mean.

Here's a short one about Hope, my older sister (I'm sure you've met her). Growing up, Hope was more outgoing, more social, friendlier, smarter, and prettier. She listened better, told better stories, smiled more than me—she was everyone's favorite. The unfortunate truth is I feel very lucky to be her younger sister. Every year, my homeroom teacher would call my name the first day and say, "Oh, you're Hope's little sister. I'm so pleased you're in my homeroom—we have very high expectations." It didn't leave much room for me to be me. Instead, I was an inferior version of her.

Last year, Hope and I did something that got her in trouble with the law. She may even have a record.

This boy in my class, Tom, was blond and a doctor's son and good looking and friendly. Everybody loved Tom, and he went out with all of the prettiest girls. He and I had been friends for a long time because we're both smart. Like everyone else, Hope liked him, and, like everyone else, he liked Hope. Tom and I were talking after band practice about how we were going to get to the football game, where we have to play the halftime show. Neither Tom nor I had our driver's license. Hope came up, and nice girl, offered to pick Tom up and drive him to the game.

We took him to the game, no problem. I don't remember if we won or not, but there was a party afterwards. Hope offered to drive us. Another boy Scott, who is nice looking but not nice, came. I wasn't having anything to do with him. Scott suggested we stop and get some beer, and Tom really wanted to. Hope wanted to impress Tom, so she agreed. We stopped and Scott bought a twelve pack, I don't know how, and we went out to a lake to drink it. It was dark and nice by the lake. We drank and talked and I started to think high school wasn't going to be all that terrible. I mean, we were out with two boys, one nice and the other okay, and Hope was being really nice to me even if she did have her tail feathers up a bit trying to impress a boy I didn't have a chance with. Of course, Hope wasn't drinking because she had to drive us, but she was having fun anyway.

After about twenty minutes, a car drove right up and flashed blue lights! It was a cop! The officer asked how old we were and poured out our beer. He took Hope to the patrol car while the rest of us waited in our car. She got a ticket for "Contributing to the Delinquency of a Minor". He couldn't give us tickets because we were too young—we were the "minors". He didn't give anyone a "possession" ticket. I felt terrible on the way home. Hope didn't want to go to the party, and none of us wanted to make her (except maybe Scott) because we felt so bad. She was so nice and responsible by not drinking, and was actually treating me like a friend, rather than an annoying little sister.

I told her I'd go along with whatever she wanted to tell Mom and Dad. She smiled seriously and said, "Just tell them the truth, but let me talk with them first." Mom asked how things went, and if we had a good time at the party. Hope told her she had something serious to tell them, and they talked for a long time. I went to my room.

Later, Dad asked me what happened, and I told him the truth. I told him how bad I felt because Hope was being so good and only wanted to impress Tom. He was kind and not mad at all. I didn't get into any trouble for having beer. Hope didn't get into any trouble either, but Dad made her pay for the ticket herself. After he left me he went to her room, and stayed there for at least twenty minutes.

That's Hope. She's perfect, and I live in her shadow. The one time she gets caught being slightly imperfect, she's so perfect about being imperfect that we all feel bad and she doesn't get into any trouble. Though I live in her shadow always, I would never put a spin on this to make her look bad—I love her too much.

This doesn't make sense, but it's the things that don't make sense that are truly telling about a person, that tell who she is. Those are the stories I'll put in here.

Love,
Caroline

*   *   *

Dear Manny,

I'm still in Hawaii, though I'm not ready to talk about why I'm here, yet. Uncle Paul brought me here to heal my aching soul, that's why.

Uncle Paul said when I go on a date, I shouldn't talk about myself. He said I should talk about the other people around me, and about what I care about. In a strange way this is like our third date for me, so that's what I'll do.

Uncle Paul. My earliest memory of Uncle Paul was being afraid of him. He's a big man. His big, loud laugh can come across like a wicked scientist on steroids when you're small. I love his laugh now, though. It's deep and happy and bellows from the hollow depths of his abdomen. I say he's big, but he's linebacker big, not sumo-wrestler big. Thick. Mom calls him "dense", and sometimes she means the physical not mental!

The Defining Moment: I was just eight years old, near the end of the summer, and Uncle Paul was coming to visit. I didn't want to hang around waiting for him, so I wandered off in the woods. I picked up a stick, and pretended to be on a grand hike through the woods, circling around our neighborhood to a farm at the other end. I'd only been there a couple times, both with Hope, who told me we weren't allowed to go to the farm; it was better to play in the woods—both times we left.

This time Hope wasn't there.

Split lumber held up a rusted barbed wire fence surrounding a big, green field that lumbered over a couple of hills. I wanted to play with the animals, but couldn't see any. I climbed between two wires and walked to the top of the hill. I got there sweaty and breathing hard. On the top of the next hill, I could see the farmhouse. There was a dried up creek bed between the hills, with another fence running next to it. I could see maybe twenty cows clustered in the shade under a couple trees. One cow lay on its side in the sun down at the creek, alone. It was big and round, and wasn't moving.

Hope would never have entered the field. There was nothing special there—it was better to play in the woods.

Not me.

I had to go see why this cow was laying down by the creek, why it was quarantined from the others.

I was still farther from this cow than from the fence. I felt if I saw it move, I could run to the fence and get away. I approached slowly, holding my stick out front to protect me if it charged. As I got closer, it still didn't move. I could see the cows on the other hill watching me, following me with their huge brown eyes. But this cow, my cow, wasn't moving at all.

As I came close to it, I could see flies buzzing around its head. It faced away from me, on its side, feet out. The top two feet stuck straight into the air. I'd never seen a cow sit that way before. Its belly was so big it looked pregnant. I got worried about the sick pregnant cow, and thought maybe I'd go up to the farm and tell them about their sick pregnant cow, and they would give me lemonade and a ride home and tell Mom what a good girl I was.

I walked right up to it and couldn't see it breathing. I walked around it, and saw the flies had eaten its eyes out.

It was dead.

I could smell it, too, but it wasn't much stronger than the regular smell you get from cow fields, which isn't good. The next thing makes me sick to tell.

This cow's belly was so huge; it stretched up as tall as I was. I felt like I was standing next to this great, taut leather tent attached to a tiny cow's body on one side. It didn't look real. So I held out my stick, and touched the edge of the belly. The belly indented where my stick poked in just a little bit.

I can remember every detail of this moment. There was a small indentation in the cow's skin, like you get when you push on a balloon with your finger. The field was warm and a cool breeze dried the sweat on my skin.

I held the stick there for a minute, then, still curious, I pushed harder, then harder still, and that's when it exploded.

"BANG!"

Rotting cow's guts erupted onto me from head to toe and knocked me down with their slimy impact. The smell was a combination of all the revolting things on the inside of a living being. The worst part was the maggots, wiggling between my fingers as I scraped the chunks of slimy innards from my body.

I fell down when all this stuff hit me, as much from fright as from anything else. For a second, I was stunned. Then I screamed and tried to wipe the goop off. I sloshed it off my arms and head in huge gooey chunks, but there was no getting clean. I ran down the hill to the fence, crying. I took the quickest trail to the road. When I got close to the road, I was too tired to keep running. I walked down the road, still crying.

I hadn't gone far when Uncle Paul pulled up in front of me in his truck. He opened the hatch, pulled out a road blanket, wrapped me in it, and put me in back. I fell into his arms when he picked me up, limp and crying. I didn't say anything. I was surprised when he pulled a U-turn and drove away from home.

In a moment, the car stopped. Uncle Paul led me into the bay of one of those self-serve spray car washes. He sprayed and sprayed and sprayed with the car-sprayer-thing. "You'll be as good as new in no time," he said with his mouth, but not with his face. It hurt when the water hit me, and made my skin red and almost sore. I needed that level of cleaning and scrubbing to rid both my body of the grime and smell, and my mind of the memory of being covered with what was previously the innards of a cow.

When I was mostly clean, I complained. "It hurts, Uncle Paul!"

He moved the sprayer away, pointing it at the ground. "Wait," he said. "Turn just a little—there's another maggot!" and he hit me with the sprayer again. I laughed and dodged and he made me dance with the sprayer like bad guys do to the good guys in old westerns with their guns. When we finished playing, he made me take my clothes off right there and sprayed me clean from head to toe.

He gave me one of his big shirts to wear like a dress, and drove to a Laundromat and washed my clothes. When I was dressed in clean clothes, he bought two ice cream cones. He handed one to me and said, "I'll tell them I found you on the side of the road, and took you for ice cream". That's what he did. Mom and Dad still don't know.

Uncle Paul never even asked why I was covered with cow guts. He cleaned me and fixed what was wrong and sent me off, maybe to find some new cow to explode on me. That's sort of what has happened now, and he's got me in the car wash place and he's scrubbing me. Somehow I expect he'll be there when I find my next rotting cow.

That's about enough for now, don't you think. Do you love me enough to clean the stinky maggots off me and buy me ice cream afterwards?

Ick! Love,
Me

* * *

The coldness sat thick in the morning air. A shallow snow had fallen in the night, and blanketed the earth in a great silence. I waited patiently for Caroline in the lobby of Reynolds. Outside, a cab waited. I'm normally five minutes late to everything, huffing and hurrying to catch up. Today, I was early.

Caroline walked slowly down the hall to the lobby in a heavy wool skirt, her formal shoes clomping in the dark hallway. She was bundled in a thick cotton sweater and Gore-tex jacket. I took her hand, and led her to the cab. We got in.

She sat in the passenger seat, looking straight forward. I said, "I love you, Caroline."

Her words came out slowly, quietly, but with true gratitude, "Thanks, Pete."

I turned toward her as the cab pulled away, and said, "It's not too late to turn back. I'll claim it's mine—I can do whatever you want." I paused again. "But I'll stand by you no matter what you do."

Caroline reached and took my gloved hand in hers, her grip tight. "Thanks, Pete. This isn't easy. Thanks for not telling." She rested her head on my shoulder.

The taxi moved forward slowly. It left a trail of heavy mist from its tailpipe, dissipating slowly in the cold winter air. The drive to the abortion clinic was short; we rode in silence. When we arrived, Caroline registered at the nurse's station, and we sat to wait. Caroline held my hand in both of hers in her lap, her head leaning lightly against the tip of my shoulder. When the nurse called Caroline's name, she rose, dropping my hand, and left without a word. I watched her go, and then said aloud in the empty room, "She's one brave girl."

A half hour later, Caroline walked into the waiting room fully dressed, looking as she did when she walked out. I stood and walked straight into a hug. She squeezed me tightly, and I felt her strong back muscles straining against my bulk through her sweater. She didn't cry. We got into a taxi and rode back to the School in time for Caroline's first class.

She went to class as normal. That evening, she called Uncle Paul to tell him what she had done, and what she needed to do.

*   *   *

Dearest Future Husband,

Now is the time to tell you about my stinky maggots—then we'll find the answer to that last question. I can picture myself, after you have proposed, telling you that there are some things I want you to know about me before I say yes. And I would only give you this if I planned to say yes. The things that I will want you to know are what I am about to write. I have to—these are my stinky maggots, and I want ice cream.

When I was twelve years old, Hope and I played frequently in the woods around our neighborhood, where there is a train track and a creek. I loved to play in the creek and build things. Hope liked to lead explorations. This time, we were exploring. Hope led us, and we pretended to be surveying the land near a train overpass where we suspected an Indian attack.

I chased a possum up the ravine to the train tracks, and then climbed up the hill to stand on top of the tracks. When I turned around, a man was facing Hope from behind a tree. He hadn't seen me, and I wasn't scared. Men had always been friendly, like my dad and Uncle Paul. He didn't say anything, then approached Hope. He walked fast, then even faster. When he got close, Hope screamed at me to run away. Then the man grabbed Hope and knocked her down.

He pushed her to the ground, and held her tight to his body with one arm. She screamed and cried, pounding his body with her little fist, useless little punches.

I'd been in fights with Hope. She had no chance. I ran down the embankment and picked up her walking stick. I swung it hard in a wide arc and hit the man's ear. He yelled, but held tight, so I jumped on his back and dug both hands deep into his long tangles and pulled. Hope was hitting me, but I didn't care. I pulled hard, holding his hair in two great big wads to my chest, pulling with my legs and my back.

He rolled off of Hope, and she slipped away, leaving her jacket in his impotent hands. Suddenly he faced me, then rolled on top of me. The rest I don't remember well. I remember Hope screaming from the top of the gully. Eventually, her screaming stopped, and I realized I was on my own.

The man tore at my sweatshirt, trying to kiss my shoulders with his nasty beard. He had my legs spread, and one hand reached down and tried to do something down there. I struggled and cried and yelled; I punched him as hard as I could and felt my breath getting shallower and my muscles getting weaker as I began to feel the futility of fighting this much larger man. I don't think I knew all the things he could do to me, but I knew I wanted none of it. He stopped for a second and looked down at me and I felt his blue eyes drill right into me, and then, only then, did I know he was going to rape me. A cold calmness filled me and the fear drained out of my body like dirty water from a tub. He had made me angry.

I bit him hard on the place where his shoulder meets his neck. I wanted his jugular. I grabbed his flesh between my teeth and squeezed and pulled with all the strength in my jaws and neck. He put both hands on my head to pull me off, but when he pulled I squeezed my jaws harder, feeling his flesh slice under my incisors. I felt that if I could just hold on, could keep this slowly separating chunk of evil within my jaws, that I could keep him from violating me. The taste of salt and sweat and blood filled my mouth as he panicked and shook me. I growled through the blood and he grunted and yelled as I bit harder. Then he must have realized that I was not letting go, that he could not pull me off, and he went still, and whimpered and leaned his head away from me, and I heard him cry and nearly felt sorry for this pitiful man who had just been bested by a twelve year old girl.

I let go and pushed and he rolled off of me. I ran up the gully, kicking at the rocks and feeling them grind hard into my palms and fingers. When I got to the top, I sprinted down the train tracks to the park, never looking back. I felt a dribble of blood on my chin and smeared it off. Hope was in the park with Mrs. Rosenfeld, and they took me home. I never looked back, but just ran and ran. When I got to the park, Hope said he wasn't chasing me anymore.

The guy didn't catch me, and the doctor says he didn't rape me. I don't think I would remember. I don't blame Hope for running, for not biting the man herself. She ran to get help, and she and Mrs. Rosenfeld were coming to help me when they saw me running. Considering everything that happened, it turned out okay.

Except that it didn't. I've been running from this guy for my whole life, well—for five years, anyway. That's why I love the track team. The speed makes me feel powerful, like I could run away from anything. Peter's the only man I didn't run from. I even ran from Curt, and that's part of what I have to explain later.

I'm going to leave this story for now. I'll tell the rest later. I'm going to bed—it's been a long day. Tomorrow, I'll write and tell you exactly how long a day it's been.

I love you. Or at least, right now, I want very badly to love you.

Love,

Caroline

To Faith

*   *   *

Dearest F.H.M.,

I woke up early yesterday morning, and for the first time in ages, I didn't have to throw up, or have diarrhea. I showered, got dressed in warm clothes, and went outside to the cab where Peter waited. They drove me to the abortion clinic, and waited while I was with the doctor.

I feel terrible for what I've had to do. I don't hate Curt—he was, well, just Curt. He wanted me and I didn't know any better and liked how he wanted me, and how others looked at us when we were together. But Curt is Curt and he is NOT my Future Husband Man.

Yes, this morning when I got up, I was pregnant. I spent the weekend in Hawaii with Uncle Paul trying to figure out what to do. Peter offered to marry me, which is the sweetest thing I know. But this is my problem, which came from my mistake (What's wrong with a condom again? I can't remember...), and I have to handle it my way...

...which is why I've decided to keep the baby. Sitting at the clinic yesterday, I couldn't let the doctor put those things inside of me and kill something. I chickened out, I guess. I think of it more like this. I've been running from that man in the gully for four years. I've gotten faster, stronger, more powerful. It was my quest for power over men that got me where I am. I'm going to stop running. If I don't make this decision now, how can I be the person it's going to take to catch someone as wonderful as you?

I called Uncle Paul last night, and he has a plan. I'm not going to tell anyone else, not even Mom and Dad. But you have to know, because there is going to be a piece of me out there, and someday we may have to deal with it. I have made a mess of things.

I'll be putting the baby up for adoption.

So, that's that. I've told you, and this book is hardbound, so it's here. I feel very empty right now, but not panicky. I'm going to stop running from men right now, starting with the one inside of me. Hopefully, by the time I meet you, I'll know how to not run, to not be afraid.

I'm tired, and, if you can believe it, hungry. I'm going to go eat. Till next time...

Love,

Caroline

*   *   *

Hope read this part of Caroline's diary to me aloud. Her voice was musical, and I could hear in it her love for Caroline, and also an echo of Caroline herself. I was lying on my side on Caroline's childhood bed, in the reading room, watching Hope as she sat in the alcove reading, the afternoon sun coming in behind her. *I do love her,* I thought. Then, *Which one? Well, both of them. There's nothing wrong with that, is there?*

Hope finished and then sniffed as she turned the page. "Caroline wrote her next entry at New Years, in her senior year."

"Oh," I said.

"You've still got a lot to tell me about your senior year," she said. "Dad's never been as angry as he was at your graduation."

"I know. I guess I've gone this far, I may as well tell the whole thing."

"I'm going to have to tell Dad, you know."

"I know. There's not much he can do now. Cut me off from my nieces, maybe."

"He can't do that—they're too devoted to you."

"Yeah," I said. I was pensive, not feeling talkative.

"Tell me about the rest of your junior year."

"Not much to tell. Caroline and I studied with Alexander and Julia almost every day. We studied, we played, we went to movies—the four of us were inseparable."

"—but you and Caroline weren't dating."

"The subject never came up again. When she said no to me the second time, I figured my best bet was to enjoy myself, and see what would happen in ten years."

"How long was that before she married Kevin?"

"It was our junior year, nine and a half years before her wedding."

"Aaahh." She made a face at me which is characteristic Hope, one side of her mouth turning down in a sad frown, the other turning up in a smile, with her eyes mirroring the ambiguity of her mouth. It was the right face—it's how I felt: bittersweet.

"So tell me about the end of your junior year. Was Caroline showing?

That's the year she went off to California with Paul, right?"

"Yeah. None of us knew. I thought she had the abortion, and the whole thing was over. She never ate much, and that spring she started going to the Y to swim, and then in the pool outside Wyche when it got warm enough. She never really showed, though I do remember one thing was very different by the time she left."

"How so?"

"I took Caroline to prom that year—"

"That's right …"

"Do you remember her dress? You helped her pick it out."

"Yeah, sure …" she said, closing her eyes. "Pink, with ruffles on the shoulders and hips …" She stopped. "Oohh. Yes, I see. Big ruffles on top of the hips, and the skirt spread out … nobody would know she was pregnant in that thing."

"What else?" I asked. "You're missing something."

She closed her eyes again, and I could tell from her breathing she was trying to picture Caroline in that dress.

"How was it cut on top?" I asked.

"I remember big ruffles around the shoulders …"

"… low on the shoulders, right?"

"Yes, big pink ruffles, low on the shoulders, and low in back …"

"… and low in front."

"Mmmmmmmm." She smiled. "Now I see what you're talking about." She kept smiling, thinking back. "Anything special happen at the prom, or graduation?"

"No. In fact, it was one of the best springs ever, and nothing special happened. Me and my friends, hanging out, learning as fast as that place could cram things into our heads."

"Doesn't sound so bad," Hope said. Then she looked at me with a little mischief in her eye, "So tell me about your senior year."

Chapter 7: Sacrifice

Students at the North Carolina School of Science and Math wear the place like a worn out sweatshirt. It fits and it's warm and soft and can take the abuse of being really close all the time. When I left and went back to Hendersonville for the summer, back out into the real world, it was like the first fall into the pool at the bottom of Sliding Rock. The School is more than good teaching and smart students—it's a whole value system built around pushing as hard as you can, learning as much as you can, and then being completely unselfish with the results. The things valued by high school students back in a town like Hendersonville—who's friends with who, what kind of car you drive, or what position you play on the football or basketball team—couldn't be less important.

As a result, I withdrew from my friends back home. Sure, we went out or went to the mall occasionally, but mostly I kept to myself. Most of the other Science and Math students did also.

I wrote a few letters to some of my friends from school. This was before the internet, so we had to use paper, which was weird, because we had an email system at school we used all the time. It wouldn't be strange for me to get two or three emails a day from Alexander or Julia or Caroline. Then, away we go back out into the "real world", and nothing for three months.

You would think it would be weird going back to school after three months of withdrawal, but it's not. Rather than the bottom-of-Sliding-Rock experience of leaving, it's like taking your first swim of the season in a swimming pool. A little uncertain at first, but as soon as you're all the way in, you're eager to let go of the wall (say, send your parents home) and in no time it's as natural as, well, swimming.

When I showed up on campus, I was a little worried about seeing everyone. I saw Alexander first, when Vince brought his stuff into our room. He was going to be the "Dormitory Assistant"—the poor schmuck who calls roll at curfew and enforces the housecleaning rules—so we got a special, big room with a balcony. Vince was unpacking Alexander's clothing into his dresser when I walked in, and Alexander was around the corner, looking exactly the same in his sport coat and tie, briefcase closed on his desk. Nothing had changed, and I don't know why I expected it would.

We walked together to find Caroline and Julia before lunch. Julia had gone a little earthy crunchy over the summer, and sported a tie die shirt and shorts. I saw a tattoo peek out from the bottom of her shorts, which told me they wouldn't be passing the dress code for long, as I'd never seen that particular tattoo before. Her piercings were the same, or at least the ones I could see.

Caroline looked different, and, well … marvelous. Her hair was longer, and her face a little rounder, but her smile was fuller and both dimples came out in force, and the wrinkles around her eyes nearly hid her scar. She wasn't fat, but was a little fuller than she had been, and, I guess most noticeably for a seventeen year old boy, her breasts were much, much bigger. I struggled to look her in the eye and was relieved when she stepped directly into a hug—relieved because I wouldn't have to concentrate on not looking at her breasts. I felt them against me as I lifted her off the ground and swung her full circle, and then, when I put her down, things were just as they had been and I didn't have to concentrate on anything.

*　　*　　*

All the seniors had to go to the assembly hall that afternoon to meet our new principal, Dr. Samuel Ledbetter. His reputation had preceded him. He was a Citadel graduate that had slid effortlessly into their faculty after graduate school at Stanford. I fully expected to be wearing uniforms and saluting before the end of the day, and wondered how he expected this rowdy crowd of geeks to adjust to his idea of discipline and excellence. He got his first taste as he stepped on stage, and a young boy in front said

"Please welcome Dr. Bedwetter!" just loudly enough for everyone to hear, including the good doctor himself.

Dead silence filled the room as Dr. Ledbetter entered from the side, and walked to a lectern at the center of the small stage. There was no microphone. Samuel Ledbetter was a tall man, with a thin frame and red hair gone blond and grey with age, cropped close around his ears and neck. I chortled as I noticed his eyebrows, big bushy beasts reaching out to meet his sideburns, not quite making the turn at his temple. He wore a dark blue suit with a yellow tie, and his shoes had been polished to nanometer smoothness. We sat down in a hush as he looked us over, then began to speak.

"I see that you all know who I am, and want you to know that I'll take the time over the next weeks to get to know each and every one of you." He paused, and several of the students looked up, deciding to listen to what this red haired general had to say.

"I'd like to welcome you back for your senior year at the North Carolina School of Science and Mathematics. This is a very special place, and for each of us a wonderful privilege to be involved this, its sixth year.

"You will all have a lot of homework to do this year." A collective groan rose up from the audience. "Before I came here, I did my own. This is what I found: you, this year's seniors, have the potential to be the best the School has ever had." He paused, and his words sank in a bit. "First, every one of you who had the grades to qualify was invited back. There were no disciplinary cases. The teachers agree this class is one of the best ever, on par with the first class, and, I might add, a breath of fresh air after last year's seniors." Applause rippled the auditorium.

"As most of you know, last year's seniors set the record for the most scholarship money ever in one year at a single high school. Even though they started with forty more students than you, I expect you to beat that record. We'll work closely with you, and I encourage you all to stretch, to take classes you might not be able to handle, to work a little harder to get that elusive A.

"Let me share some statistics. Last year, in classes where there were both juniors and seniors, the seniors averaged a 2.91 GPA, and the juniors a 3.14. Remember, the seniors were a year ahead. Also, last year was the first year we had no suicide attempts, no pregnancies, and no students in

150

trouble with the law. Drinking was minimal, and I've talked to the few participants and gotten commitments from them. You skipped fewer classes, and had fewer disciplinary actions. That's normal for juniors, but this year I expect to give fewer to the seniors than the new juniors. I want you to set a stellar example for them.

"Because of this, I have a surprise. If you can keep up the good work—and I'll be measuring it—if you do, then I will personally will kick in an extra $5000 for your prom this year. Spend it on decorations, food, entertainment—anything you like as long as it's legal. Additionally, if your class proves you can handle the responsibility, we'll let you take your dates to the prom in cars, rather than busses as in the past. And if any of you has trouble finding a date, you might find some candidates among the juniors, who, unless they are accompanied by a senior, will still be bussed.

"I hope that will motivate you. Take this as a challenge—I want you to be the best class this school has ever seen!"

The students gave him a standing ovation, the crowded little room rocking with noise. He stood proud and smiled over the noise, his two yellow note cards still held forward in front of him, as if he had more to say. He smiled and turned sideways and walked off stage with a quick, precise step. I mumbled "Bedwetter," as he stepped off the stage, and pictured him in his dark blue pin striped suit with a large cloth diaper underneath it, held fast with two gigantic safety pins with pastel heads.

Caroline and Julia hung on me as they left, "You've got to help us through Calculus and Physics again, Peter," Julia said.

"Control your urges to break into the cafeteria, too," Caroline added. "If you get hungry, just let me know, and I'll order you a pizza."

We dropped the girls off, and then Alexander and I walked back to Wyche. "He certainly has laid down the gauntlet for us," Alexander said.

"He's got it all wrong," I said. "But I'll take that challenge. I'll take it, and I'll beat it. I'll get the highest grades I can in the toughest classes, but I won't live up to any of his other expectations. Everyone else will wonder who the big senior prankster is. You'll know, and I'll know, and somehow I'll make sure he knows. He's not leashing me up that easily!"

Alexander looked stunned, then recovered. "My, Peter, I don't believe the roommate of 1st Wyche D.A. is saying such things! You will have to control yourself, or I'll write you up."

"Write me up, and I'll tell Julia you broke into the craperteria and got an eyeful of Caroline's naked boobs," I said.

"Perhaps silence would be more prudent," he said, and we changed the subject.

That speech set the tone for my whole year, and the others rallied around me. I took the most classes, the hardest classes, and worked hard to get the best grades. Visibly, I was the picture of what Dr. Ledbetter was asking of us. What they didn't know was what I was doing behind the scenes, which was all well and good, until it cost me my friendship with Caroline.

*　　*　　*

"I'm getting the best education I can, both in and out of the classroom," I said one afternoon, after the group had ribbed me about studying too much.

Caroline smiled, "You're too intense, Peter. Lighten up or I'll find another friend."

She caught me by surprise, but not so fast I couldn't come back. "One who can help you with your physics homework?"

"I'll seduce some brainy junior," Caroline replied.

I laughed, looked down at her breasts, said, "at least now you've got the equipment!" and the whole group broke down laughing. The subject turned to lighter things, and soon we went back to our dorms for study hours.

Alexander and I hung out in the lobby with some other students and Chris Clary, our Resident Assistant. Chris was a friendly, rolly-polly RA who was everybody's friend, but also managed to enforce the rules. He told me, "I'm glad you're taking Dr. Ledbetter's challenge seriously, Peter, and adding classes. Let me know how I can help."

Turning to the rest of the group, Chris said, "Over the summer we found a problem with the back door and had a new security system installed. You should feel safer now." There was a sarcastic lilt to his voice, and I wondered if he knew he was addressing the right audience. Chris could be clever. I kept a straight face, but my abdomen fell two inches.

Late that night, I slipped into the hall and studied the electronics on the large metal door. I didn't see any sensors; the whole door looked wired. A camera was installed above the door, too small to hold a tape. A red light on the camera blinked every thirty seconds. I wondered how long it would take Mike to figure it out, but didn't want to ask. He was too honest and naïve to keep a secret.

Two days later while jogging past the dorm, I had an idea. I got my wallet and, still sweaty, went to the sporting good store and the hardware store to get what I needed. When I got back, I locked my door and put a sign out saying, "Do not disturb, studying for calculus exam". Alexander was out with Julia, and would stay there until curfew.

After Alexander had gone to sleep in his newly pressed pajamas, I walked down the hall to the bathroom in a robe, carrying my shower kit and towel. I timed my entrance to the bathroom to coincide with the blinking light on the camera. Counting slowly to thirty, I dropped the robe and put my stuff in a shower, turned it on, and slipped into my wrestling shoes. I had a rope tied around my waist, and a rock climbing harness snug on my hips. At the count of thirty-one, I sprinted to the end of the hall and ducked into the kitchen. The kitchen window was not wired, and a narrow ledge led to the fire escape. Four quick steps on the ledge, a quiet lunge, and I hung onto the fire escape with both hands. I lowered myself to freedom.

I ran to the woods and ducked into the darkness. Security patrolled campus irregularly. I made my way to the old power plant on the other side of campus.

Next to the power plant were two huge brick smoke stacks, each reaching over four hundred feet high. The community had made several attempts to remove them, complaining they were eyesores. Resistance from sentimental alumni and the town historic society, and the lack of money to remove them, kept them in place.

The surface of the stacks was rough brick, but there weren't enough hand and foot holds to climb. A row of iron rungs started ten feet up. The rungs were made from rebar, about eighteen inches wide, each covered by a thick layer of rust. They would be enough for me to get to the top...after I got to the first one. I looked up, jumped half-heartedly, and then backed up to study the situation. If I didn't move quickly, this could be the longest shower in School history.

I backed up, lowered to a sprinter's stance, and took off right at the stack. Before I got to it, I planted my right foot and sprang up, catching my left foot about ten bricks up on the stack and springing up farther. I reached with my right hand for the rung, caught it and pulled myself up, hand over hand. My hands were covered with large flakes of rust, and already sore from how the rust dug into my soft skin. Once I stood on the bottom rung, I began the climbing ritual I had worked out on my jog.

First, I pulled a length of rope out of the sack on my back. I tied two short lengths of rope to the rope around my waist, then pulled out two carabiners and hooked them to each the rope. I locked one into a rung a head level, and climbed until this one was at waist level, then locked the other one in at head level, and unlocked the one at waist level. This way, I was always tied to the stack. I couldn't predict if one of the rungs was loose, or broke, but as long as that didn't happen, I could only fall a few feet.

Fifty feet up, I broke a sweat. My legs burned at one hundred feet, and my muscles quivered uncontrollably at two hundred and fifty. I climbed ten rungs, rested, and then climbed ten more. It took me nearly a half hour to reach the top rung. When I got there, I locked both carabiners so I could lean against my harness and use both hands. I pulled a large sheet from my bag and tied it to the first and third rungs. Ten minutes later, I was at the bottom of the stack and headed back to his dorm.

I timed my sprint to the bathroom with the blinking light. I turned off the shower, gathered my things, and walked back to my room.

The next morning, campus was abuzz with talk of the flag flying gracefully atop the smoke stack. In bold letters it read, "Class of 1988: In Pursuit of Excellence"

*   *   *

For days, the school was abuzz with talk about the banner. I overheard people talking about it in the halls, and got emails from students describing elaborate conspiracy theories, some leading to the destruction of the school, others just to the ousting of the current administration. Dr. Wilkins, a beautiful grey haired lady who taught us World History, gave us an overview of civil disobedience throughout history, starting with John the Baptist, then the Boston Tea Party, and ending with all the stuff in the sixties. I bet she carried her share of banners in the sixties.

Some people took the banner as a challenge, to really "pursue excellence". Others took it as mockery of Dr. Ledbetter's speech. The best part was nobody, but nobody, knew how to get it down. An individual can take risks an institution cannot, and this was no exception. The risk of climbing a four hundred foot smoke stack, using only the row of rusted iron rungs, was out of the question. A fall meant certain death. Even the fire station didn't know what to do. So the banner hung for days, shouting to the world the standard being set by this senior class. It was on the local news, with pictures taken from traffic helicopters that buzzed by and got overhead shots of groups of students studying and throwing Frisbee. The class rallied around it, making contagious my spirit of, "Yes, we're going to do the best we possibly can. But on our terms, not yours."

I didn't tell anyone I put up the banner, not even Alexander, Julia, or Caroline. Some people thought I was the most likely, but only a few juniors thought I had the guts. The administration didn't know who to blame, and that irked them greatly.

Finally, over the weekend, the National Guard brought a helicopter, and a soldier rappelled down a line, locked into one of the rungs, and removed the banner. I stood with the whole student body on the grounds for a half hour, looking up at the huge hovering ship. When the man brought the banner to Dr. Ledbetter, he said, "It was slip-knotted—a cinch to take off." Dr. Ledbetter was not pleased, but thanked the man anyway.

* * *

A week later, I noticed the lights on the cameras blinking faster, now only ten seconds apart. Later, Chris called me into his room.

"I want you to help me with something, Pete."

"No problem. What can I do you for?" I said, grinning.

"More than you could afford," replied Chris. "I'd like you to keep your ear to the ground. Dr. Ledbetter wants to catch our flag-raiser. He thinks he's going to try something else, and someone may get hurt. He wants to make an example of him."

"What do you want me to do?" I asked.

"Keep your eyes and ears open," said Chris. "People trust you, and don't think you'd side with the administration. Dr. Ledbetter thinks if our flag-raiser were going to brag, it would be to someone like you. He's been really impressed with your turnaround and wants you on our side. He wants to put a stop to it early."

"There's no telling if anyone would talk to me, but I'll let you know what I hear."

"Thanks. I knew we could count on you. Anything I can do to help you ace your classes? Ledbetter's checked with your teachers, and they're all double thumbs up."

"Nothing I can think of. I've got to keep focus. Not too tough, so far."

"Let me know if I can help, and keep an eye out for us. We want to nail the guy."

"You bet," I said as I left Chris's office.

That night, there were two memos in my mailbox. One was a form from the senior class government, telling of a t-shirt being printed. It had the School mascot, a unicorn, in the center. Above and below the mascot, it said, "Class of 1988: In Pursuit of Excellence." I immediately ordered two shirts. The other memo was a letter from Dr. Ledbetter to the student body, and wasn't nearly as exciting. It read:

Dear NCSSM Senior,

At the beginning of the year, we expected this to be the best year ever. I challenged you to work harder, learn more, and raise your standards to the highest level possible. In the words of Brad Walker, your class president, "Next year, we will be paying good money to take classes like these, and many will be less challenging. I suggest everyone learn as much as possible now, while it's free." Most of you embraced this, and I see visible results in the academic performance. The faculty is very pleased.

To reward you, the Parents' Council is subsidizing a Senior Class T-Shirt. The design represents all we ask from you this year: to pursue excellence in everything you do. Raise your standards in the classroom, on the sports field, and in performances.

Some of you know there is at least one person twisting this challenge to gain personal notoriety. While the School has no official response to the placement of the flag atop the smokestack, we will undergo a slight change in policy.

Defacing School property is either a misdemeanor or a felony, depending on the severity. For a minor infraction, we would normally deal with it internally. However, because correcting the defacement involved bringing in the National Guard, we have had to change our policy. In the future, at the discretion of the School Principal, any violation of rules in the Student Handbook that also involves a violation of local law may be reported to the local authorities and dealt with through the court system. The Parents' Council fully supports this policy change.

For those of you who have risen to this challenge, I salute you. To those who have not, it's not too late, and only you will benefit. For the very few who are mocking this challenge, beware, it may be out of our hands to protect you.

*　　*　　*

Caroline sat next to me at dinner. "Did you get the memos, Pete?"

"Yeah, I got them. I ordered two shirts!"

"Be careful—I want you to graduate with us. Don't do anything stupid."

"I'm too busy to do anything stupid." I grinned, and then gave my wrinkled face attempt at a wink.

She laughed and said, "I'll need help with physics before the next exam."

"I know, I know. All I am is a cheap physics tutor," I said, grinning.

"No, you're also a good dancer, and you give great hugs."

"It's good I've got something going for me."

She grabbed my arm as I started to leave. "Everybody thinks we're going out."

"We are—we go out all the time. Movies, ice cream, whatever. We do everything you and Curt did, except what got you in trouble."

Caroline looked down. "I wouldn't mind if you went out with someone else."

"I will, if anyone comes along. I've got too much work to spend much time looking. Besides, I told you how I feel, and it hasn't changed. I know what I'm doing."

Caroline still held my arm, looking up at me. I sank deeply into her sea blue eyes, noticing for the first time how the flecks of yellow looked like the beginning of a sunrise. Her hair was blown slightly out of her face, and her t-shirt hung loose on her sturdy shoulders. The scar at the corner of her eye looked dark, almost like a tear, sad. She squeezed my hand and said, "I love you. I just can't show it right now."

"I know," I said, and walked away.

*   *   *

I had gotten in way too deep to have time for girls, or getting in trouble. I took ten classes. A normal load was six or seven, and some seniors took only five in their second semester. Eight met three times a week; three had labs. Two were independent studies, one in Economics, and the other in Third World Mythology. The Econ class involved lots of reading about macro- and micro- economics, and exploring them through computer simulations. Third World Mythology had a lot of reading, plus one evening session a week. I barely kept up with the reading.

Once or twice a week, Alexander and I met on the mat for a workout, and then we went to the gym to lift weights. Sparing the time was difficult, but the exercise exhausted my body and renewed my mind at the same time. I returned from my workouts to a long, hot shower, and then hit the books reinvigorated.

I barely kept up. Sometimes I studied up on my balcony of 1908, but often locked myself in my room, a sign "Don't disturb, studying _____" written on the door. The subject changed, but not the resolve. This was where I was one Friday evening in October, during the Fall Dance.

My room was the only room in Wyche with a balcony, and I sat out there, reading about bird-headed gods from ancient Egypt, looking up occasionally to see two students walking hand in hand, or an overthrown Frisbee sail past the edge of the dorm. October brought new smells. Tobacco, drying in the nearby warehouses, gave a ripe aroma, like drying tea leaves, sweet and pungent. The leaves on the trees had begun to turn colors and fall, giving a dry dusty smell when they were blown in the wind.

Caroline walked toward Wyche from her dorm. She wore a sweatshirt with the letters NCSSM sewn in, only she wore it inside out, the letters backwards across her chest. The wind blew hard through her hair, her cheeks pink with the cold and the wind. Her hair blew freely in the wind, forming short tangles behind her head, a few stray strands blowing across her face. She squinted, but the cold wind brought a tear anyway.

This was Caroline at her most attractive. She had a fine womanly shape, but her beauty came from her naturalness, from her genuine heart showing through on her face and in the clothes she wore. She was much more attractive in a sweatshirt than a slinky dress. Makeup and earrings couldn't adorn her unsmiling face, and added only a hint of color and sparkle to her smile.

She kicked a pile of leaves as she walked past it at the base of a tree, sending her shoe flying. She stared at her shoe in frustration. When it landed, she laughed and ran to retrieved it. She walked to Wyche and yelled my name down the hall. I didn't answer, and then there was a knock at my door. She opened my door then stepped in and closed the door.

"Your half of the room is a pig-sty," she said.

"We could get in a lot of trouble!" I said, my smile betraying my pleasure at this surprise.

Caroline locked the door and said, "So let's not get caught." She smiled, and then said, "You can still get out the back, can't you?"

"You can't use the door anymore—the alarm works now. You can use the kitchen window, but it's tricky."

"That's how you got out."

"Got out? I've been too busy." I fell into a heap of cushions on the bed, and pushed one to Caroline as she sat on the other side of the bed. For all the clutter in the floor, the bed was the only place to sit comfortably.

"Like they could keep you in."

"Yeah," I said.

I wore my "In Pursuit of Excellence" t-shirt and shorts. Caroline squeezed me around the biceps and triceps, first with one hand, then two saying, "When did you become 'Mr. Cut Wrestling-Boy'?"

"I just worked out, that's all. I'll be 'Mr. Calculus Wimp' in an hour or so."

She let go of my arms and laughed, smiling into my eyes as I laughed back. "How come you're not at the dance, Cut-Boy?" she asked.

"I was gonna to go in a bit. What time is it?"

"Almost eleven—too late to pick up a pretty junior. They all hooked up with soccer players, anyway. Most girls think wrestlers are gay..." Caroline said, smiling.

I smirked. "How come you're not there? Some juniors have bigger arms than mine, and might have time to spend with you, which I don't."

"I was there. I didn't want to compete with Lindsey. She's in hog heaven. Alexander and Julia came for about three dances, then left."

"Maybe they're in a chair in front of the elevator," I said, grinning.

"Or in a chair in front of an elevator," repeated Caroline sarcastically. She pulled her pillow closer to me, slipped her arms around my neck and laid her head on my chest. She lay there for a minute, and I breathed in her clean smell. "I don't want to fall in love now, not with anyone new," she said. "We only have seven months till college. Why invest seven months in somebody, then have it end?"

I held her close. I sniffed her hair, then whispered, "Lucky me." She reached farther around me and squeezed me hard, burying her head deep into my chest.

"You really do have more cleavage than Lindsey," she said, a smile cracking her face. I pulled my hand from around her shoulders, and cupped one of her breasts through her sweatshirt, feeling both its firmness, and its weight. At first, she didn't resist, but then pulled away. "What was that for?"

"I wanted to see if you had more than me, or less, like Lindsey," I said. "Did you make it to a c-cup?"

"I did for a while, but they came down."

"Came down?" I asked. Caroline paused, and I felt her head move slightly against my chest. "Even after an abortion?" I asked, a bit naïve to feminine biology.

Caroline spoke into my chest, saying, "I didn't have the abortion,

Pete." It took a minute for that to sink in, and then it sank only part way.

"Did you have a miscarriage?"

"I had the baby at the beginning of August, Pete. I put it up for adoption."

I whispered, "Oh my God" and hugged her hard. She put her head into my chest and breathed hard. I couldn't tell if she was crying, or just burying her face, hiding from the world in a place where maybe she felt more safe, less threatened. She grabbed me, pinching the muscles behind my back. I held her hard with one hand, and stroked her hair with the other. With uncharacteristic insightfulness, I didn't speak, only held her.

After she stopped, she said, "You're the only one who knows besides Uncle Paul, and Aunt Savannah. You've got to keep it secret."

"Really? I thought I'd hang a banner from the smoke stack."

She stopped, and then said, "Was that you?" She waited for an answer, but I only smiled. "My God, it was you! We all thought you'd turned into a super goody-goody, and you're still living on the Dark Side!" My face was plastered with perma-grin.

Caroline looked worried. "You could have fallen! How come you didn't fall? Don't do anything like that again." She hit my chest with her little balled up fist.

I got out the rope and the carabiners, then showed Caroline the maneuvers I had done while I climbed the rungs. "It was only dangerous before I got to the first rung. It's worse climbing out the back window than climbing the tower. Speaking of which, you'd better go before people start to come back."

She hugged me good-bye. She looked up and started to say something, but pulled me down and kissed me instead. It started friendly, then became more passionate. In a minute we were laying on the bed, holding each other tightly and kissing hard, like two people who needed kissing more than anything in the world.

When we stopped, Caroline looked deep into my eyes and said, "I needed that."

"Me, too," I said, staring at her bright smile that beamed both dimples at me.

Caroline looked away, "Don't let it mean too much. I don't have a lot to give and I can't take the gossip. Can we just be friends?"

I knew the right answer. "No, we can't 'just be friends', but we can be best friends. You'll never be just a friend." She smiled, kissed me quickly on the lips, and then buried her head in my chest again, pulling herself to me.

"You'd better go," I said. We got up. I checked the hall, and then Caroline crossed without being caught by person or camera, and left by the kitchen window.

Neither of us thought about her walk down the hall to my room, which had been recorded on seven frames of the video camera, with no evidence of her leaving.

* * *

Caroline was very melancholic for the rest of the semester. She did her work, and spent her afternoons with Alexander and Julia. Alexander never did give up his practice of wearing sports coats and ties, and carrying his briefcase. I diligently read the technology section of his Wall Street Journal, and every three weeks or so Vince would show up to take us all out to breakfast. I never did meet Alexander's parents, and Julia said they were "very nice," though she wouldn't go into details. They talked openly about "when we get married," and, according to Alexander, he still got his one kiss every evening, as they were saying good night. "If it weren't for my sinful nature, I'd be very happy just as we are," he said.

"It's not sinful to want to get married and have sex with your wife. It is sinful for *me* to want to have sex with your wife, but I can't help it!" I said.

"I understand," he said. "But don't. She's got a weak spot for you, you know."

Julia kept both of us memorizing Bible verses up until the day we graduated. She worked me through the Gospels, and then chose some key phrases out of Paul's letters. I learned how the Bible was put together, and what it said. I didn't really believe, though, not like she wanted me to. Sure—I knew there was a God—the signature of a creator of some kind is all over, and even though I was turning into a pretty good scientist, I couldn't buy the "cosmic accident" theory of creation. I memorized, and Julia tolerated my questions. One of my favorite verses was 1 Corinthians

9:26-27, "So I do not run aimlessly, nor do I box as though beating the air; but I punish my body and enslave it, so that after proclaiming to others I myself should not be disqualified." It spoke a lot about what I was doing back then.

I wonder, if I had believed in Jesus Christ the way Julia did, the way she wanted me to, maybe she might have left Alexander and fallen in love with me. When we talked, I sometimes saw a glimmer of hope in her eyes, hope that I could change. But I didn't, and we continued down the same paths we had been on.

I think back on that fall, and it makes me wonder about the nature of stress. It was one of the happiest times in my life. Once swim and wrestling seasons came, I awoke every morning to long swims with Caroline. We were both on the team, and both chose to swim the long races, 500m and higher. Our work outs were normally about three miles, one for warm up and one to warm down, with wind sprints in the middle. We didn't talk much, but swam next to each other, and enjoyed the silent companionship. I had class all day, studied in the afternoons, and in the evenings after dinner, I went to wrestling practice with Alexander. We sparred, and worked hard to improve each other's skill. Caroline had joined the tae kwon do club, and sometimes she joined us after practice and we showed each other moves on the mats.

I remember the whole time I felt as if I were so busy, that I had so many things going on and was putting myself under so much stress, that I didn't have time to enjoy life. And yet, when I look back on it, those really were the best days of my life.

I blew through exams, and promptly went home and got sick. Caroline sent me a letter that Christmas, which surprised me a little—I thought I was closer to my brother than that.

*　　*　　*

Hi Pete,

How's your break going? Did you ace all of your exams?

Things are fine here. I've been shopping four days in a row, and I've bought some great gifts. I love Christmas, if only for the shopping. Hope and I are actually getting along great, as long as we are spending money.

She and Edward are getting along famously at Georgia Tech, so she's much easier to get along with. I could almost like her, except I know when they break up, she'll go back to what she was before. Though who knows, she actually used the words, "when we get married," and when I asked her, she just smiled and shrugged as she looked up into the sky. Someday, you and I may even be related!

I've been thinking a lot, Peter. You've been so special to me since Curt and I broke up—you carried me through it. I know I can never even things up. I hope with everything I am, and pray, nothing ever happens to make you need me like I needed you this year. But also, I pray if something ever does, I'll be there for you.

That's all I wanted to say. I know my secret is safe with you. Good luck this semester—I hope to see you a bunch...if only to get some great backrubs!

Lots of love,
Caroline

*   *   *

Entry in Future Husband Diary

December 28th, 1988
Dear Manny,

I need to make a promise to me and to you: I promise if I don't write any other time, I will write each New Year to tell you about my year, and how I've grown.

I spent this summer in San Jose with Uncle Paul and his new wife, Savannah. I got fat and very pregnant, and at the end, only wanted to get the baby out of me. When it came out, it hurt like crazy, and then it was okay. The baby is gone, and I didn't even look at her. I went home and cried. Uncle Paul promised me the adoptive parents will take good care of her, but if I found out who they are, I'd try to take her back. I named her Faith.

Last night, I dreamed I took Faith to the beach and she wanted to get out of her stroller and walk, so we walked, both of us pushing her stroller. I dreamed about taking her little shoes off and walking into the water holding her little hand. I dreamed about the way her skin felt when it was dry, and when it got wet, and when it got sand on it. Then I woke up and got some water and read before I went back to sleep. I love those dreams, but they make me sad. I hope this dream will come true, that I will have a wonderful baby girl with me on the beach, seeing all those things and feeling all those things. You are the one I've chosen to be by my side. You are my dream come true.

The year has been pretty good, but tough at times. Not because of schoolwork, or boys, or anything like that, but because I have a secret nobody knows. I told Pete; I had to tell someone. He told me a secret of his, too, though different from mine.

Peter has been great. I know he wants to date me, but though I love him, I don't have it in me right now to be anything for him. I have nothing to give. I'm being very selfish, spending a lot of time around him...but the truth is, I NEED him. He is the only person who has seen the real me...the dirty, pregnant, stupid me...and still loves me.

Don't get jealous, because he's still Pete. I love him because his heart is so big, and because he is so giving, so non-judgmental and accepting. Truthfully, he's annoying, too. He always picks arguments; he needs to be right all the time. Sometimes, he knows he's wrong, but argues because he wants to win, and doesn't care anymore about what's right. But when it's just the two of us we never argue. Maybe someday he'll grow up.

Why is it the people who can be what I need are also annoying, unattractive, obnoxious BOYS, and not good looking, comfortable, confident and relaxed MEN? Oh, yeah, because they're not you, and I've got to wait for you to come find me.

Manny, I meant it when I said I was going to stop running from men. It's important for me to open up to Peter, tell him everything I'm scared of, and learn to trust him. That's more important than kissing him and dancing with him. Next year, we'll go off to college and start over. I don't want him attached to me when he could meet someone without the baggage I have. Maybe by then I won't need to run, and I'll find a good guy and date him to see how it goes. I've got to start somewhere.

Oh, yeah—I punched my fist through a board this year. I did it in November, in tae kwon do. When I started, I never believed I would, but we kept practicing and working on strength, and I did it! The first couple times I tried, it didn't work, and hurt my wrist and knuckles. For two weeks I was scared to try, and just kept working. When I tried again, it broke, and I've done it a couple times since then.

Don't try anything stupid, because I pack a whopping big punch!

Caroline

*　　*　　*

I rode back to school on the bus with Caroline. She didn't have anything more to say about Hope and Edward, and I told her when I confronted Edward, he said it wouldn't be until after college, and a lot could happen between now and then. In any case, it gave us a lot to talk about on the ride back to school. We also exchanged Christmas gifts. I gave her a pair of gold earrings, in the shape of small wreaths, and she gave me a copy of *Great Expectations*, by Charles Dickens. "I haven't read it," she said, "but the title fits what I have for you."

When I got to my room, I saw an envelope in formal cream colored stationery taped to my door with my name typed on the outside. The note, also typed on the same stationery, read, "Peter, Please come see me in my office as soon as you get to school. Dr. Samuel Ledbetter"

I read the note again after settling my things, wondering if I should go now or wait until Monday. I decided to make sure Dr. Ledbetter wasn't waiting for me.

I entered the dark hallway, and saw Dr. Ledbetter's office door open. I knocked quietly on the door. Dr. Ledbetter stood when he saw me, and said, "Good, Peter, welcome. How was your vacation?" After the pleasantries, he said, "I'd like to show you something. It's just a short walk." He took his coat from a rack behind the door and steered me out by my elbow. With his coat on, he looked like a giant red haired Abraham Lincoln, and his firm but ancient grip on my elbow felt as if it were from another age.

My upper lip was sweating. "Sure," I said.

Dr. Ledbetter headed in the direction of a small house behind Wyche. "Your grades were good, very good considering your classes. I doubt anyone learned as much as you last semester."

"Thank you, Dr. Ledbetter."

"Call me 'Dr. Ledbetter' like everyone else when we're in public, Peter. Call me 'Sam' when we're alone."

"I'll try," I said, then added, "Sam," tentatively. It sounded a little strange, and I felt like I should at least call him "Mr. Sam."

"I can see a lot of me in you, Peter. Full of energy, curious, you want to understand everything, to be a leader, to make a difference," he said. "You are a leader, you know. And you are making a difference." We climbed the stairs to the small house. Dr. Ledbetter unlocked the door, and we entered, pulling the door closed against the cold.

Dr. Ledbetter turned on the lights to reveal a large room with a low table in the center. A model of the school was on the table, showing all four dorms, and the classroom buildings. There was another dormitory where the Big Woods was. The ruined 1908 building had a new wing, parallel to one of the girl's dorms. There was another large building which looked like a gymnasium by the smoke stacks. Behind it were baseball and soccer fields. The Big Woods was much smaller, but still afforded some seclusion from the neighborhoods nearby. The smokestacks stood tall.

"This is the School in ten years. Seven years ago, when we started it, we had nothing. Every building needed to be gutted, and we had no money. We walked to I. C. Powell for meals, and bussed to Duke Library to study." I was still looking at the model, studying the differences between it and the campus I knew so well. "We started with nothing but a vision of what we wanted this school to become."

I looked up, attentive. "It's fragile, Peter. It scares me it's so fragile. It could fall apart any time. If the wrong girl gets raped, or the wrong boy tries to kill himself, it's over. Sixteen year olds don't want to leave home. Then you tell them they're going to take hard classes, study hard, get locked in their rooms, have no cars, and limited sports...I don't have to tell you how hard it is to recruit great students."

"Everyone loves it here," I said.

"Many, but not everyone," said the redheaded principal, the lines around his eyes deep canyons that sank deeper under the flow of growing something so new, so unusual.

Dr. Ledbetter continued, "You know what the hardest part is?" He paused, making sure he had my attention, then continued, "The hardest

167

part is the parents. They have to be convinced their child will get the same attention he'd get at home. Hell, most get more attention than they got at home. We have to convince them our women's dorms are like vaults. The boys' moms want girls here, and sports. Everyone's worried about college entrance and scholarships. We get more scholarships than anywhere else, including the other magnets—Stuyvesant, Bronx Science, you name them—we beat them every year with fewer students. But the parents have to be convinced.

"That's why we have rules." Dr. Ledbetter crossed the room, his heel clopping on the wood floor. He turned on a television, and pressed play on a VCR. I saw Caroline walk down the hall to my room. Dr. Ledbetter rewound the tape and played it again. I remained silent, and he played it a third time.

"How can I be anything but disappointed in you for this?" He paused, and I could not answer. The silence cut into me, narrowing my esophagus, making me want to blurt out that she had a baby over the summer, that she needed me, that I was doing more good for his precious campus that night with Caroline in my room than I had in any classroom, during any test, in any sporting event. Bitter bile pooled at the back of my mouth, and I remained silent.

"You probably didn't do anything wrong. You've known Caroline a long time, and that's your business. I was your age once. You may not have done anything *wrong*...but you broke the rules." He paused. I stood perfectly still, waiting for the hammer to fall. Dr. Ledbetter continued, "The rules aren't here for you, or people like you, Peter. You don't need them, and they don't need you. They're for the cut-ups, the people who shouldn't be here in the first place. Every time I send someone home, I check their admission file for something we could have seen, some way we could have let in a more deserving student. The rules are for them, and the politicians and the parents."

I felt like my world was coming apart—like everything I had been building was crumbling around me. On the inside, I was living in a volcano in mid eruption. On the outside, I was calm and attentive. I wanted to scream "We didn't do anything—we just talked!" but I knew it wasn't the truth, and it wouldn't work anyway.

"I made a deal with Chris," Dr. Ledbetter said. I listened. "You get a two week detention, like normal, except self-enforced—only you and Chris know. Caroline gets nothing—she won't even know you were caught. Also, you switch advisers—I'll be your new adviser. We'll meet every two weeks starting tomorrow at three. We'll lighten your course load, and I have some other suggestions.

"Last, Peter, I'd been thinking about having you make one of the student speeches at graduation. Any more stunts like this and that's out. Any questions?"

I was having trouble breathing; the room had become very stuffy, and my fight or flight instinct was screaming "Flight!" I managed a "No, sir," before walking out onto the porch, where I felt a little better. I shook hands with Dr. Ledbetter, his bony knuckles and cold skin pressing into my own, and then went to my dorm. I put on sweats and went running around the lake and back, then around campus. I kept pumping my legs, kept moving. The cold air in my lungs was like nectar. I didn't understand why Dr. Ledbetter paid me this much attention. I didn't want to be treated special. Worst, two weeks detention meant two weeks without seeing Caroline in the evenings.

That night, I sent her an email:

*　　*　　*

Caroline,

I have to beg off our nightly meetings. It's nothing about you, and there's not another girl (I wish there was!). I can't talk, but it has to do with the secret you're keeping for me. Just keep keeping it, and everything will be okay.

There is some good news, too.

I can start again in two weeks. You should understand what that means.

Love,
Pete

*　　*　　*

For two weeks, I studied. I worked ahead on my syllabi, getting my homework assignments assigned early, and finishing early. I was a student machine.

Caroline and I planned a big night for Sunday, the first night after my detention was over—pizza, then rent some movies to watch in the lounge with Alexander and Julia. That's why I was pissed when the School brought in an outside speaker and required attendance, and Chris decided this didn't count as a night of detention. It put our celebration off for a week.

The speaker was a Nobel Prize winner, Dr. James Watson, one of the people who discovered the structure of DNA. It was a surprise visit, scheduled when he was in the Research Triangle Park visiting Burroughs-Welcome, one of the pharmaceutical giants with a research facility there. In honor of the speaker, we had lectures in all of our classes about the science of their discovery, the social implications of the discovery, and the role of DNA and chromosomes in history and literature. They even put up a special display model in the library of the DNA molecule including the x-ray patterns and examples of the calculations they did to solve the structure. A brass plaque in front of the display read:

DNA – Deoxyribonucleic Acid.

The double helix structure was determined by James Watson, Francis Crick, and Maurice Wilkins, for which they won the Nobel Prize in 1962.

Black = Carbon
Red = Oxygen
Blue = Nitrogen
White = Hydrogen

By the time Dr. Watson came to talk, we were all DNAed out, though many of us did realize the significance of having a Nobel Laureate come speak at our high school.

Because the speaker made my detention go on to Sunday night, and I had wrestling practice all week, I had to wait until the next Saturday before I had my fun night with Caroline, Alexander and Julia. I decided I needed to get even.

When we all finally went out to celebrate the end of my detention, I told them about Dr. Ledbetter thinking of me to give a graduation speech. "That's great," Julia said, and Caroline took my hand under the table.

Alexander, ever perfect, said, "Oh, what a wonderful opportunity to share your wealth of knowledge with the rest of the class, and their parents and brothers and sisters, too. I'm sure you'll work hard to make sure you say the right things."

"I've already got some idea of what I might say," I said.

"Oh do tell, do tell," he said.

I shook my head no. "Let's wait and see if it's going to happen, first," I said, and Caroline squeezed my hand before letting go.

*   *   *

When my detention ended, I changed, studying in public places instead of my room. I spent study hours in the library in Bryan Hall, silent under the watchful eyes of the librarian Mrs. Lobensky, a large grizzly-bear of a woman. On Saturday mornings I and the work study student were the only people in the library. Many Saturdays, I was waiting when the library opened, hair still wet from my shower. When the library closed, the work study student had to ask me to leave.

Every day in the library, I had a small bar of hotel soap in my pocket, both sides sanded smooth. I was waiting for the chance to use that bar of soap.

The semester passed quickly for all of us. With no boyfriend, Caroline joined many school activities, and became everyone's friend. She was at every sporting event, helped on the yearbook and on the school newspaper. She joined the Student Activity Council, or SAC, which organized the dances, vans to sporting events, and other social events. She spent less time with me, but passed me a special double-dimple smile when she saw me, and that was enough.

Our group of four still met every night after study hours. We took walks; we talked; we griped and gossiped. This was my escape, my one social hour. I loved these friends, and felt us forming bonds like Kevlar. I believed we would be friends forever.

Alexander and I went to Sectionals that winter. I finished the regular season with a 0.500 record, plus a 5-1 record in a preseason tournament, which was enough to make the cut. I won three matches in Sectionals, then lost, and eventually finished fourth. Three wrestlers went to the state tournament, and that was fine with me. I could claim a little fame, but didn't have the extra two weeks of practice, nor give up the weekend for the tournament.

There were eight weeks left in the semester when I got my chance to use the bar of soap. During those eight weeks, I was frequently asked to watch the library when the work study student needed to use the bathroom or check her email. Those breaks lasted five or ten minutes, and I couldn't risk being caught.

One Thursday at the end of study hours, a junior library worker came to my table. "Pete," she said, her hand resting lightly on my shoulder, "I need a favor." Beth was thin, with an almost boyish figure, shoulder length hair and large, overly fashionable glasses. She smiled shyly, "I want to go home tomorrow night. Could you open the library for me Saturday morning?"

I looked up, my heart galloping. I tried to keep a still, calm face. Her hand was still on my shoulder, but her smile faded. "Only if you planned to be here anyway. Most Saturdays, it's just you and me. Nobody wanted my shift so I'd owe you."

"No problem," I said, thinking of a lonely Saturday morning, alone in the library with the keys to everything.

"Good, I'll give you my keys tonight, and you can give them back Saturday."

"Okay," I said, "I'll bring your keys to the dance Saturday night."

When Beth closed the library, she went over my responsibilities, and told me what key was for what.

"Don't worry," she said. "Conan doesn't come in on weekends."

"Conan?" he asked.

Beth giggled. "Sorry," she said. 'That's what we call Mrs. Lobensky. 'Conan the Librarian.'" Mrs. Lobensky was a large bull of a woman with a gravelly voice and biceps used to heavy lifting. We laughed, and Beth touched me on the arm. I noticed.

Later, at two am, I slipped out of Wyche, and then slipped into Bryan through a door at the back of the laundry room, then into the library using Beth's key. I locked the door, and sat in a shadow and watched. I timed the security guards' rounds. I repeated this on Friday night, until I was confident of their schedule.

Saturday night, I came to the dance about an hour after it started, keys in my pocket. Beth was waiting. I had never seen her in a skirt before, and she had a little more body in her hair, and color on her face. After talking for a few minutes, I asked her to dance.

"I don't dance to fast songs," she said shyly. I looked down, rejected. "We could dance to the next slow song," she added quickly. We talked and I took her hand and walked out onto the dance floor at the beginning of the next slow song.

Her hand was soft and moist in mine, not quite like a child's, but definitely welcome and ... dependent. At first, she was stiff and tense, holding her body away from mine, but after I smiled and our eyes met, she relaxed and her body moved a little closer. By the end of the dance, her head was on my chest with one arm draped loosely around my neck. I buried my head in her hair, and smelled and felt things I hadn't expected, not with library-girl Beth. Later, we took a walk, and ended up kissing in the darkened corner of a lounge.

* * *

I bought a set of calipers, and measured exactly the size master key needed to copy each of the keys. I recorded the dimensions in a hardbound, pocket sized notebook, and made two impressions of each key in the hotel soap. I bought a set of jeweler's files, and went to work duplicating keys, working two hours each night after curfew. I napped in the afternoons.

I also wrote to my friend, Freddy, asking him to do a big favor.

I woke early each morning and zipped to the cafeteria and ate Lucky Charms, separating the marshmallows. I concealed the marshmallows in zip-lock bags in my pockets. It was going to take six large boxes of cereal to complete my model.

I couldn't accurately predict when security would come by the library first, but felt confident once they came by, I would have an hour of freedom before they came by again, which was enough.

I made keys and separated Lucky Charms for four weeks. I spent time with Beth, and she joined the group of friends, now five. She was quiet, but claimed she enjoyed it, and I didn't care—she was great to me, and I needed my friends.

With four weeks left in the semester, all I had left was exams, which were given a week early for seniors. Leaving time to study, I had two weeks to work on the model.

I entered and exited by the window in the kitchen. The first night, I watched security again, to make sure of my hour of freedom. When they had passed, I checked my keys. They all worked, except one, which went to a storage closet. The second night, after security passed, I gave them ten minutes, and then went to work. I mixed epoxy glue in a small Tupperware container, then carefully removed five little balls of one color from the model, and replaced them with Lucky Charms marshmallows. I replaced carbon with blue stars, oxygen with pink diamonds, nitrogen with yellow moons, and hydrogen with the four leaves off the green clovers. I took five balls each time and replaced them. I could replace about 150 balls in an hour. Slowly, night after night, I made progress.

I spent less time in the library—only when Beth was there, and even then sat with my back to the entrance, so I wouldn't have to resist staring at my slowly morphing model, resting in its display case.

I met with Dr. Ledbetter on Monday two weeks before exams, when I was about halfway finished with the model. As normal, I talked about my assignments, what was easy, and what was difficult. The conversation turned to exams. "It's a tough exam schedule. You've done well keeping up, but I'd like you to finish your independent study projects before you study for exams. That's the smartest thing."

"You have no idea what you're asking me to do," I said.

"Sure I do. I asked your instructors to move up the due dates."

I remained silent, trying to mentally rework my nocturnal schedule.

"There's something else. We expect the usual end-of-year pranks and vandalism. Your class is special. Some of you will try to outdo stunts from last year and before.

"Keep your ear to the ground. Let petty stuff pass by—drop me an email. If you hear of anything major, I'd like to have a chance to stop it."

"What's major?" I asked.

"Some things can't be replaced—lab equipment, scientific displays. Please tell me if we're going to need a helicopter. I can't believe we didn't catch that one."

"It may not have been a student. I hear alumni come back for pranks."

"Why? They get a great education! Just keep your ear to the ground. I don't want anything major this year. This class has potential...I want to steer it the right way."

"Count on me, sir."

"I know I can, Pete. Last thing."

"What's that?"

"You get ten minutes at graduation—you were selected on my nomination, by vote of the faculty. I expect you to be impressive."

"Thank you sir. I'll do my best," I said, my heart racing.

"We're gonna miss you next year, Pete. Knock 'em dead at Ohio State!"

"Thank you. You know I'll try."

*   *   *

For the next five days, I hardly slept. I worked on my final projects for Macroeconomics and Biology, putting together a shoddy, barely passable job. It didn't matter to me anymore. What did matter was the two nocturnal hours I spent replacing the little atom-balls with Lucky Charms marshmallows.

I finished the model late, the Thursday before exam week. After I replaced the last atoms, I replaced the little brass plate with one I had had Freddy make for me back in Hendersonville. It read

DCA – Deluckycharmuleic Acid.

The Pursuit of Excellence was achieved by 172 hard working, diligent students, for which we received our high school diplomas on May 29th, 1988.

Yellow = Moons

Pink = Hearts

Green = Clovers

Blue = Diamonds

I slept in on Friday, but didn't miss any classes. I took Beth out for dinner Friday night, and we shared a very tender moment in a lounge before curfew. Saturday, I studied for exams, minus a short trip to the mall to buy a new white bed sheet. I couldn't pass up the opportunity, though in hindsight the price I paid may not have been worth it.

*   *   *

After nearly five hundred telescoping days of intense study and intense friendship, seniors at the North Carolina School of Science and Mathematics are ready to graduate. We approach graduation the way a sailor, long at sea, approaches the shore. As it grows closer, we stand on the rails, longing for the new life it offers. We leap off early and sprint through the shallow waters of the days just before, and then dive into it and kiss the first land we touch.

Then, not days after we have gone home, we miss the sea; we miss our School. It has shaped me like no place, no group of people, no singular event has before or since. I love it; I miss it; I am forever grateful for the memories it gave me and the changes it imparted to me.

Perhaps through uncommon wisdom, I knew as the last days of school ticked by that I would sorely miss everything I had grown to love there. I stole time from sleep and from Beth and Caroline to research in the library, searching for inspiration to include in my graduation speech. I wanted to somehow capture everything I had learned, everything I had loved, had appreciated, and use it to propel myself and my classmates into the future, into the world waiting for us to create it. I found my inspiration in a great poet, and his namesake, a great leader. I spent hours crafting my speech, and then more hours practicing it in front of Beth, Caroline, Alexander and Julia. With their help, I honed it into seven minutes of perfection, and I longed to deliver it.

*   *   *

A little known but well publicized discovery at the North Carolina School of Science and Math is how to get information to travel faster than the speed of light. Physicists everywhere will argue it can't be true, that the entire space-time continuum breaks down if an object moves faster than the speed of light. And likely that is true; however information can travel faster than the speed of light, and here is how you can do it: Go to the school, and start a rumor, especially one against "the administration."

176

Several students noticed the plaque over the weekend, and by Sunday night everyone had "discreetly" walked by to see it. There was a buzz all over campus, but because it was done so tastefully, and with such attention to detail, and because all of the missing pieces were found in a cardboard box underneath the display area, there was a tacit agreement to report it to the School administration after graduation, so proud seniors could walk their parents by the display and tell them the story of the flag, and how hard they had worked to live up to its ideals. So, while students, faculty, and basically everyone with a heartbeat on campus knew about the display model, it went unreported and stood proud on the evening before graduation.

Caroline came by to see me during exam week, with my yearbook in hand. She gave me a hug, and then handed it to me. "I didn't know what to write. You mean much more to me than I could describe in words." A tear fell from the corner of her eye, and her scar was dark.

I hugged her close and then we sat down and I handed her yearbook to her. "You'll have to do some work to understand it—it's in code," I said. She opened it, and squinted her eyes in confusion at the jumble of words in front of her. She shook her head, and looked up at me with a confused smile. "Here's a hint," I said. "'Olive juice, is how I feel about you, and 'tissue' is what I'm going to do when you're gone." She shook her head, still smiling, but not understanding, and kissed me on the cheek and left.

* * *

Caroline spent all night working on the code, and the next morning, came to show me what she had, written out in the margin. "Elephant shoe," she said. "Olive juice," I said back.

Dearest Caroline.

Olive juice. Elevator, tissue. *(I love you, and later, miss you.)*

Mule essays gravitate inimitable. Essay wombat samarium apart. Mecca war mess ends éclair. Sitcom portable mega foam. Blue army foam.

(You'll always have a place in my table. The same one as from the start. Make a warm nest and stay there, get comfortable, make a home. You are my home.)

Elephant shoe. *(I love you.)*
Peter

* * *

After we were locked in our dorms at curfew and devoured a literal "leaning tower" of pizza, I excused myself, saying I needed a little sleep. Most guys with girlfriends, at least those who could "borrow" a ground floor room, were getting some "sleep" also. I walked to my room. It was three a.m. the night before graduation.

I changed quickly into dark sweats, and gathered a small bag filled with items I would need. I crossed over to the kitchen, and left via my normal route. There was lots of nocturnal activity in the woods tonight— security was busier watching the dorms than the Big Woods. I heard at least two couples in various stages of passion on my trip to the smoke stacks. I gave them a wide berth, and made it to the stack undetected.

I watched the routes the security guards took, and, when I had a break, jumped at the bottom rung. On my second jump, I was up, and attached myself as before. A strong breeze blew, especially up high, which made my balance more important, and caused my carabiners to clink against the rungs. That worried me.

The noise from the carabiners was way too loud. I leaned back against my harness, arresting the tinkling noise. I tore a strip from the bed sheet in my bag and wrapped it around the bent ends of the carabiners. It made the attaching and detaching of the carabiners more difficult, and made my flag a little less than "Excellent", but quieted my climb considerably. I continued up, breathing heavily, concentrating on safety.

When I got to the top, I unfurled the flag, and used bailing wire to attach it. I wanted to get down before someone from security saw the flag and came over to investigate. What had been a forty-five minute climb was going to have to take only a few minutes on the way down. I'd be caught if I took longer. I decided to climb down without the safety of the carabiners.

I climbed several steps down, holding the bottom of the flag as I climbed. My soft wrestler's shoes hugged the rungs tightly, but the balls of my feet ached where they had been holding my weight, unsupported, on the climb up. In one motion, I let go of the flag and began to climb down, deliberately, yet quickly. I gripped the rungs hard, and concentrated on moving only one contact point at a time. I moved an arm. Then I moved a leg, then another arm. I climbed down much quicker than if I were moving my protection each time, but still infinitely slowly. It would be very quick, though, if I fell.

The wind picked up, and it unfurled the flag. I looked up—it was beautiful in the wind. But it also made a clicking noise as it blew back and forth, the bailing wire banging against the rungs. To me, each collision between wire and rung was like a gunshot. I scanned the ground below, but couldn't see any security personnel outside. They would finish their rounds inside soon enough. I had to get down.

The noise made me nervous, my hands sweaty. I climbed down quickly, still moving only one contact point at a time. My feet ached with each step, but each step brought me closer to freedom. A little more than halfway down, my foot slipped on a rung. Holding tightly, I raised myself with my arms, got both feet secure on the rungs again. I scanned the ground below. This time, I saw security making their rounds.

They were on the other side of the dorms, but the flag could be seen from anywhere on campus, and to me, was making a huge racket. I knew the noise would carry. I began to descend again, trying to be careful, but increasing my speed.

As I got to a level just above the tree line, I saw the security personnel turn the corner of the dorm. It was Tommy, a fat, friendly black man who took a special pleasure in protecting the "good kids" from "the bad eggs." I knew I had time because Tommy was a slow runner, though I was sure Tommy would see the flag as he turned around the building. Sure enough, as I went below the tree line, Tommy broke into a lumbering run and put his walkie-talkie to his mouth. I climbed down helter-skelter, disregarding safety. I was close enough to survive a fall, most likely.

When I got to the bottom, I heard Tommy's heavy breathing coming toward me, his gun and handcuffs banging as he bounced through the woods toward the smokestack. Ten rungs from the bottom, less than twenty feet from the ground, Tommy broke free of the woods, looking up at the flag. I sprung away from the smokestack, twisting myself as I did it. I hit on my feet and rolled. I hurt a knee and an ankle, but got up and made a break for the other side of the clearing. Limping, I was still faster than Tommy, and tore through the woods as Tommy told his walkie-talkie he had seen someone jump off the tower.

I ran through the woods, this time not avoiding the passionate couples. I owed them a warning, at least. To the first couple I whispered, "Get going—security's coming right now!" They looked up in surprise, and when they heard Tommy crash into the woods, pulled on clothing on as they ran. They were not quiet.

Tommy's thrashing and the skipping, running couple roused the other two couples. One boy asked, "What the hell?" as I ran by. I didn't answer, concentrating on being the quietest, fastest runner in the woods.

When I got near to Wyche, I stopped, surveying the grounds. Behind me, six students and three security people ran almost randomly in the woods. The security guards all used high powered flashlights. One of the couples had been caught, and stopped running. Another made a break out of the woods, a security guard rumbling behind them. The third couple stopped moving, deciding to wait it out.

I made my break as the fleeing couple pulled the security guards towards the main end of campus, away from Wyche. I jumped, then climbed the back side of the fire escape to the ledge, and climbed into the building. Sticking my head out into the hall, I saw students at the end of the hall in the lounge, talking.

I thought quickly, then stripped to my underwear, stashing my sweat clothes in a cabinet under the sink. After the camera blinked, I crossed over to my room, opened the door, then stepped out and walked down the hall to the bathroom. My heartbeat was like a sledgehammer going double quick. When I got back to my room, the voices down the hall hadn't noticed me.

An hour later, when all was quiet, I retrieved my clothes from across the hall unseen, and spent the rest of the night getting well needed sleep.

*   *   *

The RA's woke all of the seniors at 6:45. Most of us had only gone to bed an hour or two earlier. I stepped outside and saw the other seniors collected in the stands set up on the lawn for the graduation ceremony, looking up at the flag. Each one, as he first saw where everyone else was looking, then looked himself, joined in a huge collective smile. I took my place silently beside Caroline, and Alexander and Julia each joined a moment later. Dr. Ledbetter stood on stage, glaring down on us. Some students yelled, and shook their fists, "Yeah!" "In your face!" "We sure are!" they jeered. The range of emotion displayed among the students ran from joy of victory, to almost tears as some students were ashamed of their classmates. When we had all collected, Dr. Ledbetter began his speech.

"I had great expectations—that could have been the title for this year, 'Great Expectations'," he began. He took out some notes, and I saw the students stir quietly. "Some things I'd planned to say: 'This class has broken a lot of records. Highest attendance. Highest grades in Calculus. In physics. In chemistry. Most college credits, per student, in the United States. National Debate Championship winners. National Chess Tournament runner's up. Highest scholarship money ever received in a single year, passing much bigger schools.'" Dr. Ledbetter paused after each phrase, the crowd visibly deflating after the last. Some students were still defiant, proud of their class. Other students hung their heads. I looked directly at Dr. Ledbetter, never blinking. Caroline held my arm, her fingers digging small divots in my biceps.

"I'm not going to say any of those things today, because there will be no graduation ceremony with that flag flying over this campus." He paused for this to take effect. As it sank in, the reactions grew animated. Some students cursed, many just got angry. One or two of the girls put their heads down and began to cry. Scattered parents had begun to gather near a tree beside the ceremony, and their faces tightened.

"Not only that," continued Dr. Ledbetter, turning to the group of parents. "We will sit here as your parents collect until one of you takes the flag down. None of you are permitted to talk with your parents. Let them see what kind of student is among you." The few parents already there grew restless, whispering to each other.

Dr. Ledbetter watched from the podium as the emotions of the class went steadily south. While many of the other students either cried or cursed, I remained resolute. Dr. Ledbetter locked eyes with me, and spoke again.

"All but one or two of you are innocent. To keep our standards, you all have to suffer," he looked straight at me. "You earned the things I was going to say. You worked incredibly hard. I never expected perfection, but some of you came close.

"If anyone knows who did it, you can save your graduation ceremony," Dr. Ledbetter said. He looked straight at me. "It would save a lot of trouble." He paused, then, softly, "Do you know who did it, Peter?" I looked straight at him, unblinking, as Caroline dug her fingers harder into my arm. The immense tension in my temples began to flow into the rest of my body as I felt my muscles tighten. With my thumb, I rubbed the raw skin on the pads of my fingers, from climbing the rusty rungs. I remembered my helter skelter descent, and thought about the danger if I had fallen. While I could make any sacrifice myself to make my statement, I could not let others suffer for me. My speech was important to me, but not that important.

It must have been an eternity, then, slowly, I leaned forward, preparing to rise. As I did, Caroline pulled down hard on my arm with both hands, and then stood silently. I screamed, "NO!" and tried to hold her as she pulled away, but an invisible force held me to my seat. She moved through the crowd, heading in the direction of the smokestack. The crowd, including Dr. Ledbetter, stood still as statues as Caroline made her way toward the smoke stack.

We all held our breath as she stood for a couple seconds at the bottom of the stack, looking up. My palms grew sweaty, and again I thumbed the sore skin. Caroline's first attempt to jump to the bottom rung was clumsy, but she quickly mastered the method I had described to her, and caught hold on her second jump. She slowly pulled herself up until she was standing on the bottom rung.

She began her slow ascent. She climbed, one rung after another, holding each one tightly, pausing before she mounted the next. I sat in tense agony until she had reached a third of the way up, then jumped to my feet and ran to the smokestack. Several members of the crowd, and then the whole crowd, joined behind me. Dr. Ledbetter came behind, walking quickly. "I can't believe it," he said as he came to the edge of the crowd. "Caroline! Come down now!" he yelled. "I don't want anyone getting hurt," he said to the crowd, which now contained a few parents.

Caroline continued climbing. She had passed halfway, and I could see her stop to wipe the sweat off of her hands at each rung. Red rust stained her shirt where she wiped. The crowd was buzzing below, in frenzied paralysis.

Then I heard the familiar voice of Caroline's father. "What the hell is going on here?" he demanded. "Caroline, get down from there right now!" he yelled up at her. Then he walked straight up to me and turned me around by my arm. "What kind of shenanigan is this, Peter Bennett? In Possession of Excellence? This is not some stunt Caroline pulled by herself." He left me and went for Dr. Ledbetter. Donna stayed behind and took hold of my arm as we both watched Caroline's ascent. Hope and Edward held hands, staring up at our brave Caroline.

Caroline's forehead was wrinkled in determination as she pulled herself up the last few rungs, standing even with the flag. She worked with the bailing wire, her hands clumsy with fatigue. She loosened her belt, looped it through a rung, and then leaned back cautiously, holding on with both hands. It held.

Working with both hands while leaning back, she untwisted the bailing wire quickly. The crowd let loose an audible gasp as the top of the flag flew out of her hand, streaming like a ribbon in the wind. She moved down to the other tie, hooked herself in and did it again. When the second tie came undone, the flag blew away from her in the wind. She smirked as she watched it fly away.

She loosened her belt. "Don't give up, Caroline!" I yelled up at her, and realized I had been holding my breath. "You have to get down!" The crowd, which had been watching the flag drift gently to the lawn, echoed my concern. To her classmates, Caroline had become a class hero, soon to be class martyr. "Take it easy, Caroline!" "Rest if you need to!" "Be careful!"

When she came to the bottom rung, her entire body shook. Her legs, in good shape from her swimming and tae kwon do, had held strong. I waited below the bottom rung. As she stepped down past the last rung and tried to grip her tennis shoes on the vertical brick wall, I reached up and held her foot and her calf, carefully lowering her to the ground.

She had not said one word during the climb, and held silent for the rest of the day. Her father, who had whispered something to Dr. Ledbetter and then stood silent as she loosed the flag and descended, started screaming, first at Dr. Ledbetter, then at Caroline, me, and anyone else who stood close enough. Caroline was whisked off to a conference room with her parents, Dr. Ledbetter, and a few other administrators, while Hope, Edward and I waited outside. Alexander gathered up the flag and folded it neatly. He carried it cradled in his arm, military style, until the graduation ceremony ended.

Outside the conference room, we could hear Caroline's father yelling. At one point, he threatened to sue the School, but that didn't get anyone's attention. After nearly an hour, Edward went to get us all drinks. When he was gone, Hope asked me, "Peter, do you know what's going on?" I nodded my head. "Did Caroline put that flag up, and do all the other things they're saying?" I looked at my shoe laces, then shook my head slowly, almost imperceptibly, no.

"Do you know who did?" I looked up, and looked dead in the center of her brown eyes, and nodded.

Hope didn't ask the next, obvious question. When Edward came back, she opened the door to the conference room, and I saw her walk behind Caroline and stand beside her. "May I have a moment alone with my sister? I may be able to help." There was silence for a moment, and then both Dr. Ledbetter and Mr. Novak nodded, and everyone except Caroline and Hope filed out of the room.

We all sat in the School lobby in stunned silence. The adults had spent their anger in the conference room, and were enjoying the proverbial eye at the center of the storm. None of us knew what Hope would accomplish, but we hoped for more than a stalemate.

A few minutes later, the door opened and Hope stepped out, leaving Caroline sitting alone, in the same wooden chair she had been sitting in for over two hours. I could see the rust stains on the palms of her hands, and thought about her suffering and the danger as she climbed that stack without the aid of protection.

Hope walked up to Dr. Ledbetter and her father. "She isn't going to tell you anything today, and her wish is to not participate in the graduation ceremony. She won't talk today. You'd better just both go with it."

Mr. Novak had a few more words with Dr. Ledbetter, but eventually, Dr. Ledbetter and the administrators left and went out to organize the ceremony proceedings.

I tried to go into the conference room with Caroline's family, but Hope turned around and said, "You have to give your speech, Peter. Get out there," and closed the door in my face.

* * *

The ceremony started a half hour later, and when the time came, I took the stage, took a deep breath, and surveyed the crowd before me. Our class sat in alphabetical order, and I looked to the empty seat where Caroline would have been sitting, I began.

"Two roads diverged in a yellow wood,
sorry I could not travel both
be one traveler, long I stood
looked down one as far as I could
To where it bent in the undergrowth;

Then took the other, as just as fair,
having perhaps the better claim,
Because it was grassy and wanted wear;
Though as for that the passing there
Had worn them really about the same,

both that morning equally lay
In leaves no step had trodden black.
Oh, I kept the first for another day!
Yet knowing how way leads on to way,
I doubted if I should ever come back.

I shall be telling this with a sigh
Somewhere ages and ages hence;
Two roads diverged in a wood, and I—
I took the one less traveled by,
that has made all the difference.

I paused for a moment after I finished, and then said. "Those words, from my great great uncle Robert Frost, have been read in thousands of high school graduations, and written in millions of yearbooks. They are no less apt for us today, as we finish this leg of our life, as we realize one more step on our ladder in pursuit of excellence.

"I never knew Mr. Frost. My grandmother knew him. He was quiet, withdrawn. His name was Robert Lee Frost, and he was a natural nonconformer. My grandmother said he was embarrassed by the attention, but was nonetheless driven to write his poetry, to share his wisdom with others through his craft.

"He told us why in one of his poems:

"My avocation and my vocation
As two eyes make one sight.
Only where love and need are one,
the work is play for mortal stakes,
Is the deed ever really done
For Heaven and the future's sake."

Again, I paused, and for a moment I could breathe in the freshness of spring and feel the new growth, and the scent of chlorophyll and sunlight combining filled my senses. I saw the class, sitting below me with their chins held high, our juniors sitting behind them and a crowd of proud parents in the stands to the sides. Then I continued, "Robert Frost did not know much about being ordinary. In this poem, he did not tell us how to be ordinary." I changed my voice to the same one I had used to quote the poems. "'To be ordinary,' he might have written, 'do as others do, satisfy your greed or your laziness. Get angry when things don't go your way, and practice your passion alone, never to perfect it.'" A light ripple of giggles passed across the crowd.

"His words are quite clear, 'Only where love and need are one, and the work is play for mortal stakes is the deed ever really done for Heaven and the future's sake.' I couldn't find any better words to take us to college, to guide our search for our vocation and our avocation, which should be 'as two eyes make one sight.' We should find one where 'the work is play for mortal stakes.'

"He told us how he viewed himself,
"'If an epitaph were to be my story
I'd have a short one ready for my own

186

I would have written of me on my stone

I had a lover's quarrel with the world'"

I took a large lungful of air, sucking in the spring morning, then began again. "Robert Frost's namesake shared his wisdom not through words, but through deeds. He was a great general, an idealist, a leader, and someone who stood up for what was right. There may have never been an American with more character."

"After he surrendered at Appotomatox Courthouse, he returned to Richmond. We can only imagine how he felt—lonely, defeated, as if he had let down the world. Wondering if on the day in 1860, when he chose not to take the position of General of the US armies, and instead fight for the South, he had chosen the wrong 'Road less traveled by.'

"In Richmond, he went to church at St. Paul's Episcopal Church. He sat in a pew near the front, with his wife. His presence caused a stir among the other churchgoers. They certainly noticed him. He chose another 'road less traveled by' that day, one clearly done 'for Heaven and the future's sake.'

"Normally the white church-goers received mass first, and the blacks, who sat in the back, came up only after the whites had finished. Most whites, and many blacks, thought this normal and proper. There were two that day who did not.

"As the priest made preparations, before anyone else came forward, a stately black gentleman rose from the back and walked slowly down the aisle. The church was silent as he approached and took his knee at the altar, opening his hands to receive Mass.

"The priest was confused, and for a long time, nobody moved, or said anything. I can only imagine the deafening reverberations of the silence in that church," I paused, and saw interest in this largely southern bred group of students. "Before it ended, Robert E. Lee stood, dressed impeccably in his Sunday suit, walked to the front and took his knee beside the black gentleman to receive Mass."

I folded my notes, diverting from my planned speech, and said, "So do actions speak louder than words. Be patient, then, and perhaps ignore my words, but heed my actions." I looked straight at Alexander, and saw the flag cradled proudly under his arm.

I walked off the stage. A few claps popped around the crowd, but the applause died as I passed my seat. Alexander walked to the end of the row, handed me the flag, and I walked toward the smokestack.

I made the climb without protection, the same climb I had made twice before, the same one Caroline had made that morning. For the second time, Dr. Ledbetter and a stunned student body watched as someone climbed the smokestack. The seniors stood together, and cheered loudly when I unfurled the flag and began my climb down.

Later, when everyone gathered for the end of the ceremony, Dr. Ledbetter spoke before the diplomas were given out. "Peter," he said, "you have given each of us a graduation speech we will always remember. I'm afraid students will be talking about this for the rest of the history of this School.

"This class has achieved excellence this year, and deserves to graduate under that banner." The seniors again cheered, this time joined by their families and the juniors, who watched from behind. Dr. Ledbetter went on to list their accomplishments, each one receiving a standing ovation from the parents, before the diplomas were passed out.

Caroline did not graduate.

*   *   *

Dear Faith,

I haven't spoken more than seven or eight words to your mother since that day. There was, of course, the big stink about whether I could be invited to Hope and Edward's wedding, but Hope made a stand since Edward wanted me as his best man. Her father did manage to prevent me from walking her down the aisle, though. Late that night, at the reception, I managed to corner her when I thought her father wasn't looking. She stopped me before I could say anything. "You have to go," she said. I started to protest, but she stepped in and took my hand in hers and put a finger to my mouth. "Stop, Pete," she said. "It's okay. Nothing has changed. I'd do it again today, if I had to. But you have to go." I nodded, and stepped away. She still wasn't married, and I was waiting for ten years. I think she knew it, also.

Hope and Edward went to her wedding, of course. They said it was beautiful, but Edward wanted to know who this Curt guy was, who was the best man, so I assumed he got a little too friendly with Hope. No surprise. Evidently, Curt and the other guys in the wedding got drunk, and tried to throw Kevin into the pool, but screwed it up and dropped him on the concrete poolside and broke his tailbone. He had to sit sideways on the airplane all the way to Jamaica, and then wasn't much good at performing his marital duties, or so I'm told. I can take a little joy from that.

Somehow, Faith, Caroline and I fell so deeply in love with each other that we were beyond love, beyond needing each other and beyond just companionship. I would do anything for her, make any sacrifice. Raising you—well, that would have been no sacrifice, nor would have marrying your mother been one. What she did for me—well, that was a real sacrifice, and a real risk. She did it so I could make a speech, which may or may not have been any good, but was important to me, and what was important to me was important to her.

Caroline got engaged nine and a half years after I made my penultimate proposal to her, and was married six weeks later. I never got to make the last one. I know the full story now of her marriage to Kevin, because it was in her diary. If you've read this far, then you'll get to read it also, on the next few pages. I wish that could have worked out better, but it didn't. And Josh? Well, I don't know. It's been okay, at least up until the accident. Honestly, I kind of like the guy, if only because we share similar disfavor with her father. You might also ask me what I think of Mr. Novak, and I'd have to be honest with you. He's a grumpy, power mongering old son of a bitch, but his motives are true, and I can't fault him for anything he does out of love for Caroline.

Alexander and Julia got married in Martha's Vineyard just after they finished at Yale and Princeton. Alexander went on to work at Morgan Stanley while Julia was at med school at NYU. Caroline didn't go; evidently her father told her he wouldn't pay for medical school if she saw me, and they all knew I would be there. I got to sit at the head table with Alexander and Julia, and Julia again gave me a verse to memorize. It was a long one, James 1:22-25. "But be doers of the word, and not merely hearers who deceive themselves. For if any are hearers of the word and not doers, they are like those who look at themselves in a mirror; for they look at themselves and, on going away, immediately forget what they were like. But those who look into the perfect law, the law of liberty, and persevere, being not hearers who forget but doers who act—they will be blessed in their doing."

Whatever it is she's got that enables her to give her life over so freely, without any reservations or doubts at all—I was starting to get it then, at the wedding. I don't think I'm any further along the road now—there's still too much that doesn't make sense. Though I want to believe everything she says, everything the Bible says, and believe it without question and act on it, I haven't gotten there yet, and maybe I never will. I have to take each morsel and stick it in the corner of my mouth and chew on it a bit. So far, I've accepted every one, and maybe with time the consistency of my acceptance will grow, but then yet maybe not; maybe I'll always be a doubter.

I am married now, and Jen fits me like a good wrestling partner. Where I am weak, she makes me strong; when I lose, she is there to help me to learn to be better. She is my home base in this lifelong game of tag; when I am with her, I can never be "it." At our wedding, a good friend from graduate school wished on us "active and argumentative" children. Luckily, though I have both a son and a daughter, only one lived up to his wishes. My son is my mirror image (the parents' curse!), and my daughter is the spitting image of Jen, and I could not love her more.

Should you ever enter my life, Faith, I will transfer immediately to you all of the love I ever had for your mother, and also every unpaid debt. Come into my home, to visit or to stay, and you will be welcomed and loved. There are a few stories I've left out, and I long to tell you of them. I am generally not hard to find—go where the action is, and look out front—that's where I'll be. Come find me.

Love,

Peter

Chapter 8: Marriage

Caroline swept into my life like a wave rolling onto the beach, and I—I was the sand crab, first fleeing, dancing sideways to save myself from her turmoil, and then, as she slipped away, chasing her down the warm sand until she returned again, this time with more force. Eventually, the seduction of her descent and the force of her approach overcame me and I tumbled in the waves of our friendship, where I have been ever since those first two years, when we were roommates at the North Carolina School of Science and Mathematics.

When I first met her, she stepped into the doorway of our dorm room, and stood frozen in space, smiling down on me like a crescent moon on a starry night. I should have opened up to her then and entered into her waiting friendship, but I was scared. I had just left home; my parents had driven away in tears, leaving me with one small suitcase of clothes, a pad of paper and a few pencils, and my Bible. I did not want any friends, and certainly not friends of the sort I was sure Caroline would be.

She smiled at me from the doorway, holding a large suitcase in each hand. Peter was behind her, holding three large boxes stacked up to his chin. He was a muscular boy back then, the kind I knew I wouldn't have the will to resist, so instead avoided. Behind the two of them were Peter's parents, each carrying more of the effects Caroline needed to make this room, our room, into her home.

Peter's family left quickly to get Peter moved in, and, looking back, I know that Caroline tried to be friendly.

"Where are you from?" she asked me.

"Kitty Hawk," I said.

"Wow. That's great! It's where the airplane was invented, right?"

"Flown. It was invented in Ohio."

"Oh. Well, it must be exciting."

"It's nothing special."

Our conversation went on like that for a few more minutes. I didn't ask her one question about herself, and didn't answer any of her questions with more than a minimum of information.

She moved in quickly; her side of the room became an altar to her life. She had a small wooden box that she kept locked, and on it were pictures of her family, of her with friends, of old boyfriends. Ribbons, hair combs, hiking boots, mirrors, books—all these things populated her side of the room, while my side remained Spartan. When other girls passed by in the hall, they peeked in and asked about her things—about the boy in this picture, or about a book she had open on her dresser. Little did Caroline know that when she wasn't in the room, I shut the door and studied every feature of every person in each picture, that I memorized the titles of the books she had read, that I looked jealously at every adornment of her life.

*　　*　　*

We probably didn't say two hundred words to each other that first week, and I expected her to ask for a new roommate once the mandatory one-month trial period had passed. Things changed before that time came.

Of those two hundred words, I think fifty were "Peter." "I'm going to meet Peter at the cafeteria." "I'll be studying with Peter tonight." "Peter and I are headed out to the mall. Do you want to come?" My answers were "Okay," "Alright," "No, thank you."

*　　*　　*

There was a dance on the second Friday night, and I was determined not to go. I came back to our room after dinner and planted myself on my bed, leaning back against my single pillow, my Bible opened across my knees. I was reading, studying the life of Job.

Caroline came into the room. "Do you mind if I turn on some music?" she asked.

"No," I said, and she pulled out a vinyl album and played Loverboy's "Working for the Weekend." Not one of my favorites. My lips tensed and

I continued reading.

Caroline was not one to let my attitude become contagious, and she danced around the room as she pulled off her clothes one piece at a time, leaving them hanging off the edge of her bed, or curled up in the corner of her desk chair. I could never get over her lack of décor, of shyness, in our room. I saw more of her body in that first week than she has ever seen of mine, and yet inside, I am to this day insanely jealous of the ease and nonchalance with which she passes through life.

I watched as she transformed herself from a casual, nice school girl, into a moonlight diva. She pulled her hair back, left one more button unbuttoned on her shirt, wore slightly larger earrings, gold, and applied just the right amount of make-up to accentuate the way her smile magnetizes a room.

I watched through the corner of my eye, my mind detouring away from the story of Job, and as she started toward the door, I waited, expecting her to say she was going to meet Peter, as if I needed to know. Just as she was about to pull the door shut behind her, the silence of her departure screamed through every pore of my mind and I asked, "Are you going to meet Peter?"

"No, of course not," she said. "Peter and I aren't like that."

I am cursed with a curious mind. "Like what?" I asked. It was the first time the iron clad grips of my discipline had let go in Caroline's presence, the first time I had asked her a question.

"Peter is..." she paused. "He's like a brother, but different." She turned back into the room, then sat on her desk chair, brushing her underwear into the floor, and smiled in reminiscence. "He was the first boy I kissed, back when we were fourteen. But even then it was, you know, very virginal. I've known him since I was four, and now he's my best friend. Like a worn out sweatshirt—too comfortable to throw away, but not nearly nice enough to wear where anyone will see us."

That was, I think, the longest statement she had made to me in the two weeks we had lived together. I don't know if I was tired, or lonely, or hungry or just scared of what the next two years would be like, but my defenses were down and I asked her, "How did you meet when you were four?" After she told me, I asked her another, "Tell me about your first kiss," and then "Why did you break up?"

We talked for two hours, and sometime in the middle, she began to ask me questions, and I answered. I was amazed that Caroline, the social debutante, was giving up her time on the dance floor to talk with me; so I talked.

Nearing ten o'clock, I said, "You'd better go—you're going to miss your dance."

"You're coming with me," she said.

"No." The word escaped my lips, but the lie was betrayed by the whole essence of my being, and Caroline saw through it.

"Yes, you are. And you're going to knock them all dead," she said, as she opened a drawer and pulled out a sky blue satin shirt that I never would have worn by my own choice, on any day before that one, or that has passed since.

* * *

Now it is important to tell you something about me, something that I believed was the root to my being misunderstood my nearly everyone I had ever known.

Back when I was four years old, during the same summer that Caroline and Peter met, I made a decision to give my life to Jesus Christ. My father walked down the aisle with me at our church on a sunny Sunday afternoon, in a special service they were having. We climbed together into a swimming pool, small and round but deep enough for the water to be up to my waist. Then, my father asked me if I wanted to give my life to Jesus Christ, and I said "Yes," and leaned backward into his waiting arms, and felt the cool water cover my shoulders, neck, and then head as he lowered me slowly into it, saying, "I baptize you in the name of the Father, the Son, and the Holy Ghost. Amen." When I arose and stepped out of the pool, dripping wet, I felt in every pore, every orifice the water had touched, that I was not my own, that I had given my body over to Christ.

That doesn't mean I'm not like everyone else. It doesn't mean I don't lust, or have daydreams, or get jealous or want things or have dreams of myself in grand places. I am in bondage to those thoughts just like every other child of Adam, which is all of us in case you don't believe in all that. But I have segregated that part of me, my sinful nature. I have imprisoned it in a cage and have locked the gates and thrown away the key, though at times it takes every ounce of discipline I have to keep the gates closed. The prison for that part of me is within the warm, dark, fleshy part of my body that resides between my ears and behind my eyeballs. There it is, and there it shall stay, for the rest of my body does not belong to that part of me.

What does that mean? How can I do that? It's like this. Everything I do, everything that touches my body—that becomes a part of me—all of it is there only to glorify Jesus Christ. Every tattoo, every earring, every bit of polish on my toenails, every piece of clothing, every touch of gloss on my lips and curls in my hair—each is there only to glorify the life, death and resurrection of Jesus Christ my Lord. I have seventeen piercings, in my ears, my nose, my eyebrows, my navel and even my nipples. Through each one is some sign of my love for God, whether a fish, a cross, a crucifix, the torso of the Mother Mary, or his own likeness. I have seven tattoos in places that do not see the light of day, that depict the seven I Am's from the book of John. They are on my hip, my shoulder, my breast, the back of my thigh, and inside my bikini line, all of them in the most private and personal places I have, as my signal to Jesus that he owns me, every cell and every milligram.

I could never have resisted my sensual impulses if I had to do it alone. The temptation was every bit as strong in me as it was in everyone else, maybe stronger. But my will to obey God was even stronger still, and those tattoos and piercings were my way of giving my sexuality over to the Holy Spirit, of ensuring that, should I be tempted to expose them, He would be there to remind me to invoke His protection from my temptation. They are my yellow sticky notes to myself, left where I or someone else will find them, to remind me to call on the protection of the Holy Spirit. I am ashamed to have to have them, but know that there was no way I could have retained my purity alone.

There were times that I hated those tattoos, those piercings, that I wished for them to disappear for only an hour so I could experience the things other girls my age enjoyed on a regular basis, but they wouldn't go away and I couldn't be so false as to open up the pictorial love letter I had written to Jesus Christ on my body in the name of lust.

*　　*　　*

Soon after Caroline fell into her coma, and everything else happened, Josh called me and asked me to annotate Caroline's diary, especially through her college years, and up to her marriage. "You knew her best back then," he said. "It's important. It's to Faith."

I agreed, of course; my only stipulation was that he publishes every word just as I wrote them, without a single change, a single edit that might in some subtle way make either my person or the events of Caroline's life more palatable to the masses, who have mostly misunderstood both of us. I love her nearly as deeply as I love my God, and this is my chance to let the true depth of her character show. I will, and here you have it.

*　　*　　*

December 22nd, 1989

Dearest Mann,

I'm at college now, at the University of North Carolina. High school, and all that happened there, is behind me. I'm learning to love Carolina, and of course basketball.

This last year was hard, maybe harder than the year before, if you can believe that. Does life ever get easier? I've got to know—I can't do this by myself. When are you coming to help me? Hurry!

It's time to tell you about Peter. I loved that boy. He's at Ohio State now, ranting and raving about their football team. I get only an occasional letter—he's distracted by school, and the girlfriend he left behind at NCSSM.

I would love to tell you everything about Peter. He was my first kiss, my first boyfriend, my first friend, and my first love. When we graduated from high school—well, when he graduated—he knew everything about me. He knew about my pregnancy, about my intention to get an abortion, and about my cowardice when I got to the clinic, and through all that, he still loved me, accepted me as I was, and wanted nothing more than to make some sacrifice that would make me whole again.

He couldn't do that, and I couldn't let him. He proposed to me my junior year, after he found out about Faith. One night, when I was crying because nobody knew, I asked him to come up to a secret spot that Curt and I used to go to. I sat in his lap, crying, and when he asked me what was wrong, I placed his hand on my belly and held it there until he understood. A minute later, with not a trace of hesitation in his shiny blue eyes, he asked me to marry him. I said no, but spent the next hour kissing him, nearly delirious with relief that I was no longer alone. He proposed again a week later.

I wanted to say yes to him so desperately that it nearly consumed me. I wanted to take my lousy life, my mistakes, my insecurity and inadequacy and load it into the ambulance he offered—but when it came time to do it, I couldn't. I could not, and never will, make a commitment to marry out of pity, or obligation, or remorse. Though I hope in the center of my heart that in many ways you are like Peter, I could not say yes to him, not because of who he was, but because of who I wasn't.

Peter is gone now. He did some things during his senior year that would have gotten him in trouble, and at the end, I took the blame for him. Dad found out the truth, and forbade me to see him, threatening to withhold my tuition if I saw him. My dad—well, he has influence over me. I'm his little girl, and had just done something very bad. I decided to listen to him. Peter never understood, but I'm sure he forgave me. That's who he is.

I hope you can forgive me for the depth of feelings I've felt for Peter. If it's any consolation, I never slept with him—somehow our relationship went straight past sleeping together to a much deeper, much more sacred place; not the same place, but one very much like the one I'd like to share with you someday. However, I would like to sleep with you also, frequently and energetically.

Love,

Caroline

PS: Before I quit, I have to tell you about a very sweet Carolina tradition. I was in my dorm room one night studying and talking to my suitemates. The suite door was open, and we heard singing. One of the girls, more in touch than I was, said "It's a panty raid" and ran out on the balcony. I went too, curious. When I got there, a bunch of guys, maybe a hundred, all walked toward our dorm wearing coats and ties (Carolina boys, normally t-shirt and jeans boys, will use any excuse to put on a coat and tie!), singing one of the Carolina serenade songs. Every girl in the dorm came onto the balcony to listen to the sweet song they sang. We all laughed and cheered, and then they sang another song. After the fourth sweet song about beautiful Carolina girls, the songs turned a little "south", if you know what I mean. They sang "My Ding a Ling" and a few parodies on old songs—"Put Your Legs 'Round My Shoulders" to the tune of "Lay Your Head on My Shoulder." They kept singing, and all the boys and all the girls laughed their heads off at the words—me too! Then they sang a good-bye song, again very sweet which made me want to love every one of them. All us girls—me too—ran to our rooms and grabbed our favorite underwear and bras—the "nice" ones—and threw them down to the boys! It was like a ticker tape parade, with the underwear filling the sky and all the boys boxing out and leaping to catch it, all the while singing about the sweet sorrows of parting! They left singing sweet ol' alma mater, and we all cheered and went back to studying. I dreamt of marrying one of those Carolina boys with his full voice and his tie and my underwear. We had a mixer with them Friday night, and Doug Clark and the Hot Nuts sang all those dirty songs. We got to meet, and they were all duds, but it was great fun anyway!

* * *

Caroline led me by the hand straight onto the dance floor, the two of us dancing with each other, flowing with the music and not caring about the swirling masses around us. Though many think I am a prude, I am gifted with a bit of rhythm, and I'll admit within the confines of my mind that when I give my curly mane a toss and smile at the crowd, I can get a little attention. I wanted it that night.

Caroline introduced me to Peter, maybe thinking we would find an attraction to each other. And maybe I would have ... except Peter was, as I said, a little too ... I think "dangerous" is the right word. Yes, Peter was a little too dangerous for me. On the other hand, I knew at first glance that Alexander would understand me. He wore a sport coat and tie to the dance; he was the only one dressed that way; most of the other students wore shorts or blue jeans. I saw it as a sign of discipline, of a willingness to stand out because of what he believed. Over the next several weeks, I would learn that was true, and Alexander and I never looked back.

*   *   *

First Day of College

Dearest Caroline,

You're taking a giant step. Today you start making decisions for yourself, and, unfortunately, you have to bear the consequences with less help from your family.

I told you in a letter if there were anything in this world you want, if it was within my power to give it to you, I would.

In another letter, I said, "No matter what choices you make, no matter what methods you choose to learn life's hard lessons, I will be there for you. If there is a material thing in this world, I will give it to you. If there is a spiritual lesson, I will help you learn it. You can always come to me for a hug. Sometimes that's all you need."

I can see in your tiny little eyes, and the way you follow your older sister around, you are going to be just like me. Constantly pushing the edge of what you can do. Too proud to ever ask for help. Long on appreciation.

You understand, actually giving you things isn't why I made the offer. I want to be a person you can trust to come through, who will pick you up when you break a bone, who will hold you when you lose a boyfriend, who will be there in the hospital when you wake up after a car wreck. I do want to be like that for you.

But not for the times when I actually have to be that person. It's for all of the other times. I want you to know I will always be there to give you a soft landing when you fall hard. Here's the important part. Knowing that, Caroline, I want you to jump just a little higher on the trampoline. When you're up in the air and scared and sure you're not going to come down straight and terrified of doing a flip because you're going to be UPSIDE DOWN, I want you to flip anyway, because you know when you fly off and hit your arm or your head or your shoulder on a tree and break something, I'll be there to get you to the hospital, to nurse you as you heal, and to train with you as you work to regain your strength and get back on that scary bouncy thing.

The trampoline may be a bad example, but you know what I mean. I mean swim to the other shore, though it's far. I mean talk to the cute new guy, though you don't know what he'll see in you. I mean punch through the guy's face, though you're scared he'll punch back. (I hope you haven't grown this old without me or your father teaching you how to throw a punch.) I mean dance, though you're scared what you'll look like. I mean for you to try things you're not sure you can do. I mean for you to love, even when you are sure there is nothing left but hurt on the other side of love. Because I want you to know, from me, there is love that doesn't end.

I want to be very special to you, for the times I'm not there, for the times you step a half step farther because you know there is a cushion. Some people build nests and are happy sitting in them getting more and more comfortable. You and I aren't like that. For us, life is lived on the edge. We live, we learn, we grow on the frontier, where it is a little wilder, a little scarier. Go skin your knees—I have plenty of band aids.

Love always,

Paul

PS—I know I'm not the only person filling this role in your life. The rest of your family is, especially Hope and your father. They would do anything for you. When they are there, I don't need to be. Sometimes you need more than one spotter on a trampoline.

*　　*　　*

Caroline, Peter, Alexander and I became frequent study partners, and fast friends. I didn't take to Peter very quickly—in some way, he threatened the shallow veneer of discipline that I wore over my sinful mind. Perhaps he could see through it. Perhaps I wanted him to. So I made up a game of forcing him to memorize Bible verses every time he joined us, or when we moved say, from the library to the cafeteria. I thought it would keep him away. Rather, he took it in stride, and had me up late reading my Bible, looking for the next dozen or so verses I was going to force him to memorize. I love him for that. Sometimes I even hope I might have changed him.

Curt was another story. He was dangerous in the same way that Peter was, but exponentiated. He didn't give in to memorizing verses for me, and so we didn't have to tolerate his presence in our study group, and I hardly saw him. Caroline split her time between us; when she was with Curt, I was not there, and the opposite was true as well.

While it was clear from the beginning that Curt and I would never be friends, Kevin was the one in high school who rode both sides of that fence. Sure, he always had some young girl he was seeing, usually from another high school, or back home, and when this girl wasn't around, he allowed others to call her his "bitch." But after Curt and Caroline broke up, Kevin came to the dorm room with a vase of flowers he had picked along the banks of the South Ellerbe Creek. "Tell her there's more," he said as he handed me the vase. "If she ever wants them, I'll go get some for her." He did, too, dropping by new flowers to put in the vase several times that spring. More than once, I'd bump into him after class and say, "Not too sunny in our room lately," or some such thing, and not long after he would show up with more flowers. He never asked for her, and as far as I know they never talked more than casually, but the flowers kept coming, and they did help, that spring when Caroline had Faith growing inside her.

*   *   *

December 28, 1990

Dearest F.H.M.

There are times when I break down and cry, wishing you were already here for me, wishing I could bury my face in the safety of your warm substantial chest. Then I realize in order for you to find me and love me, I have to be strong, because no man I could love could love a weak woman. So I shake it off and face the day.

I joined a sorority. What a stupid thing to do! I'm just not the bouncy, "Hi, I'm Kappa Chi Caroline!" type. As they say, "A sorority is the best friends money can buy!"

Pledging was terrible. As one small example, picture me in sweats, with my bra and underwear outside my sweats and my face painted up like a little girl with big rosy spots on each cheek. I had a big lollipop in one hand, and a nipple hanging around my neck. Now picture me with three other girls pushing a hot dog cart up and down Franklin St. selling hot dogs for $1. That's not the worst, but it's the worst I'll tell.

I have to tell you about one party, at Wake Forest in Winston Salem. A Wake fraternity chapter hosted a mixer with us and their chapter at UNC. Sarah, a girl in my pledge class who was dating the President of the UNC fraternity, was talking with her boyfriend and the President of the Wake fraternity early on. Next thing you know, two Wake brothers come up and need her boyfriend for something, and she's left alone with the Wake President. Later, they danced. I like dancing and joined in, and some other Wake brother joined us. When they played a slow dance, I left but Sarah danced with this Wake boy, and the whispers started. They stayed together on the dance floor for an hour or so, dancing fast, slow dancing. I even saw a kiss. All the time, her boyfriend is standing over by the keg, fuming and drinking. I ended up taking a walk with a boy I knew I would never see again, but who was nice anyway.

Sarah wanted wine, and the Wake boy was going to get some for her. She went with him. A block or so away, they came to a major intersection, stumbling to it, holding hands. When they got there, Sarah's boyfriend ran up behind them, his feet slapping sloppily on the pavement as he slowed down. "Where you going with my girlfriend?" he slurred, out of breath, and shoved the Wake boy's shoulder.

The Wake boy stepped back, eyes wide and hands in the air. "What girlfriend?" he asked? Sarah's boyfriend looked at her, and I saw real fear cross her face. "Sorry man," the Wake boy said, "I thought she was just another sister."

"Yeah, whatever," her boyfriend said. He looked at Sarah with tight jaw and tense lips, then ran off as fast as he had run up, and Sarah started crying.

My boy and I had followed and saw the whole thing. I went to Sarah. I held her and listened and told her it would be okay. I took her back to the house and got a glass of coke to drink on the bus, and we talked. She was emotional, and told me her whole history, which included a pregnancy, but hers ended differently from mine if you know what I mean. I didn't tell her my story; I just can't. But I told her I knew how she felt, and she believed me because I really did.

The next day, Sarah and her boyfriend each got half of a hundred dollar bill delivered by Federal Express from the Wake chapter, with a note telling them to go out to dinner. Neither one wanted to but I talked with both of them and they reluctantly agreed. Eventually they forgave each other and dated for the rest of college.

Sarah and I are good friends, as I am with lots of the girls. I've become the sorority mom, and I like it. I'm the person all the fraternity boys hate, because I won't let my drunken sisters go home with them. I tell the boys they are drunk, and send them home with a dry penis. That's our word for un-sexed guys. I also keep condoms in my pocket at every mixer and every party, in case one of my sober sisters thinks she might need it. They all know this, and get one if they think they might end up with a guy, because not having one is a sure fire way to make sure you want to have sex with him. I give them out like candy. Most come back the next day, tossed at me in the breakfast room with a "Thanks," a look of disenchantment, and chuckles from the rest of the girls.

As the sorority mom, I'm the one everyone talks to when some boy is a schmuck or some sister is a witch and steals the schmuck boy. I listen, I hug, and I tell them my story is much worse, but I never tell them my story. I love the way I can help the girls.

I haven't used any of my condoms myself, though I probably will someday. I just haven't yet met a boy I'm interested in being close to. I don't drink, either, mostly because of all the stupid things I've seen people do when they drink. No thanks. It's not a moral thing, and I don't mind other people drinking. I just don't want to deal with it.

So, I did something stupid, joining a sorority, and I hate the actual sorority part of it. But I love the girls, and they love me, and that's what sisterhood is all about. We're all going to Galveston, Texas together this Spring Break. They swear they are going to find me a man, there. Hardly!

Love you, and miss you already.

Caroline

*　　*　　*

Caroline and I retreated to our room on graduation night. We packed boxes. We read each other's yearbooks, and signed the back for each other in flowing blue lines touched with the salt of drying tears. We laughed at the memories, at the pictures of the beauty contest that we had entered Peter and Alexander in, the two of them standing on stage with eleven other boys, all dressed in dresses, with make-up and high heel shoes and nerf footballs sliced in half and crammed into bras.

Endings make you ask big questions. Knowing all that I am, and all that I have failed to be, I asked her, "Caroline, how can you ... or anyone ... love someone like me?"

"It's simple," she said. "Because you try so hard."

At midnight we ordered a pizza, joining every other student on campus in our last prank on Domino's pizza, who still had a 30-minute guarantee. Rumor has it that our student body ordered over three hundred pizzas between eleven and eleven thirty that night, most of which were delivered after midnight, free of charge. Unlike many of the others, Caroline and I did go to bed sometime after three, and we slept for four blissful hours before the alarm dragged us into the events of the next day.

*   *   *

Being a Christian is the hardest thing I have ever done. I hear others talk about how easy it is, to just let God into your life and let him take control, and suddenly, somehow, there is no more sin and no more strife, no temptation, no bitterness, jealousy, rage or lust. By my experience, those people have quite the imagination, and a well developed capacity to believe in the fictional. In other words: malarkey!

There was one time, during our senior year at Science and Math, that to think about even to this day will cause my face to flush, my ears to burn, and my forehead to tingle. It is perhaps the meanest thing I have ever done, and certainly the meanest thing I have ever done to someone I care about as much as I do about Caroline.

We had gathered one evening in the cafeteria, the four of us. It was normal for us to talk about school work, about teachers and other students and the trouble they got in. There was one particular teacher, Mr. Romero, who some of us called by his first name Robin. He was tall and athletic, and normally had a tan from coaching our soccer team and sparring with the team members on weekend afternoons. All of the girls who had Calculus with him knew he was single and working on his Ph.D. in mathematics; some of us called him "Romeo" because he was such a hunk.

Robin also led the campus Fellowship of Christian Athletes, and I knew from our meetings he was truly genuine in his love of our Lord and in his real giving affection for the students around him. Nonetheless, on a small campus like ours, rumors would fly.

And so it happened that Peter and Caroline had seen Robin on a walk around campus with one of the most attractive young girls in our class. They were alone, walking very slowly, several feet apart, and obviously talking about something that had them distracted from anything else going on around them.

Another important thing to remember about this night was that it was early in the year, and I had not yet found out about Faith. I still don't understand how I could live with a pregnant roommate for five months and not find out, but I did. Sometimes God gives us blind spots, and I am not going to question His wisdom.

Peter piped in, "Romeo wants her body. There's no other reason to hang around her."

"That's not fair," I said.

"You're sticking up for him because he's cute," Peter said.

"I am not," I said with partial conviction.

"Look, he's no different from Kevin or Curt or any of the other soccer jocks, only a few years older. What makes you think he's different?"

"I know him, that's all." Alexander was watching now, and Caroline was silent. "I've seen him at the FCA. He cares about us, what's going on in our lives."

"That's a charade to make himself attractive to naïve young girls, and you're living proof it's working. He wants to check her lubrication, like everyone else." Alexander was getting angry, but before he could come to my rescue, I popped.

"Look, Curt may be trying to 'check the lubrication' of every girl on campus, and Kevin might be doing it with the rest of Durham, but Robin is a Christian, and he knows that through God there are consequences for behavior like that. God doesn't let that sort of thing go unpunished! If you act like a harlot you get to reap the rewards of a harlot! Robin knows that, and he wouldn't do it. Curt will get his someday, and with the amount Kevin has been scratching lately, he might already have his!"

I'm flushing now, as I write. The whole table got silent after I said that. Caroline stood silently, said something about studying, then walked quickly to the front of the cafeteria, her nose pointed at the ground and her shoulders slumped. Alexander, who had tried to take my hand halfway through my monologue and been brushed away, now let his palm cover my fingers in warmth and his fingers curl around mine. Peter sat, his lips motionless, but his blue eyes ablaze with anger, shooting white hot lasers into my own, softer hazel eyes. Peter stood silently and left.

All four of us normally met in the library during study hours. Caroline had gone out running, and came back to the room just before study hours. She showered and the two of us left for the library. She was friendly, as normal, if perhaps a little quieter. Alexander met us in the library, but Peter wasn't there. "He's back in the room," Alexander said. "He'll be here later."

Peter did show up later, and when he did, I gave him a Bible verse to memorize, as normal. After he committed it to memory, he said to me. "Tonight, Julia, I have one for you, too." I smiled and looked at him curiously, ready to accept the challenge. "It's from Galatians, 5:22. 'By contrast, the fruit of the Spirit is love, joy, peace, patience, kindness, generosity, faithfulness, gentleness, and self-control. There is no law against such things.'" He delivered the verse with unmasked anger, and while I knew that he was referring to my outburst at dinner, I wondered why he was suddenly sticking up for Curt and Kevin. I prayed about it before I got to bed, but never felt I had gotten the whole story.

Of course, that night is a big part of what I was asking Caroline about on graduation night. How could she love me, when I am someone who can say something as hateful and judgmental as that, right to her? It's true, I didn't know about Faith, but I knew she and Curt had slept together. Why should she love me? I still don't know, though I am sure it says much more about her than it does about me.

Today, as a surgeon who sees sick cancer patients every day, I keep that list in front of me on my desk, and in each of my consultation rooms. Love, joy, peace, patience, kindness, generosity, faithfulness, gentleness and self-control. That is the most important part about being a Christian, not whether or not I let Alexander touch me in a certain way, or whether I let myself act on some of my other urges. To hold myself pure as I was doing, and yet not have those nine words present in my heart and in my mind, that is worse than the harlot who cares about everyone she comes into contact with. That Caroline could love me despite my bitterness and anger, my jealousy and my envy; that says much more about her than it ever will about me.

*　　*　　*

January 3, 1992

Dearest Manny,

I'm finally starting to date again halfway through my junior year. Foster is a goofy guy in a fraternity so nerdy we won't even mix with them. He's a chemistry major, on the club football team, double majoring in business. Normally, I would never look twice at him.

It happened like this. Some of my sorority sisters went to "Late Night", a weekly Thursday night party that I normally avoid because it's full of drunks and professional partiers. Late Night starts at 11:30, and…well, I've never seen the end. Gina, one of the sisters, is a beautiful freshman who shows her naïveté. Sitting on the porch before the party, she said, "Hard liquor just doesn't get me drunk. I can drink as much as I want and never feel it!" I went along as "mom".

The band had a good beat, and at least in my corner of the host fraternity house, I was surprised not to find the usual layers of dirt and grime. Foster came over to talk to Gina. "I remember you from our History class," he said. Everybody "remembers" Gina from somewhere. She was excited at first, but then got bored and next thing I know Foster was talking to me. I could tell by his accent that he was from up north somewhere. We people-watched together, and had fun stereotyping all the other party goers with the characters from "Animal House." I had my guard up—I know what Carolina frat boys go to Late Night for—but it was okay talking to him.

I'll skip the details. Gina got very, very drunk. Later, she was off in a corner leaning on some guy. I'm so short I lost her in the crowd. I had explained to Foster I was the sorority "mom", and he must have listened, because he pointed Gina out to me. She looked as if she were about to pass out, and her boy seemed eager for it to happen.

Foster, by listening to me, had already set himself apart from most of the other Carolina boys I'd talked to.

Foster took my hand, and we went into action. The next few seconds are a blur. Foster walked up to Gina, me tailing him. When he got close, she had a second of lucidity, and threw both arms around him as if he was a long lost brother, home from the war. "FOSTER" she yelled, hugging him. Foster hugged her quickly, stood her up, and then passed her to me. He still had his drink in his hand. Just like that, the other guy tossed his drink in Foster's face. Foster looked confused for a second, then he turned to me, said "hold this", and handed me his drink politely, like nothing had happened. He reared his right fist way back, and punched the Carolina boy on the cheek. Nothing cracked, but the boy fell down. Foster jumped on top of him, punching and punching, and people backed away. Then it turned into a melee. A couple of the "house" brothers jumped in, pulling Foster off. Then a couple of his brothers—nerds—jumped in, pulling them off. The band stopped playing, and everyone yelled and screamed. Two or three other houses got into it, just for fun.

Foster slipped out of the melee, retrieved his drink, took Gina by the other arm, and we carried her out. "Let's get her home," he said. "That'll go on for a couple hours." As we left, his fraternity brothers caught up and asked him what happened. "I don't know how it goes down here, but up north, when someone pitches a drink in your face, you deck him. So I decked him." The frat boys left and we took Gina home.

At the sorority house, the sisters had all heard about the "gang fight" between two "of the biggest houses on campus". I passed Gina in to them, and thanked Foster. I was stunned when all he said was, "Great adventure—maybe I'll see you around," and turned to go. I didn't answer. Then, when he was halfway down the stairs, I said, "Call me," which got him to turn around. He looked at me, maybe for the first time, and said, "Okay", and left. He called the next day. We studied and played pool, had a real "date" on Saturday, and the rest is history.

Three weeks later, he broke his leg playing intramural soccer. I stayed with him a lot in the hospital, and his friends kept coming to see him.

Friends from classes, fraternity brothers, club football teammates, chemistry geeks—lots of them. All those friends are one reason I like him so much—it lends credibility. His broken leg has delayed anything sexual happening between us, which is convenient. I drive him around to class, study at his apartment in the afternoons and evenings, getting him cokes and stuff, and we play pool and rent movies on the weekends.

I've decided to go to med school. That's taking the "mom" thing a little far, but I want to help people. I've decided to go into family practice, and donate half my time to battered women's homes and orphanages. I can live easily on half a doctor's salary, and I'll feel tired when I get home at night, which I love.

I love you, Manny. I hope you don't mind me telling you about Foster. I don't think Foster is you, but I could be wrong. I'm too young. Foster would be sad to hear this, but if he ever reads it, it means he is you, and that would make it okay.

Love you, and miss you always.

Love,

Caroline

* * *

November 24, 1992

Dear F.H. Mann,

It's no surprise nobody understands me, since I have this big secret I won't tell anyone. How could they? It frustrates me.

I wrote a New Year's resolution a few years ago, and now I do it every year. In the first one, I decided to work on everything. I was going to be thriftier, more caring, more diligent in my schoolwork...you know the story. Last year was the first year I focused on only one thing. I settled on love. I wanted to make all my choices, everything I did, every word from my mouth, aimed at loving others.

It worked. I have more friends than ever. The whole sorority turns to me when they need help. Foster's fraternity adopted me as their little sister, and named me as their "Sweetheart" at their Fall Formal. Then there's Foster. More about that boy in a minute.

There is still an emptiness inside. I'll lie down to bed, and the emptiness will swell. I feel alone, even when Foster is there. I've prayed for God to tell me what is missing, why I feel like I have some fatal, unfixable flaw that keeps me from being happy. God hasn't answered. He's still answering the one I prayed at the beginning of the year, when I asked him to help me to love, and to be loved.

I applied early admission to medical school. I was accepted at UNC, so I'm staying here. I've been volunteering at Student Health.

Next year, it'll be a little different. Though I loved this year, it was selfish. I wanted my sister's love, the adoration of the fraternity brothers, and the care of my sorority sisters. I wanted Foster to be selfless and giving. I'm sometimes empty inside, and it's because, even if I'm loving externally, internally I'm still very selfish.

Next year, I will love selflessly. I will go to bed tired every night, knowing I gave my all to what was in front of me. I will never refuse a request for help. I will work to become the best doctor I can, and to help my classmates become the best doctors they can. I will keep my energy high, and devoted to giving to others, regardless of whether I expect to receive something in return. That's my resolution.

Foster. What a boy. I knew he was a keeper after our third date. It was still the first weekend, Sunday, and his fraternity was playing flag football like they do every Sunday. He invited me to play. We were on opposite teams, and I could tell he was some kind of a stud in the fraternity (bunch of nerds—smart, but nerds). He played behind the guys rushing, and made most of the tackles. Took the flags, that is. I caught the ball once, and he ran at me, but I swiveled my hips when he tried to take the flag and he missed, then I ran for a touchdown. He said, "Fine, I'll just tackle you," teasing, smiling.

I caught most of the balls they threw to me, so they kept throwing them. The second time I caught one, Foster came from across the field— he's FAST—and tackled me. I expected it to hurt bad, but when we hit the ground, he was on bottom and I landed gently on top of him—in his arms, really. That happened over and over; he tacked me and I landed on top, unhurt, in his arms. Once, when I was running away from someone else, I actually ran TO him to get tackled. He never let me win—no way would he stoop that low. But at the same time, he protected me. Staring into his blue eyes over ice cream afterwards, I decided to stick with him. I hope he sticks with me.

Our future is uncertain. I'm staying here for medical school. Foster is looking for a job. He loves me, and if we're close, he'll stay with me. If he goes away, then I don't know. He says I don't have the attention span for a long distance relationship.

I haven't told him my secret. I haven't had sex with him, either; I know he is frustrated. He pressured me for a while, but we had a big fight and I almost broke up, and he hasn't pressured me since. Since then I've been making him at least a little bit happy, anyway. I guess I'm not ready for sex, given my first experience, and he understands and doesn't ask too many questions. I can't imagine college without him, but I'm not letting him close enough to hurt me, not until we know our plans for next year. He knows I won't get married until after med school, so maybe that's that.

There are times at night, even when Foster is there and we're sleeping apart, that I curl up and imagine you're spooning me, holding me, and keeping me safe. I guess that's how I know Foster isn't you. He's there, keeping me safe, and yet I am still dreaming of my imaginary Future Husband Mann. Or maybe I'm a little crazy, and find comfort in my imaginary friends, like little children do.

Life can be confusing when I spend most of it thinking about me. That's why next year I'm focusing on other people. I'm going to give, because that's easier than trying to figure myself out.

I love you.

Caroline

* * *

Caroline came to visit me once at Princeton during her senior year in college, while she was dating Foster. Alexander was at Yale, and reluctantly agreed to let Caroline and me have the weekend to ourselves. Normally, he drove down from Connecticut to see me, if only so we could stay up all night studying together. Being loved the way he loves me is the one thing that is right in this world.

The leaves were changing and Caroline and I took a long walk around campus. One of my favorite things about the Princeton campus is the gargoyles, and so I took her past my favorites. As we passed one, the Monkey with a Camera, I told her a joke I had used to rib Alexander periodically. "Said the ape as it swung by its tail, To its children both female and male, 'From your children, my dears, May evolve a professor at Yale.'" Alexander told me it was from a couple of Princeton Alumni, John Armstrong and Anatole Kovarsky.

"I thought you didn't believe in evolution," she said.

"I don't believe in *random* evolution," I said. "I believe in entropy, and the Second Law of Thermodynamics, which preclude such nonsense."

"I thought you were a creationist."

"You mean do I believe the world was created in 168 hours, compete with dinosaur fossils? Read Romans 1, 'For what can be known about God is plain to them, because God has shown it to them. Ever since the creation of the world his eternal power and divine nature, invisible though they are, have been understood and seen through the things he has made.' Look around. The world will tell you its story."

"Explain," she said as we turned to walk down another long sidewalk blanketed in the fallen leaves of another growing season past.

"Look, the Second Law of Thermodynamics says that any system evolves toward a state of compete disorder, in the absence of a driving force." I went on, and on, talking about how God was the driving force, but we had to believe both our observations about the world, and the Bible. She argued with me, saying evolution was the driving force. In the end, neither of us knew with a certainty the truth about creation, or about God, but through the whole thing we did know for certain about our enduring love for each other, and, whether Caroline does or not, I find God to be present in that love, at least.

* * *

That night, we climbed into bed together, Caroline in her cotton shirt and running shorts, and me in one of Alexander's shirts and a pair of sweats. She had been talking much of the day about Foster, but even as she did, I felt something missing.

"What's the bottom line about Foster?" I asked, after we had turned out the light.

"We have a great time together," she said. "And I feel ... relaxed, appreciated—unjudged."

"Yeah," I agreed. I expected her to say something else, but she just stopped. I waited, then I said, "There's a 'but,' isn't there."

Her voice was high, almost squeaky, and quiet as a single cricket singing alone under the stars. "Yes," she said.

I waited, feeling her body warmth only a few inches away. When she didn't speak, I said, "What is it?"

"I don't know," she said.

"But there is something, right?"

"Yes."

*   *   *

College Graduation

Dearest Caroline,

Now you are graduating from college, and becoming a woman. I will be there—there is no question. I've already got the date on my calendar. Like everyone else, I've got some advice for you. Here it is:

Live life.

That's it. The rest is just details. Here are a few of the things I've done when I knew I was living—don't check them off one-by-one—rather, make your own list.

1. Walk hand in hand down the banks of the Seine with someone who can make you laugh, and who is good to kiss.

2. Get in a fistfight with someone who is much bigger than you. Remember to punch *through* their face, not at it.

3. Climb a mountain—a really big one, with glaciers. Use crampons and Gore-Tex. Leave a note for a friend at the top, and tell them it's there only after you get back down.

4. Visit the Louvre. But don't walk to it—take the subway right to the Louvre station. When you come out of the subway, look around. You'll feel like you're in another time.

5. Sneak out the window to meet some friends and go skinny-dipping in the middle of the night. (Somehow I'm guessing I'm a little late on this one...)

6. Speak at a funeral.

7. See a Broadway play.

8. Score points in front of a really big crowd.

9. Publish something you've written. Preferably somewhere a little better read than the Monthly Patent Journal.

10. Go running in lots of different places. Especially when you vacation, and when you travel. You notice so many things on foot you never see in a car. Run by the lake in Chicago, by the harbor in Baltimore, down the Seine in Paris. Jog down Biele Street in Memphis, and past the Café du Monde in New Orleans. Look around.

There's more. Like I said—make your own list, and then check them off, one by one, as the years go by. Add to the list if you like, but whatever you do, don't just sit around in front of the TV waiting for life to end. Live it!

Love,

Paul

*   *   *

December 29, 1993

Dearest Manny,

This spring was easy, and Foster and I had great fun. For a while, not knowing our future hung like a cloud of uncertainty over our relationship. Then Foster started joking about it. "I can't wait until summer, when I don't have to give so many backrubs," he'd say. Or, "Another night on the couch with YOU? Next year I'm gonna date someone a lot more fun." I'd give him a punch after he joked, and we'd fall laughing into a hug and it would be okay for a while. We'd seen some friends get married after college, because they didn't know what they wanted (but didn't want to break up). They were miserable. A few are already divorced. We decided to break up at the end of the year, but keep in touch. We even set a date— a big deal with candles and everything—for our breakup. We believe God will bring us back together if that's what's right for us. Foster is up in Manhattan doing computer something-or-another for a big company. We talk and write a lot. I'm getting email, which makes it easier.

214

I've lived up to my promise—I go to bed tired every day. At night, when I first close my eyes, I review my day and thank God for my blessings, and for the lessons. I go to sleep concentrating on the lessons, trying to make them stick.

Medical school is swamping me. Many of my classmates are smarter, and it's easier for them (though it's not actually *easy* for anyone). Some do it for the money. "Think of how our lives are going to be when this is all over." They already talk about which specialties make the most money, and work the fewest, or easiest hours.

My motivation is different. I keep thinking about Faith. Maybe I will never find her. I don't know. But I can find some other girl living without her mother, and can care about her, and make a difference. I use my mental image of my lovely daughter to keep me studying late at night, and to get me out of bed to study again in the morning.

I go to the gym incessantly, and I've started wearing spandex workout bras and shorts. My body is okay for someone who has had a baby, but doesn't compete with the workout freak undergrads. My stretch marks have faded. I still haven't told anyone, but it feels good not to hide my midriff anymore.

Sorry to be so distracted this year. I'm afraid it's going to be at least four years until I meet you—at least until we settle down—I won't have the attention you deserve. I know I'm going to love you—be patient for the next few years—it's for a good cause!

Love,
Caroline

* * *

Alexander and I got married right after graduation. The independent side of me didn't want to, but, honestly, Alexander was about to explode and I wasn't sure I could hold onto him any longer. I think maybe I had grown accustomed to it. "It," of course, is a life without sex, with almost no intimate contact at all. We stuck to our one-kiss-a-day ritual right up until our engagement party, where I let him get a little sloppy with me when our guests, most of them Science and Math alumni, clinked their wine glasses. The whole night was a night of spoons tinkling on glasses, flushed faces and us trying to act casual about something we had almost never done.

The wedding was not big—I insisted that my parents pay for it, which didn't go over well with Alexander's mother, as she had different ideas about the guest list. I was an only child, and my father a factory worker. Their dream, and mine, was that I go to medical school.

I chose Caroline to be my maid of honor, and she came to visit me for a week before the wedding. After our third trip to the florist, trying hard to consider my future mother-in-law's newest idea about how much greenery needed to be around the altar, I nearly lost control, and Caroline whisked me off into her car, then drove me first to McDonald's for a chocolate milkshake, and then home for a good cry.

After I finished crying, my mucus and saliva forming sloppy dark spots on Caroline's blue shirt, she said, "Let's try on our dresses!"

My wedding dress and my bridesmaids' dresses were the only places I didn't skimp. I only had three bridesmaids, each more beautiful than me, and I wanted them to shine. Each was in her best color, with Caroline in a pastel blue. Jennifer, my best friend from home, was a natural blond, and I put her in yellow. The best was my grandmother, who hadn't dressed up in years and fought not to be in my wedding until I begged and begged and told her she couldn't come to the wedding at all except as my bridesmaid. Mamaw wore pink. All of the dresses were satin, off the shoulders, low in front and lower in back. Alexander swore he would marry Mamaw if I backed out.

And my dress? Well let me tell you.

We pulled the dress out from the huge box that stored it. I had only tried it on once, when I picked it up, and I knew the work we were about to get into. "Are you sure?" I asked. I wanted to—I had never had anyone as close to me as Caroline, and in a way she was becoming the sister I had always wanted.

"I'm dying to see you in it," she said. "Maybe I'll try mine on, too, and we can take some pictures."

I opened the box and pulled the dress out part way. She reached down and pulled it away from me and said, "I'll get this. You get undressed."

There it was, laid right before me. I hadn't even considered it. How natural, of course—two close friends, nearly sisters, going to play dress up one last time with a wedding dress—of course the one who was to put on the wedding dress would have to undress.

In the two years I had lived with Caroline, and all the time since, I had never undressed in front of her. I never went swimming, never wore revealing clothes. Nobody had seen me in anything less than shorts and a t-shirt in a dozen years except my doctor. And Jennifer's mom, who works on the beach as a tattoo artist.

I had talked about them—most people knew they were there. Once or twice, in rare daring moments, I had lifted my shirt to show the one on my belly, which had a shepherd on one side herding sheep, with one lost lamb down around my bikini line. That was as brave as I had ever been.

*   *   *

I got the tattoos all at once, when I was fourteen. I had been dating a boy—it's always a boy, isn't it? I met him in Sunday School. He seemed to be the right sort, and he nodded at all the right times and gave all the right answers in church. On our first couple dates, he was very sweet, opening the door to the theater, and getting me popcorn and a Sprite then holding them when I had to go to the bathroom halfway through. He called me every night, and we talked—only for a few minutes, but enough to make me feel remembered. Then, on about our sixth date, he took me to a party. One by one, the other couples disappeared into side rooms, out onto the porch, or out to "take a walk." He asked me if I wanted to take a walk, also, and I said yes.

I will skip the details, but let it suffice to say that, what he wanted, I wanted also, and before I knew it, he had me up against a tree, and then down at the base of the tree. Kissing turned to holding, and then caressing…his hands were like magic on my skin, guiding electric sensations all over my body. But in the back of my mind, Paul began to speak to me, and, even as we were kissing, I realized that this was the seduction of the flesh that he had written about in his letters. I stopped kissing and pulled away, and that's when it got ugly.

He was aggressive, holding me hard and telling me I didn't mean "no." I was conflicted, shoving him away, then a moment later yanking him to me and grinding my body into his. Despite his best efforts, I did not lose my virginity that night. I freaked out, panicked—I don't know exactly what—but I hurt him, ran away into the woods, and then walked the three miles home. Four days later I visited Jennifer's mother with all my savings in my pocket. She didn't take my money, but she did listen to me for two hours, then got on her knees and said a prayer with me, and over the next two weeks, decorated my body as I requested.

*   *   *

Caroline pulled the dress away from me, and I stepped away, trying to appear calm. My hands shook as I undid the buttons on front of my shirt. Caroline wasn't even looking as I slipped it first off one shoulder, then let it fall behind me to my elbows and slowly slipped each arm out. Four of my tattoos were now visible.

Caroline was nearly lost in all of the satin and lace, and didn't notice as my hands reached down and fumbled first with my belt, then snaps, and then pulled my shorts over my hips and let them fall to the ground. I stood nervously, clad only in my heather grey cotton underwear with "Victoria's Secret" sewn into the French cut waistband, waiting for her to look up and discover what almost nobody had ever seen.

I think she saw me first out of the corner of her eye, because she stopped moving, and then looked up at me very slowly, her eyes wide, but a warm, friendly smile on her face. I had goose bumps on every inch of my skin, and the rings sticking through my nipples hurt like they sometimes do when I get cold.

Her eyes rose over my body, but quickly settled onto my eyes, and her smile closed into a warm, loving grin. "What do they stand for?" she asked me.

"It's silly," I said.

"No, it's not," she said, and after a moment, I nodded my assent.

"Seven times in the book of John, Jesus says the words 'I am,' followed by something. I have a tattoo for each of the seven 'I am's.'" She looked at me, and saw the sun rising on the slope of my breast, and a gentle shepherd with a lost lamb on my flat stomach. On my hip, only partially covered by my briefs, was a gate, halfway open along a stone fence. I was nervous, and could feel a long bead of sweat appear across my upper lip as she looked at me. Slowly, I turned around, and she saw a vine, life sized and real, gathered around the top of my left leg, snaking up into my underwear. A loaf of bread stuck out from my panties on the other buttock. On my shoulder was a cave with a stone rolled away, while in the middle of my back was a book on a stone pedestal at the end of a road.

*   *   *

She got me in my dress and we played dress up without further comment, and once I was clothed I was no longer nervous. That night, as I lay in bed, with her in her sleeping bag on the floor, she said, "You've never shown those to me."

"I never showed them to anyone."

"Had Alexander seen them?"

"Only the shepherd." She stopped, and I'm sure the rest of the implications of that thought slowly made their way through her mind.

"Are you nervous?" she finally asked.

"I ..." I stopped, uncertain what to say next. "I don't want to disappoint him," I said, my voice choking as a tear slipped down my cheek.

She reached up and found my hand lying on top of the covers, and pulled it down to her face where she pressed it to her lips and I could feel the warm tears press between my fingers as I tasted the salt from my own tears. "You could never disappoint anyone," she said, and we both cried, and then I laughed and said, "Oh yes I could!"

Later, I asked and she told me what to expect, and I was glad that God had given me such a girl to be my sister in this special time in my life.

*   *   *

Engagement

Dearest Caroline,

I'm glad I can take part in this special moment. The good part is you're getting married. The other good part is I have three really good stories for you.

I'm not married. Both my brothers are…despite the way they proposed.

Let's start with Travis. He lived with his wife for two years before he finally proposed, and dated her for a couple before that. It's not like he didn't have the chance to get to know her, to get over his fears. But fears he had, and they nearly overcame him.

Finally Brandi told him he had to. He bought the ring—a nice one, with a big central stone centered in a beautiful arrangement. He took her to dinner at the Poplar Lodge, their favorite restaurant, at the top of a mountain. They have no menu, but show you the cuts of meat, and prepare them any way you like. The food is fantastic. They had wine, they had candles, they had great food, laughs, romance … the perfect situation. Travis had hidden the ring in his sock, and he chickened out each time he reached for it.

After dinner, they took a walk. Some sections of the trail overlooked the lights of good old Hendersonville. Again, they had soft conversation, dim lighting, soft kisses, romance. Travis had butterflies. They finished their walk and went home.

They got home, and Travis faced two conflicting fears. One of proposing, the other of getting ready for bed, or undressing in a more compromising situation, and having her see the ring fall out of his sock. That would earn a lashing. The proposal won out, and he proposed and she said yes and loved the ring and now they have kids and a great home and it's been happy-ever-after so far.

Your father did even worse. He called me four times a week for two months as he shopped for the ring. He was terrified. As an lawyer, he tried to maximize the four C's of diamond buying: cut, clarity, carat, and color. He read books. He negotiated with a bunch of jewelry shops. We talked through all the details. I loved it, though I occasionally got bored, and was frustrated with his inability to make a decision. I'd never seen him humbled before (my perfect older brother), and I was enjoying it…just as I've enjoyed seeing him constantly humbled in his marriage. Finally, he bought a ring.

After he bought the ring, he called his future father-in-law to ask permission, and received it. Then, the waiting. Your mother came to visit one weekend, and he carried the ring in his pocket for the entire weekend.

He was waiting for the perfect moment. By the end of the weekend, there was no perfect moment, so no proposal. I respect his decision, because you only get one chance to do it right. Or to blow it.

He called me Sunday after your mother left. I asked if he had proposed, and he said no, it wasn't right. Then he gave me every intimate detail of every moment of their weekend, with a long, analytical explanation of why each one was imperfect. When he finished, I was *exhausted*! But he was right. No perfect moment, so no proposal.

Donna visited again two weeks later. He called me every night to talk—I was as nervous as he was. Normally, I might drink a beer with some friends, or go out with a girl, but I made a point to be home when John called.

John agonized and agonized and agonized, and Donna never had a clue. Finally the day arrived. She rang the doorbell. John greeted her with a kiss, then took her bags and set them in the living room, turning away from her. He walked away, toward the kitchen to check on something he had cooking. As he entered the kitchen, he tossed the ring box at her, and said, "Here," then continued into the kitchen.

Donna caught the box and figured what was coming. Then she said, "Is there something you'd like to ask me?" He didn't get on bended knee or anything, but he did deliver a proper proposal, and she accepted. After they'd called both sets of parents, I got the phone call I'd been waiting for.

Third story. I have once in my life proposed to a woman—sort of. I didn't have a ring, she wasn't in the room, and I wasn't ready. She said no. Good grief!

Despite that one nebbishly attempt, I have known since I was sixteen what real my proposal would be like. Let me describe it to you:

I will ask Miss Wonderful to picnic with me on a beautifully sunny day. The ring, a simple solitaire, will be in my left pocket without the box. We'll drive into the mountains and take a secluded exit halfway up. I'll hold her hand, talking softly, stroking her fingers with my thumb. I'll play with her wedding ring finger, though she'll never notice. I'll turn off and continue down a winding paved road, peppered sparingly on both sides with cute houses in well kept yards. Eventually the road will turn into a dirt road. Miss Wonderful will grow quiet as she wonders where I am taking her.

The dirt road will wind, but eventually, we'll stop. A couple hundred yards off the road, Miss Wonderful and I will stop at a clearing by a small creek and eat cheese, fruit and fresh bread while sipping wine and watching the sun sink behind the trees. Time will be unimportant. When we are done, I'll stand, take her hand, and tell her I want to show her something. Pulling her up, we'll walk to the Perfect Spot. We will cross a creek by walking on a fallen tree, and I will appear chivalrous as I guide her across.

Further on, we will see a valley open up before us. I'll pull her to a side trail and we'll walk to the edge. Letting go of her hand, I will step off onto a ledge, invisible to her. I will lift her down to stand beside me. I will sit beside her, our legs dangling off the ledge, holding her hand and talking gently. Below us the valley will drop three hundred feet. Bradley Falls will be in front of us, slightly to the left. The water tumbles over worn rock formations into several pools on its way down a four hundred foot cliff. At the bottom is a large pool of water, good for swimming and diving. We will return here many times to go swimming, and sometimes to sit and talk, and remember. The sun will set to the right, and we will arrive just as it goes over the hill, leaving the sunset above us, and nothing but the birds and the waterfall to interrupt what I will do next.

I'll reach with my left hand into my pocket and pull out the ring. Not showing it, I'll pull her hand into my lap, and turn to look into her eyes. I'll say, "Miss Wonderful, I want to spend the rest of my life with you. Will you marry me?" As I say it, I will let her glimpse the ring in my hand as I tease the end of her wedding ring finger with it.

I expect her response will include tears, smiles, hugs, a kiss, and a "yes".

I expect, Caroline, the proposal you received was somewhere in between the real ones your father and uncle delivered, and my imagined one. Cherish every detail, good or bad. It's special, and special doesn't have to be as you dream it. My real proposal will be nothing like the one I've dreamed. But I love the dreamed one anyway.

I love you, Caroline. Congratulations!

Love,

Paul

222

*　　*　　*

Caroline and Kevin had been dating for two years, and living together for one, by the time they got engaged. When Caroline called to tell me, it was as if she had bought a new blouse. "Oh yeah, Kevin and I are engaged now," she said.

"Really? Like with a wedding and everything? Or just another big party?"

"I'm not sure," she said, and I detected a little something in her voice.

"What?" I asked.

"I think Dad put him up to it," she said, and there it lay, an empty carcass, and we didn't know if it was a fantastic filet, or road kill.

*　　*　　*

I went down to see her a month or two later. Hope and I rented a cabin in the Blue Ridge Mountains for four days. It was late spring and the afternoons were hot, but the breeze blew in the evenings and cooled us off. We spent our time hiking, taking pictures and, like any three girls will when they are alone, talking.

I learned to love Hope that weekend. She took care of everything, finding the cabin, planning our menu, our hikes, buying the groceries, buying the things we would need to put together our project for the weekend, which was to build a scrapbook of Caroline's life as a gift to Kevin. Somehow, she has a sense for what is needed, an innate ability to predict the voids that might occur, and fill them before they do. I've never had that, and never will, and it was wonderful to place myself into her loving care for the weekend, as if I were lying myself in a soft down bed to be pampered.

The scrapbook was great, and filled our mornings and our evenings as we pored through pictures, yearbooks, newspaper articles and theatrical programs. Caroline didn't save any of this stuff herself, but Hope and her mother had been thinking ahead since Caroline was just a child, and there was plenty of material for us to work with.

The cabin was spacious, with a pool table in a room off the living room, and a hot tub on the screened-in part of the back porch. After we finished the scrapbook, on the night before we were to leave, we headed out to the hot tub with a double-sized bottle of champagne and a gallon of cookies and cream ice cream. Hope set it all up for us on a side table as Caroline and I slipped into the hot bubbly water. We were sore from hiking and had a great sense of accomplishment at having finished the scrapbook.

After spooning out three obscenely large bowls of ice cream, Hope handed us each a tumbler of champagne and then raised her glass and said slowly, majestically, "To Caroline, my sister and my one true love, who through her courage and her tender heart has made more of a difference in my life than everyone else combined." I watched, and as the words fluttered from Hope's mouth, Caroline stopped breathing, her eyes riveted on her sister, unable to comprehend all of the different meanings bundled together in this one simple toast.

We each took a swallow of champagne, and the moment was dissipated as Hope handed us each a bowl of ice cream and a huge spoon, and we sank into the hot flowing comfort and spooned chilled nirvana into our mouths. "This is the last fattening thing I will eat until my wedding," Caroline said, her tongue numbed by the cold ice cream filling her mouth. We laughed and let the water and the champagne melt our sore muscles and turn us into warm jelly.

I'm not one for toasts, or public speaking of any kind, but I could not let this evening pass without saying something. As Hope poured the last of the champagne, I knew my time had come.

I rose out of the water and felt the chill mountain air on my skin. I saw Hope look at me and knew that she would never understand my tattoos, or why I had put them there. Caroline looked also, but in her eyes there was love, laced with a hint of pity.

"Caroline, you are the sister I never had, and Hope, I can never thank you enough for sharing her with me."

"You can't have her," Hope said, then smiled as she brought her glass to her lips and sank lower into the water.

"I just want to share," I said, and Hope nodded, smiling even more deeply.

"Caroline," I said, and then paused, salty bile filling the back of my throat. "Paul said this about love. 'If I speak in the tongues of mortals and of angels, but do not have love, I am a noisy gong or a clanging cymbal. And if I have prophetic powers, and understand all mysteries and all knowledge, and if I have all faith, so as to remove mountains, but do not have love, I am nothing. If I give away all my possessions, and if I hand over my body so that I may boast, but do not have love, I gain nothing.'" I stopped to gain my breath.

"You have proven to me, Caroline, that though you are a noisy gong sometimes, and sometimes have no faith and can be materialistic—." As I said this, I waved my arm to show all that we had enjoyed over the weekend. "Because you have love and give it so freely, you have become to me the best woman I know." I stopped and Hope sniffled and wiped her eye, and then I sank into the cold water and the three of us gathered into the center of the hot tub and drew our arms around each other.

*   *   *

Day before Wedding Day

Dearest Caroline,

I'm thirty two, and still suspect I'll get married someday. Some things will have to change when I do. I won't store my belts on the floor anymore. I will clean the grill, and maybe Sammy won't climb in bed during thunderstorms. Or maybe she'll sleep in bed all the time, and I'll have to bathe her more often. I'll come home earlier. I'll become a better listener. (Maybe I'll do that before I get married.) I'll drink less, and probably eat more (seconds are the best compliment, after all). I'll kiss more, and if the stories are true, there won't be much sex. Despite all that, I am looking forward to it.

The way my parents met and got engaged is a wonderful story maybe you've never heard. It's one I can hardly believe, but know to be true.

They met at work. Mom worked in the technical library at Dupont; Dad was an engineer. Dad had been introduced to Mom by a friend, but Mom forgot him as soon as he left the room. Dad didn't forget her—she was quite the looker back then. Several weeks later, after coming off the night shift, Dad had a couple drinks and got the courage to call Mom at work.

She picked up the phone expecting a literature request. She had forgotten who Dad was, and so was a little flustered on the phone. She wasn't desperate, but since he asked her for dinner and dancing, rather than a movie and smooching, she said yes and gave him directions to her place. That was Tuesday.

They went out on Friday night. While they were having a great time, Mom managed to learn Dad's first name, but not his last. She still didn't know who he was.

They were to visit his parents on Sunday, an hour and a half away. They talked and joked and laughed all the way there. Mom, thinking she was clever, asked Dad what side of the road they lived on when they turned onto his street. He said the right, and Mom scanned mailboxes to see the name on the mailbox. Dad turned in and Mom panicked—the mailbox was on the left! Needless to say, Mom made a lot of eye contact with Dad's parents, but never once called them "Mr. This" or "Mrs. That". She left still not knowing his last name, but things were clicking along pretty well anyway.

They met for dinner on Tuesday. After dinner, Dad asked her to marry him. According to Mom, foremost on her mind was her ignorance of her potential new last name! She fussed and told him she'd answer when they saw each other again.

They saw each other next on Friday, one week after their first date. Mom played a dirty trick—she asked him if she could see his picture on his new ID from work. When she got a look, she finally saw his last name. She tried it, repeating her name with his a few times in her head. Later, she accepted his proposal.

I'd say that was it, and they went on to live happily ever after and raise three beautiful boys, but things are never "happily ever after" in my family. Dad still had to meet Mom's parents.

One month after they met, Mom brought Dad home for Sunday dinner. They hadn't told Mom's parents they were engaged, so Mom kept her ring in her pocket. In those days, meeting a girl's parents was a big deal, so Dad got spiffed up in a sport coat and tie. He sat with Mom's father in the living room having a drink and talking while the women prepared dinner. Mom's little sisters spied on them from the top of the stairs.

When dinner came, all the girls helped bring it to the table, and Dad and Papa joined from the living room. Dad cordially followed Mom to her chair, and pulled it out for her to sit down. Just when she reached the point of no return, when her center of balance was too low and too far back to stand up again...he pulled the chair out from under her, and she fell giggling on her hind end, skirt tossed everywhere and legs sprawled out in front of her. Dad and Mom were laughing hard as he helped her up.

Mom tells this story with glee on her voice and love in her heart. My grandmother, however, told the story quite differently. For her, this was the beginning of a long relationship of disapproval and disdain. From my vantage point, Dad spent the rest of her life trying to live down that moment.

The happy ending is this. Mom and Dad have been married for forty years, and raised three beautiful boys. About Dad and my grandmother: after Dad's mother died, his attitude about Mom's mom changed completely. He doted on her nonstop from the moment of his mother's passing until her own death. I think she even began to like him. I know she loved him his entire life; she was just slow to admit it.

That's the happy ending. I'll have another story for you tomorrow. You're very special, and I can't wait until you walk down the aisle. I promise I'll be the second or third happiest guy in the room!

I love you,
Paul

*   *   *

Alexander and I flew in just before Caroline's rehearsal dinner, with just enough time to get from the airport to our hotel to change, and then over to the Grove Park Inn in Asheville for the dinner. We walked up the long, stately brick walkway to the entrance and I thought to myself that all was finally going to be right in Caroline's world. I was relieved and so very happy to see her joining her life with one of our childhood classmates, albeit perhaps the wrong one, and finally settling into a marriage that would certainly be blessed with every material blessing a couple could wish for. I wished in my heart that Kevin had changed though I had no evidence.

The rehearsal dinner was a reunion of sorts, and Alexander and I very quickly got lost in the embraces of old friends from high school. I stopped early and spoke with Curt and met his wife, and as I did Alexander left to bring me a glass of wine.

Caroline and Kevin had not arrived, and Peter was not coming. He had not been invited at the request of Caroline's father—fallout from the graduation fiasco, and the law suit that followed. I think John reasoned that he wasn't going to buy a fancy dinner for someone who had cost him $20,000 in legal fees.

Hope and I gathered together and she introduced me to her two girls. John and Donna, Caroline's parents, had joined us when we saw Kevin walk in through the two open doors. He looked very sophisticated in a royal blue shirt, grey jacket and navy tie, with black wool pants and black wing tip shoes. John stepped away immediately. I saw John pulled Kevin close in a crosswise grip, and John grabbed Kevin's other arm around the biceps in a manly, yet very affectionate, embrace.

I slipped through the crowd, and as they let go, I slipped my arms around Kevin's neck and kissed him on the cheek as I said, "Congratulations, Kevin."

His arm around my waist pulled me a little too closely as he said, "Thanks," and tried to kiss my lips. I dodged and he got only cheek, and I smelled a strange smell on his breath, one that I imagine must have been strong liquor of some kind.

"Where is Caroline?" I asked, slipping lithely out from his embrace.

"She went to the bathroom to touch up." As I tried to slip away, he took my hand and held it tightly as he said, "She'll be okay—she just needs a minute to gather herself together." He smirked a one-sided, knowing grin, and said, "I think it's just the stress." Hope, who was standing behind Kevin as we spoke, turned and slipped out the door behind us, so I returned pressure onto Kevin's hand, and felt his grip lighten as he introduced me to his mother.

*   *   *

Caroline, Hope, and Donna all came into the room together a half hour later, just as we were being seated for dinner. Caroline looked radiant in a simple pine green dress. She was tanned and the neckline of the dress flattered her figure and accentuated a single diamond hanging around her neck on a gold chain. She touched my shoulder and leaned down to put her cheek next to mine as she walked past, but didn't say anything. I felt her warmth and touched her hand with my own and noticed that hers felt moist.

The rest of the night was a little bit of a blur for me—too many friends in too little time. Alexander and I were seated at one of two tables full of NCSSM alumni from our graduating class. I got to tell over and over of the surgical residency I was taking at Columbia Medical Center in New York City, and Alexander spoke of his job at Morgan Stanley as a financial advisor.

Later, Hope and Edward arranged an exercise that would turn into another scrapbook for Caroline and Kevin. "There are cards being passed around with four questions on them," she said. "You don't have to participate, but if you have something you'd like to write on any of them, then fill them in and we'll collect them in a few minutes." One question was, "What famous celebrity does Caroline/Kevin remind you of most?" Another was, "What wishes do you have for their marriage and their future?" I forget the other two.

Later, people stood to give the answers to their questions, and I can't remember most of them but remember the smiles and applause and the knowledge that here was a room full of people who had loved this couple for their whole lives.

I only remember one of the things said, and that was from Curt. When it came his turn, Curt stood at the end of the other table of NCSSM alumni. His blond hair had gone a little brown in the last few years, and his forehead was an inch or two taller than I remember, but other than that he was still the tall, good looking young buck that had swept Caroline off her feet a decade earlier. On this night, drunk on old friendships and with the confidence that comes with a wedding ring on my finger, I smiled sweetly at him and leaned back to enjoy the spectacle of his speech.

"Dog," he said, and waved his wine glass at Kevin, "You've been my man for a long time." He smiled at Caroline and said, "Caroline, you may not know it, but you'll always be the one that got away." I saw him sway a little in his stance as I glanced at his wife, whose grin had gone plastic. "My wish is for you to have children like yourselves. Children who are active," he said as he looked at Kevin, "and children who are argumentative." His glance drifted to Caroline, who was now sitting perfectly still, her smile winnowing. "Children who know how to get into trouble." He looked at Caroline. "And get out of it." He looked to Kevin, and a sly smirk passed between them. "I wish for you to have children who have all of your brains, and all of your good looks, and all the capacity for love that you both have so much of. And last," he lifted his glass of wine to his lips and turned it up for the last swallow. "This last part isn't so much a wish as an expectation. I expect your children to be a little stubborn, like both their parents."

*   *   *

Wedding Day

Dearest Caroline,

This is the happiest of days. I smile now knowing there is little I can do to make your day better or worse, more memorable or less. For a moment, I'll imagine your smile on this day, refreshing in my mind your optimism. I love you. Looking at you even now, at three years old, I know you will be a very beautiful bride.

I remember your parents' wedding day. They got married in Hendersonville, and had their reception at the Country Club where they had met a decade before at the pool. I was John's best man. We played golf in the morning, and John's sweet spot covered the whole head of the club and went halfway up the shaft. Every ball went straight and far. It was a beautiful day, with springtime blowing, literally, across the fields in great yellow gusts of pine pollen. My nose ran like crazy, but nobody cared.

We rested after golf, then showered and got ready. John asked me to take the clubs out of his car so he could put their luggage in. I forgot, and took my shower. When I got out of the shower, John was in front of the house in his underwear with elastic straps snaked around his legs, holding his socks to the bottom of his t-shirt. He lofted bags of golf clubs twenty or thirty feet across the yard and screamed at me as I looked out the window. I didn't hear the words…but I knew something had to be done.

I gathered his clothes and mine, and met him on the stairs in my tux bottoms, clothes under my arm. He scowled. I handed him his pants and started walking toward the church; he followed. "We'll dress at the church," I said. Three minutes later, we were in a room behind the altar, dressed neatly and ready for him to get married. We were two hours early.

My memory of those two hours, locked in a small room with my brother as his best man, is a very fond one. My build is such that, when I move my shoulders, my shirt untucks a bit. He kept making me unzip my pants and tuck my shirt in again. Then we would walk back and forth, he would check to make sure I still had the rings, I would move my shoulders and he'd make me tuck in again. He explained that the elastic snakes holding his socks to his t-shirt were attached to his shirt tails, holding them tucked nicely.

A few minutes before the ceremony, a kind old lady came to pin flowers on us. My boutonniere was just below my nose, a fountain of pollen. My eyes and nose began to water and run as soon as we stepped out. I had never been happier as we stood before the crowd. My brother's pride and happiness shone like a beacon over the room.

I remember most explicitly the moment Donna stepped to the center of the aisle and the wedding march began. My lungs ceased functioning, and my heart stood at rapt attention in honor of her beauty. I wasn't able to awaken them until she was halfway down the aisle. When they did I was relieved I wasn't going to ruin my brother's wedding by having a heart attack before he said his vows.

By the time they stepped to the altar, the fountain of pollen had taken effect, and my nose was running full force. A tear had escaped my left eye. I turned to face the happy couple, and everyone in the church saw me crying.

They said their vows proudly, walked out, and received. After the receiving, there were pictures. Donna was radiant, and both families stood as side ornaments beside two beautiful centerpieces. Just before they left in a genuine jalopy, John pulled me aside, handed me his watch, and asked me to have a spring repaired—he wouldn't have time before he left for his honeymoon. Thus the adventure began.

Skip the adventure—boring monotony as I went from jewelry store to pawn shop to jewelry store looking for someone to fix his watch. They waited and waited at the reception, but finally had to announce the wedding party and begin eating without me. Ninety minutes later, I showed up and was announced in the middle of the second course, broken watch silent in my pocket. Years later, I still rib my brother about why he needed to know the time on his honeymoon.

I gathered our two cousins, beautiful girls a couple years our junior, to decorate the car. I had balloons and colored tape. We filled the car with balloons and used the tape to write things that shouldn't be preserved on the sides and rear of the car. I pulled his newly decorated car out front, as instructed, then filled all of the empty crevices with more balloons. There was not an empty space left.

When the happy couple left, we greeted them with a raining shower of rice. John ushered Donna through the rice-storm to her door and opened it quickly, hoping to get her into shelter. The balloons were wedged in so tightly they were forced to remove them one by one as the rice continued to pour, and we laughed at their pitiful efforts. John made a face that I recognized as the same one I saw every time he beat me up as a kid, but this time he didn't follow through, and continued to dig a hole to plant his wife in the garden of balloons. Eventually, we ran out of rice, and he made a Donna-sized hole in the passenger side. He worked his way into the driver's seat. They had survived a storm of several dozen of pounds of rice, and John to this day maintains there was rice in his car when he sold it several years later.

Many of the memorable things that happened were unplanned. People still tell me how touching it was that I cried at my brother's wedding. John still can't explain why he needed to know the time while they honeymooned in Jamaica. The pictures of them wrestling with balloons and rice can make any one who was there laugh out loud.

My advice: smile, be charming, show no fear and roll with the punches. This is your day, a day to remember. I, like so many others, will be just one face in the crowd, all of us happy for you and your wonderful groom. Cherish the love you feel on this day, and share it with everyone you greet.

Love, congratulations, and best wishes,

Uncle Paul

*   *   *

Caroline and her father came together at the end of the aisle for her last walk as an unmarried woman, and like the dipoles in a magnet every one of the two hundred guests turned toward her radiant smile. Her dress was white and low in front showing her tanned skin and a long necklace of pearls circled twice around her thin neck. I watched from the front of the room, where I, along with seven other bridesmaids and a platoon of groomsmen and her future husband, awaited.

She made the short march up to the altar with grace, dignity, and a flowing happiness, and I saw her exchange smiles and winks over and over with people in the crowd, and I felt special to be able to share in the massive collection of relationships that were in this room, each like a spider's thread somehow connected to Caroline and her groom, and I felt sure that no matter what happened to her and Kevin in their lives, those threads would come together to hold them fast when they needed it, when they felt they might not hold on their own.

The ceremony was like many others. My voice cracked as I read 1 Corinthians 13 one more time and thought about how much love Caroline had brought into my own life. Finally, we came to the end and the music began and Caroline and Kevin walked down the aisle, arm in arm and life in life, smiling and laughing and then running out to their waiting limousine, where they circled the church a few times before joining us for more pictures, and then we headed out to the country club for the reception.

We came down the stairs after we were announced. The reception was held in a large dining room overlooking the pool on one side, and the green hills of the mountain golf course on the other. I stepped across the dance floor and saw on its other side a six layer cake next to an ice carving of a groom, sitting with his bride next to a lake, in which several small, ice ducks floated. The lake was red, which appeared a little odd, until I saw the fruit floating in it and realized that it was punch.

I found my way to Alexander, and he brought me a drink and we found a place near the band where we could watch Caroline dance with her groom, and then her father. When dinner was over and it was time for the party to start, Caroline gathered all of her bridesmaids together for one last dance, this one with no men, to Eric Clapton's "Wonderful Tonight." When we finished, we each had several suitors lining up for the next dance, and we danced nearly all night long.

The reception was a party, and while most polite company left after about nine o'clock, there were still over a hundred guests left when it all began to unravel.

*   *   *

I was not surprised when Hope found me before the wedding began and said, "Edward just told me that Kevin is in the church basement getting drunk."

I said, "Don't worry—Kevin's a happy drunk," and for the moment we let it pass. Kevin stumbled several times during the pictures, and he was loud and insisted on a picture of himself with the bridesmaids without Caroline, which I thought a little strange.

At the reception, I saw Hope bring him three separate plates of food, which he picked a piece or two off of before grabbing his drink and heading off to talk with one more of his old buddies. Caroline didn't seem to mind, but I did see Edward hovering near Kevin more than once with a glass of punch, trying to switch it with his real drink.

It was late when it all happened, maybe nine fifteen or nine thirty, and what is amazing is that Edward is the one that got it all started.

Alexander and I had settled in with some friends at a table beside the pool with a good view of the dance floor. The band was playing Mark Cohn's "True Companion," and Edward had found Caroline and brought her to the dance floor. I can remember watching and imagining that they were dancing a dance in honor of Peter, who could not be there but wanted her brother to stand in his place briefly to show Caroline how much he cared. They looked close and talked softly and I sat a little lower in my seat as I leaned back to watch.

That's when Kevin burst onto the dance floor. "Get the fuck away from my wife!" he slurred as he yanked Edward away from Caroline and gave him a shove that nearly knocked him over.

"What?" Edward said, regaining his balance, confusion evident on his face.

Caroline rushed to Kevin, pulling his arm and then his shoulder as Kevin moved toward Edward. He turned and shoved her with both hands and she slipped off balance in her heels and fell. Immediately, Hope joined her, and I made my way toward her, not knowing what I might do but knowing I needed to be near her just then.

Edward took two steps back as Kevin took his jacket off. "No man is going to put his hands all over my wife like that!" His lips were wet, and spit flew as he yelled. He flung his jacket to a table. I was certain poor Edward was going to be forced to defend himself when Curt came running up, tuxedo tails billowing behind as he ran.

"Hey, Kevin!" he yelled. "Dog, what's up?"

It got Kevin's attention, and he turned toward Curt. "No man's gonna—" he slurred.

"No way, man. No one can dog the Dog! You and me, bud, we'll take him. Now who was the rascal?" Curt smiled and brandished his fists round and round like old fashioned boxers, turning first to one part of the crowd, and then another. The rest of the groomsmen had filtered onto the dance floor, except Edward, and Curt said again, "Who was the rascal? We'll douse him for sure!"

I saw him wink at Edward, and Edward nodded, then came forward and said, "Me. I couldn't resist Caroline's beauty, and may have stepped out of line. Could you forgive me?" His voice was theatrical, overly loud and lilted with a touch of sarcasm.

Kevin started forward, but Curt pulled him back and said, "No way to forgive what you did, bud! You're going in the pool!" Edward's face turned from theatrical submission to abject surprise, and the rest of the groomsmen gathered him up and lifted him over their heads, carrying and passing him forward like a band member at a rock concert until they finally reached the edge of the pool. Edward, six feet off the ground, was scared to fight in case he might fall, and so was lofted by a platoon of groomsmen in a slow, gentle arc that landed him eight feet out into the shallow water.

He arose from under the water a dripping wet tuxedoed puppy dog, everything sagging low across his thin body. He turned and made his was to the steps on the opposite side of the pool.

Then Kevin screamed from the side of the pool, "Yeah man! Yeah!

Yeah! Teach you to put your hands on my wife! Get out of here." Kevin accompanied his yell with a middle finger jammed high into the sky, and accentuated it by banging on his bicep with his other fist. Alexander came up beside me and said, "Now, this will be a wedding to remember."

About that time, all of Caroline's cousins, plus a few of her friends from high school and other distant relatives came up behind Kevin and grabbed him and lofted him into the sky, much as the groomsmen had done to Edward. Kevin, though, was drunk and angry and fought hard to free himself, so he looked like an angry thrashing alligator in a tuxedo, barely being held aloft by a sea of hands, each clutching some piece of his clothing. He yelled and wriggled, breaking an arm free once to punch one of the NCSSM alumni in the face a couple times and sent him ducking for safety. They pulled him quickly to the edge of the pool, and as they tried to throw him he gave one final desperate convulsion toward freedom, and the throw which should have landed him safely in the water sent him sailing through the air, flopping like an angry carp caught on a line and landing tailbone first on the side of the pool, where he bounced once, then curled up in a fetal position and slid slowly into the water.

*   *   *

The ambulance arrived nine minutes later. They cut Kevin's tuxedo pants off with scissors to reveal a giant purple mark on the base of his spine. Kevin would not cooperate, and so rocked back and forth against the pain until they were forced to strap him to the stretcher before loading him into the back of the ambulance. Luckily, his injuries were limited to a broken tailbone and a nasty bruise, but he did spend his wedding night in the hospital, and was none too comfortable on the eleven hour flight to Hawaii the next day, where even the free liquor in First Class couldn't relieve the pain throbbing in his tail end.

Chapter 9: Second Marriage

When people who are fighting injure a pregnant woman so that there is a miscarriage, and yet no further harm follows, the one responsible shall be fined what the woman's husband demands, paying as much as the judges determine.
--Exodus 21:22

Kevin pulled the door of the U-Haul moving van shut after we had finished loading it for their move to Dallas. "Stay cool, Josh," he said, climbing into the driver's seat and started the engine. Caroline came over and gave me a hug, squeezing me hard in silence, and then letting go and climbing into the van. We had talked, but her silence and her desperate clutch spoke more than any awkward "We'll get together" promises ever could. The van pulled away, and took a piece of me with it. I loved her then as fiercely as I do now, and the pain of her absence stung in the hollow place above my breastbone.

For most people, I guess Carolina was the same after Caroline and Kevin left for their residency, but for me it was different. Gone were our long, slow walks at lunch. Gone were the awkward dinners when she and Kevin set me up with another young nurse or med student. Gone were the times she surprised me in the library. She was my best friend for those three years, and I believe I was hers, and when she left, my days lost some of their playfulness and became more like work.

I didn't hear from her much from Dallas. Occasionally, Caroline sent out mass emails to her scattered friends and told us she and Kevin had bought a house with a pool, or that they both worked very hard and never saw each other. I also received the annual Christmas card, with a letter copied on red paper, the print barely legible. These letters told stories of vacations in Mexico, in Paris, in Alaska. They told of her friends who got married, and of how much they looked forward to the end of their residencies, when they could go back to living a normal life.

I sent a congratulatory present when they finished their residency—a small concrete UNC Ram for them to put by the pool in their even newer house. A few weeks later, I got a short thank you note, telling me they loved it and it fit perfectly with the décor of their new house, and I must come to visit. The note was a hollow fossil of a friendship that had once been very dear to me.

Four months later, I received this email from Caroline.

Dear family and friends,

I have difficult news to share and it is awkward and uncomfortable. Kevin and I are getting a divorce. We have come to this decision together - after many months of trying to work things out, going to counseling, and still not finding a happy medium for us both. Papers have been signed and the process will be complete in the next couple of weeks. I want you all to know he and I still care about and respect each other. This is as "amicable" a decision as it could be, but one we feel had to be made. We will both go through a "grieving process," but hopefully we will grow into stronger, happier people.

At a time like this, we both need support - to remember we are not alone.

This is my email address, and Kevin is keeping the other address (for now). He will also stay at our house for the time being, so his address and phone number are the same.

Sorry if we've been out of touch for awhile, but now you understand why.

Love,

Caroline

I sent a short, supportive reply, telling her I was here if she needed me. Three weeks later, I got another broadcast email:

Just in case you were wondering, the divorce is now final. I will resume use of my maiden name. Thanks again to everyone who has expressed support and sympathy. It has meant so much. It is a rough time,

but also a time for growth - like spring coming out of winter... (There are occasional frosts, but ultimately the flowers and the fruits come...)
Love,
Caroline Novak

My next reply was a little longer:

Dearest Caroline:
I close my eyes now, and I can see you clearly. I can see you throwing the Frisbee on the day I met you, your curious "hello" grin and a strand of hair sticking to your sweaty forehead. I can see you squinting on the quad, shading those beautiful eyes behind your bangs from the sun. I can see the water drying on your skin as we drank beer in the hot tub with yet one more nurse or med student you thought I might like. What I can't see, and don't know how I'll ever understand, is your face without a smile on it.
Love,
Josh

Her reply was short, but at least not broadcast:

Josh,
If I could tell you everything, I might be able to smile again.
Love,
Caroline

I replied to her:

Caroline,
I'll listen. I'm afraid all I know of love is what has come from several young eccentrics in Paris who had an amazingly clear vision of what is should be, but could never get it right themselves. Try as I might, neither have I.
I'm a quiet man, Caroline. I work hard. I read, and I write. I don't have any magical cure for what ails you. If you want to talk, you can tell me of the love you had, and how it went wrong. Then I'll tell you of Ernie and Scott's loves, and how they went wrong. (Remember, E committed

suicide, while Scott committed Zelda to the funny farm.) I'm sure you'll feel better about yours.

Love,

Josh

* * *

I had a little cube in the Graduate Library with a desk and a locking bookshelf and a mini refrigerator I kept stocked with Pepsi. I was there often during the day, and almost every evening until after midnight, empty Pepsi cans stacking up around me. It was two or three weeks after I sent the last email that I heard a familiar voice from just behind my ear, and felt sure I had been working too long, so long in fact, that I was hallucinating. "Buy you a cup of coffee, stranger?" Caroline said, and I blinked, feeling the fatigue that had crystallized in the corners of my eyes.

Then her hand touched my shoulder, and my eyes went wide as I looked at it. I stood and lifted her in a hug, my laughter echoing around the stacks, drawing "sshhh's from a few of the more uptight students. I squeezed hard, and felt in her the same clutch she had given me before climbing into the U-Haul van four years earlier. The joints in my back made a cracking sound, but I kept squeezing.

I put her down and let go, and she grinned at me, lips together, two tears rolling slowly down her face. I cracked a smile and said, "I don't drink coffee." Her smile widened, lips apart, then she took my hand and said, "Let's go," and we walked away.

We stopped at a coffee shop near campus, and she got her double whatever tall and thin with lots of words that don't describe coffee at all. I had a glass of skim milk and a big piece of chocolate cake. Behind my back, she said, "I'll have two Quarter Pounders, fries, ice cream, an apple pie, and a Diet Coke!" sneering the last two words.

"I like the taste of skim milk," I said. It would be a while before I converted her to my dietary habits, and she never quit her coffee.

It was impossible to make small talk; old friends can be like that. After we sat down, she pulled a small hardbound book from her bag, and handed it to me, silent and definitely not smiling. Inside it began, "My Letter to my Future Husband", and continued, as you have read. I turned a few pages, not reading but looking at long, angled writing. I flipped some fifty pages, then closed the book and said, "I can read it, or you can tell me."

"I never showed it to Kevin," she said, "He found it when we were packing up to move." Her face remained stoic, and as I looked and the meaning of what she said slowly seeped into my brain, I stared into her eyes and at her smooth cheeks and all I could think was, "Never play poker with this girl." "He asked for a divorce after he read it." I reached out and touched her hand and she blinked and I saw the thin veneer of her emotions and stood, dropping a twenty on the table. I took the book and walked out with Caroline under my arm, her head buried in my chest.

We talked almost all night, or rather, she talked, and I listened. I opened a bottle of Merlot, which we drank slowly. I read her diary with her looking over my shoulder, and slammed it to the floor after the last letter. Later, I opened another bottle, and, our conversation turned to me. I knew as I walked her to her room we were going to make love. I didn't want it, and knew it wasn't God's plan, but it seemed...inevitable. I did make love to Caroline that night, and it was different from any other woman, and any other night even with her. She held me like I had never been held before. Not passionately, not like she was enjoying anything except the mere presence of my body. It was as if a great storm was pulling her away with the might of its wind, and I was the only tree she could hang on to. Our lovemaking was not tender or caring, but was the most physical, desperate exertion I've ever experienced in the arms of a woman.

She moved into the guest bedroom, and we did not share nuptials again until after our marriage six months later. We didn't even talk about it, but we both knew. That night, what we did, and how we did it—that's not who I wanted to be, and though I loved her more than love itself, it is not what I wanted from her. I was in love, and I was weak, but if we were going to do that again, it would be as husband and wife.

We both expected her to move out after a week or two, after I had been a good friend and given her a good heal. But she never did. Soon, she began working for a practice in town, and talking about buying a house nearby.

* * *

September 23, 1999

Dear Manny,

It's been so long since I've written in this thing, it's like I forgot it existed. I didn't, you know. It remained in the back of my mind, a childhood dream I'd never quite let go of. When I saw Kevin again in med school and knew we were getting married, I knew I could never show him what I'd written. But even in marrying Kevin, I never let go of you, of my dream husband, where you knew everything about me and loved me, despite my faults, despite my past, for who I am. Somehow I dreamed he could become you, though in the bottom of my heart I knew better. He never did.

This must be confusing. Let me start at the beginning. With Kevin.

I met Kevin in High School. He was Curt's roommate—we went on double dates together. He never had a steady girlfriend, but always had a companion. They came and went. Kevin was the same, and the girl played the same part; only the face changed. Kevin always had a smile, and could always make us laugh. He was bright and competitive, but I remember thinking I had gotten the winner of the two roommates. Besides being nicer looking, Curt seemed more stable, more of a family person. He was very attentive. Kevin was never attentive to whatever sidekick he brought along. I thought of Kevin as a very bright clown with great professional future, but who was destined to be lonely.

Once or twice my senior year Kevin came to visit campus, and we talked. I wondered if I had missed a good friend because of Curt. Later, I wrote it off as being lonely after the baby, and needing a friend.

Our first real date was terrible. After not seeing Kevin all through college, he came to medical school at Carolina. We saw each other in classes during our first year, also at parties and such. He again had a regular parade of faceless sidekicks. They were mostly undergrads, very pretty and vacant upstairs.

Our second year, a bunch of our classmates dropped out, and the rest of us bonded. In the fall, he had an extra basketball ticket; I don't remember which game. Very casually, while studying, he asked if I wanted to go. I said yes, and we went on a Saturday afternoon.

I dressed in blue jeans and a "GO HEELS" sweatshirt, not thinking anything of it. Kevin didn't bring a sidekick, and I liked the attention. I noticed him talking to me, noticing me, and he kept looking at me between plays. As we walked out of the stadium, he made me laugh as he guided me through the crowd, his hand on the small of my back.

About an hour after he dropped me off, he called and told me he had a nice time. That was way out of bounds, and I sensed a change. I told him I had a nice time also, and next thing I know we had made plans to go dancing that evening.

Kevin picked me up late; I had asked Lindsey, a friend, to go with us, and we had a few glasses of wine while we waited. When he finally showed up, he told us he had gotten caught speeding. We went to the dance club.

At the club, I ran into someone from college I hadn't seen in ages, and the four of us ended up dancing. This guy...I'll leave out the details...I had carried a torch for him for a long time. He asked me to dance once, the two of us, and that was it. When his friends left for another club, I asked Kevin if we could give him a ride home. The four of us went out for a late night breakfast at Breadman's. I played cool, but I hoped Kevin wasn't thinking anything special about me, and this other guy was.

I remember the trip home very clearly. Kevin drove; I was in the passenger seat, with Lindsey and the guy in back. We were quiet most of the way, then Kevin asked, "So, where do I drop you off?" The only sound was the purr of the engine. Everyone except Kevin knew of my torch. They wondered if I would invite him in. I wondered, too. Finally, Lindsey said she could give him a ride from my place, and gave directions. Kevin made a joke, laughing it off, and drove us to my place.

It was about four in the morning when we got there, Lindsey, the guy and I got out of the car. We stood in the road talking for a few minutes, and then the guy went around to Kevin's side of the car and thanked him for the ride, giving him a wink. I said good-bye to Kevin, and gave this guy a hug and my phone number as Kevin sat in the car. Kevin saw him kiss me, and I kissed back, and for a moment I got lost in his lips, in his grip, in his hands which lingered the bare edges of the places I wouldn't let him touch me, at least not until we were alone. I didn't care. I felt lucky.

Of course the guy never called. Kevin didn't look at me in class. He laughed and joked with everyone else, but wouldn't talk to me, and twice walked away when I approached a group.

That weekend, someone in our class had a surprise birthday party for her boyfriend, and we were all invited. Kevin showed up in fine form, drinking and laughing and joking. He put his arm around every girl in the room at least once, except me. Later when things started to settle down, I found him in the kitchen by the keg. He tried to make small talk, but I cried. I took both his hands in mine and looked deep into his grey eyes, bawling and apologizing. Very gentlemanly, he said it was okay, he understood. Our talk was short, but we agreed to get together in a few days to see a band and have some buffalo wings.

It turns out *Kevin* had been carrying a torch for *me* longer than I had for the other guy. He was a very attentive boyfriend, and a good friend for the next two years. He never once referred to me as, "Bitch", though people still called him "Dog". We studied together, relaxed together, and eventually when his roommate moved out while I was looking for a new place, moved in together. I loved Kevin, and really did tell him almost everything. I never showed him this diary because he was still best friends with Curt, and I didn't want Curt to find out about Faith.

Kevin never understood it when he found this book. That's the problem—along with one other. I'll write the other problem in the next day or two.

I want you to know this, Mr. Future Husband Man: I've done a lot of things in my life, and it's been tougher because of the mistakes I've made. I've never met anyone who doesn't have something in their life that needs to be forgiven. When I read this book, right now, paging through my mistakes, I wonder if there is anyone out there who can forgive me for everything I've done. If there is, I'll be lucky to find him.

I believe with all my heart I am wiser, tenderer, more forgiving and more loving because of what I've been through. There's hurt inside, and I can't pretend I'm not scarred, but there is another side, and I wanted you to know.

I wanted you to know because of the things I have to tell you next. I haven't forgiven myself for them yet, nor have I forgiven Kevin. It's difficult for me to ask you to forgive either of us, but you'll have to. I won't get married again without showing this book. No matter what. The Bible says we are forgiven for what we have done, for who we are—but I don't feel forgiven, and I am not able to forgive. I have some growing to do. I read the words every day, and they give me hope, but I am not there yet.

I love you. I know already showing you this book is going to be one of the hardest things I'll ever have to do.

Love,
Caroline

*   *   *

September 25, 1999

Dear Manny,

I sometimes wonder if I've already met you. I used to think you would be Peter—but he's so happy with JJ. Maybe someone else from high school or college—or maybe you'll never come. Maybe you were just a dream, a childhood friend I made up in a time of desperation, a time when I had to either have something to believe in, or to let go entirely. When I was carrying Faith, you were so real. And ever since I gave her away, you began to disappear, like the Blue Ridge fog in the late morning, you lingered in the low places and then were gone entirely.

This next story is hard to write, knowing I'll have to show you this someday. There is a tear on my cheek now, a tear born from my fear that this story might drive you off. Little did I know, when I started, the worst was yet to come. I'd better get started.

Kevin and I got married at the end of medical school, both board certified doctors. We were very happy with our new degrees, our bright future, and our new marriage. I loved him deeply. Our honeymoon in Hawaii remains one of my happiest memories.

We were in the same residency program, forced to work different shifts because we were married. I never saw him, and I mean that quite literally—we each worked 80 hours a week, and there are only 168. During our few hours together, we would cuddle with a bottle of wine, or sneak off on a date. We left notes, and presents. This marriage masquerade worked only because we knew it was for a short time.

We were both doctors. You would think we would know how to prevent what happened next. With only eight hours each week together, you would think I could plan. But I had lost the timing of my pill, and may have missed one—with my schedule, who knows. I had ovulated. I'm a doctor. I should know better. I was just plain stupid.

About five months into our marriage, I got pregnant. I woke up throwing up one morning, and I knew. I remembered the feeling. I waited two weeks to take the test, though, pretending it couldn't be true. After all, I was on the pill.

I took the test just before one of our short times together. When Kevin showed up, I was crying. He comforted me, and wanted to help, and all I could do was bawl in his chest. Finally I showed him the test. He looked at the test strip and asked, "Does blue mean you're pregnant?" I fell into him and bawled some more, and he said, "Pregnant. If you weren't, I'd know how to cheer you up." I laughed a little, then he made it all better by saying, "We're going to be parents."

I dried up. I smiled and squeezed him, burying my head into his chest and holding tightly to the man I loved. We had a great four hours before I went to work.

We saw each other again four days later. He had left me a pair of baby shoes and a cap so small it didn't even cover the palm of my hand. He pulled out a yellow pad and talk about the things I would have to do to take care of the baby. Child care, breastfeeding, shots, clothes, the nursery. He talked about the time I would take off from my residency—was it going to be three years, or four? I got quieter and quieter as his vision of "our" parenthood became more clear. I was to be the doting wife, greeting him at the door with his slippers in one hand and his daughter in the other, and in my spare time finish my residency and start a career as a family practitioner.

Then it happened. It was still early in the pregnancy, maybe eight weeks. He came home half tanked; he opened a bottle of wine, we made love, and he nearly finished the bottle alone. He was drunk, and we argued. He told me "how it was going to be," whether I liked it or not, and when I tried to defend myself, my career, my lifestyle, he wrote it all off as being "inconvenient."

We fought and fought until he said, "Get a fucking abortion, then! We'll have a baby when it's more fucking convenient!" It made me so mad! "Maybe I will!" I screamed. "Why wait?" he yelled.

When he said that, we both got silent. He sat down, and I curled up in his lap. We talked. He told me he still loved me, that we could do it, and that we could have another baby in a couple years, when I was done with my residency and we were both working. He talked about the trip to Europe we'd planned for the next year. He was so loving. But I told him no, I wouldn't have the abortion. I wanted that baby. He didn't understand, but how could he when I hadn't told him? No, I'd given up one baby, and I was not going to do it again, not even if I never finished my residency.

He stayed with me for a while, holding me, his arms covering me like a fog, making me feel nearly invisible. I drifted into nether-sleep, and woke only briefly when he covered me with an afghan and left.

An hour or so later, I heard him making noises in the kitchen, and rolled over, stretching my neck a little, twisting it so the crick could move to the other side. He came to me, and the smell of hot chocolate roused my senses and made me think of those times when he would bring me cocoa while we studied. "Take this," he said. "It will help you sleep." I knew he was right, so I took the cup and drank it slowly as he led me to bed.

I slept through my shift—Kevin had called me in sick. I was sick the next day, vomiting and wrenching like my stomach had a tropical storm blowing. It wasn't much better the next day, and there was some bleeding. Three days later, I realized I was no longer pregnant, and wrote it off as a miscarriage. I even thanked God for watching out for me, for protecting me from my own forgetfulness. I swore to him, if He would give me another baby someday, I would be the perfect mother, no matter what sacrifices it required, and then I thanked him again.

I'll tell the rest in a couple days. We didn't divorce for another three years, though in the back of my mind I wondered what really happened. Despite everything I've been through, I could not get my brain around a man who could do what Kevin had done. I shrugged off my fears as my own insecurity, and blamed it on Curt, on Faith, and on the man in the ravine. None of them were to blame, and nothing makes me sadder than when I think of the man I married, the man I loved.

I love you, Manny. Stick with me through this, and we can make it through anything.

Love,

Caroline

*   *   *

Dearest Manny,

I expect you're going to be smart, like me. I mean, it will take some good brains to keep up with me. Anyway, I'm smart, and have always known it. It's the way it is.

Every now and then, I wonder how someone as smart as I am can be so stupid. Have you ever wondered that? Well I was, and I have been. In this case, I was stupid over and over and over. I had a big pile of stupid, and I wallowed in it till it filled the pores of my skin and caked my hair into big, stupid clumps.

I mean, drinking can cause a miscarriage, if you drink too much, or if you drink something you shouldn't. Certainly getting sick can too, if it's bad enough, and so can some medicines. Almost anything can.

After I lost the baby, things went back to normal. Kevin took me out for a nice dinner on our next night off together, and then we took a vacation in Paris. His father footed the bill, said it was an early graduation gift. Funny, but the big Dog was scared of heights. I got him to the top of the Arc de Triumphe, but couldn't get him on the Tour Eiffel. I videoed him from the top, and zoomed in on him waving. He was very cute.

They don't work you as hard in your second and third years of residency, which gave us a chance to really enjoy each other. We went to plays and hung around with the other residents at a brew pub across from the hospital. After we finished, we both found jobs in Phoenix, and began to think about life after residency. We had loans to pay off, but living on two doctors' salaries was going to be okay. We found a house, and talked about having another child.

It happened the week before we moved. Kevin was packing boxes, and cleaning out my closet. He found this book—that's right—the one in your hand. That was the first stupid part. Thinking it was cute, he sat down to read it. I walked in just as he finished the part about Faith. I know after I saw what he was reading, I had a guilty look on my face. I know it didn't last more than a moment, but I felt our entire relationship play out on his face as he just looked at me. A storm swirled in his eyes, but I wasn't yet smart enough to be scared. He was my husband, and we had weathered fights before.

"Should I have seen this, or do you have some other husband in mind?" he asked.

I hesitated. I—honestly—had forgotten what I had written in here. It had been a decade since I'd started it, and years since I had written anything. "Why raise demons from the past?" I said.

"Yeah, why raise them?" he said, and closed the book, and I thought that might be the end of it.

I stepped forward and held out my hands for him to give me the book. "Let's get rid of it," I said, and smiled. There are ways a wife has to make a husband forget nearly everything, and I was planning to use them. I would have burned it if he had given it to me.

"You're not the type," he whispered.

"What do you mean?" I asked. Stupid part number two. What, again, did curiosity do to the cat?

"You don't get rid of things. You save them." I still hadn't clued in. "Like this diary," he said, holding it forward, just out of my reach. "You've kept it. Who knows why? Maybe you'll have another husband someday. You know, one in the future."

"Listen," I said. "We can get rid of that right now. I don't need another husband." I shook my head slowly, trying to will some love into the storm swirling in his eyes. I didn't want another husband. If we hadn't had this fight, I would be married to him today. But after what was said, there was no way. Some things can't be forgiven.

"Yeah, right," he said, and held the diary forward, within my reach. As I was about to take it, he pulled it back, and asked, "Anything else you've kept I should know about?"

I thought for a moment. I hadn't forgotten about Faith, but maybe I'd compartmentalized her, you know, put her away. I loved her, and thought about her every day. Besides, I didn't keep her. I carried her, nurtured her, and then I birthed her. Then, I gave her away, in the greatest act of faith I've ever committed. How can something you've "kept" leave such an aching hole, such emptiness?

"No," I said, and I pouted my lip. That usually gets him.

All this was stupid. Stupid acts numbers three, four, five, six and seven. I had stupid in my pores, under my eyelids, between my teeth.

"Nothing around here I should know about? No other diaries? No skeletons?"

"No."

"You don't mind if I search the rest of your closet. No skeletons in there."

I still had no clue. I thought about it, mentally cataloguing the things in my closet. Clothes, Frisbee collection, letters from Uncle Paul...

"I've got the letters from Uncle Paul. You know about them. I don't really want you to read them, though." I'd read him pieces of the ones coming up to the wedding day. I remembered.

"And you've got faith in me, you trust me not to read them."

"Right. I trust you." I said it almost as a question.

"That's a lot of faith," he said. Something sparked in the back of my brain, just a flicker. Then it went out. I remained silent.

"You've always had a lot of faith," he said. "Off to church whenever you can, reading your Bible. Never threw it in my face though. Not like this."

"What do you mean, Kevin? What have I done? That was just some stupid diary I wrote—"

"After you had your fucking baby!" he yelled at me, red faced. My heart sank all the way to my groin. "Faith. My fucking roommate's fucking baby! Yeah, you can have his, but won't have mine!" he yelled, and the world went into slow motion, my heart beating a slow metronome to an unpracticed ending.

"I wanted to have had your baby...it was a miscarriage," I said, the words drifting out in a stunned monotone.

He said softly, "Yeah. Right. Maybe you're not the only one with a secret."

I looked at him sadly. I was starting to cry. My lips and my scar get redder when I cry. I'm sure I looked like a circus clown, one of the sad ones, with make-up tears on their faces.

Every woman who has ever had a miscarriage wonders what caused it, and finds a way to blame herself. Was it the half glass of wine? Did I eat wrong? Work too hard? Exercise too much? Was it the stress? Our fight? I'd played over all the possibilities in my mind so many times, so many ways. I had considered that Kevin might have done something—he'd had access, and he'd left for an hour, and then there was the cup of cocoa. But I'd believed in his love for me. I was too scared of the truth—it was much easier to blame myself and then get on my knees and thank God. Now I knew, and I wanted him to say it. There was no turning back.

"What do you mean, Kevin? What secret?"

"You didn't want me to ever find out about this, did you?" he asked.

"No," I said.

"Something you regretted?"

"I regretted getting pregnant. But I don't regret having her. She was beautiful."

"I'll bet she was. I bet she had your eyes. Or maybe Curt's," he said. I've never seen him so sad, and never been so sad myself.

"I think about her when I'm in the hospital. I'll lay down in a cot and just daydream. Or go to the maternity ward and look in at the other babies, looking for her face. I've never seen it. She's like, twelve now. But I look for her in the maternity ward."

"Our baby would be turning three soon. Walking and getting into stuff."

"Tell me your secret, Kevin," I said, tears rolling hard down my face. Stupid act number six hundred and ninety two.

"I didn't want to do it," he said.

"Yeah," I said.

"It was so easy, though. They gave me the pill in the hospital—no questions. I put it in the cocoa and you took it. You—." He hesitated, and I waited for him to say the words. "When you took the cup, and sipped it…the look in your eyes was so grateful, so innocent, so loving. I thought maybe you'd understand."

I shook my head slowly, tears soaking my shirt. Then I sniffed, and wiped the mucus on my shirt sleeve, like I was five years old.

"I've got to go," I said.

"I know," he said. I didn't turn away. Dumb.

"I only did it because I loved you," he said.

"Right," I said, and then turned away and left.

I haven't seen Kevin alone since that moment, and my skin has not touched his. We went to counseling, but I could hardly talk. I didn't hate him. I still don't. In my mind, it all came down to his last statement…that's what I couldn't deal with.

What he did, I probably could have forgiven. I could have written it off to him being drunk, and been more careful in the future. Maybe. I don't know. But the part I couldn't get past, that I couldn't put away, and he never explained in counseling was the part about it being an act of love. We danced around it a hundred times in counseling. "I was saving you," he'd say. Or, "You didn't want it, but I knew you wouldn't have the courage to get rid of it."

"COURAGE!" I'd screamed.

"Courage." "Love." These words kept coming up in our counseling sessions, and I realized how different we were. I've heard divorced people say they didn't even speak the same language. I wrote it off as their own weakness, some kind of fault, or lack of persistence on their part. But now I know. Kevin and I didn't speak the same language. The words just didn't mean the same thing.

A few months later, we gave up on our marriage, and got a divorce. I had a lawyer handle it all, and wouldn't show up. It was the way it had to be. I read the parts of the Bible about divorce, and knew how God feels about it. But I couldn't do it. I couldn't love Kevin, and couldn't live with the lies so integral to him that they were part of his vocabulary.

God hates divorce. I could feel no other way but that God hated me, too. Pathetic, I thought about killing myself, but I guess I didn't have the courage.

I'm sorry to dump this on you, Manny. I'm a little better now…at least I can think about a future, and one with another husband in it.

I don't have anything more to say. If I show this to you, then you're in. And if you don't run off when you read it, then maybe we can make it work.

Will you clean off my stinking maggots, and buy me an ice cream? I need one.

Love,
Caroline

*   *   *

Caroline began visiting local health centers and a nearby orphanage, donating her services. After a few weeks, she took up part time work with two doctors nearing retirement and one younger practitioner. I changed my hours working so I could join her at the orphanage in the evenings.

Driving home one night, I said to her, "I've forgiven you, you know."

"For what?" she said, glancing at me sideways.

"For everything."

"What do you mean?"

"Everything in your diary. I've forgiven you for all of it." She sighed, looking down at her lap. "So have the kids. If you told them everything, they'd try to cheer you up. They'd hate it if you were sad."

"I know," she said.

I took her hand. "So why don't you forgive yourself?"

"I'm starting to think I can," she said, and squeezed my hand.

"Can you forgive Kevin?" I asked.

She shook her head. "I don't think I'm ready, yet."

"Jesus has forgiven you both, you know," I said as we pulled into the drive.

"That's what I don't understand," she said. "How could he forgive Kevin? Something about doing things to little children is like doing them to him. And then a weight around the feet and a river, if I remember. Not forgiveness." She pursed her lips white and shook her head in tiny little no's, over and over, her head shaking back and forth until the car stopped and we got out.

"When you do understand, forgiving yourself will be a cinch. So will forgiving Kevin."

"Maybe. But I'm not there yet."

*   *   *

I can remember the minute I started thinking about marrying Caroline.

We were at dinner, and I made her laugh by asking if any stinky maggots ended up in the Italian sausage in our spaghetti. We stopped laughing, and I asked, "How many other people have seen your diary?"

She said, "I've never shown it to anyone but you. Kevin found it after we bought the new house." The way she looked into my eyes stopped me cold. From then on, I obsessed with the possibility, and then the reality of my marriage to Caroline.

In those days, everybody had a dot-com business, and had lowered prices in order to "capture market share". I took advantage. A week after our conversation, I started looking at diamonds online. I studied the four C's, chose my target, and compared prices at different websites. I've always had trouble keeping secrets, and used the process as an outlet for my nervous energy. I avoided her, first so I could look for the ring, and later because Caroline and I talked about almost everything, and this secret was conspicuous in my thoughts, the proverbial "elephant in the room." Luckily, our lives were so busy she hardly noticed. Then there was the gravity of asking her to marry me when we weren't even kissing.

The ring came in a well-sealed Federal Express box, inside of which was another well-sealed box, and inside that another. Inside this last box was a lot of stuffing, and an envelope with the ring box inside. The thing looked puny. It arrived on a Thursday. My bowels turned to water the moment I saw it, and they stayed that way until Saturday.

On Friday, I cavalierly asked what she had planned for the weekend. "Nothing," she said, "hanging around with you." I said nothing else, and then took her to a movie so I wouldn't have to talk with her.

Saturday morning, I packed a bag with a change of clothes, a camera and a flashlight and stowed it in the car. Caroline awoke at around 11am, and came out showered and ready for the day around noon. "I have an idea," I said as she sat down with a glass of orange juice.

"What's that?" she said smiling.

"Let's go on an adventure." I said, then winked.

"Alright," she said. "How long's this adventure gonna take?"

"That's secret."

"Do I need to pack?"

"All taken care of. Just come along, and trust me." My heart galloped a stutter step inside my chest. Caroline could tell something was up.

"When do we leave?" she asked.

"Now." She finished her juice, and we walked out to the car.

I'd like to say the drive was relaxed; we were cozy, having fun and joking all the way there. But I'm afraid I wasn't the poised young bachelor who could deliver the perfect marriage proposal. I wasn't so much scared as obsessed. I wasn't really afraid of her saying no, but "not now" did come up as a potential answer as I analyzed, differentiated and integrated every possible outcome. I was unable to think about anything else. My thoughts were carried to the question I was about to ask by a force as great and violent as gravity pulling water down a waterfall, crashing to the rocks and slowly destroying them. I told her it was a four hour drive, turned up the music, and sang to distract myself. She listened, slept, and once held my hand.

We pulled onto a dirt road off I-26 in Saluda, and I drove down it. She said, "Almost there, I hope."

"There's a little hike up here to some places we can take some pictures." It was around 5:30, and we had maybe a half hour walk in front of us. I had predicted the sun would set between 6:30 and 7:00, so my timing just might be right.

We talked on the walk up. She had grown up in the area, but had never been here. "How did you find this place?" she asked.

"I found it in a book. There's a waterfall up there, if we can find it."

We crossed a dinky little creek that made me question the guidebook's description of the spectacular 300 foot waterfall. I took her hand as we walked across the creek on a log. On any day in the last fifteen weeks, I wouldn't have noticed taking her hand in mine, but on that day, I noticed everything.

"This is beautiful," she said, "peaceful." I felt as though I drifted along the trail, floating ten feet above us, watching her playful chatter, and there was nothing I could do to force myself back into my body. I was completely incapable of small talk.

We were winded from the climb as we reached the top. The smell of dried leaves and fallen branches filled my lungs, and I could see in the distance the sun beginning to set behind a layer of faint clouds. I could hear the falls, and saw the trail dip down to a ledge above the valley, a sheer fall below and beautiful space on all sides. I again took her hand,

and helped her down. I stepped forward cautiously, feeling my way to the edge of the sandstone, then returned to seat her on a natural step. I sat down next to her.

Across the valley, a river sprung out from a cluster of trees, flying down 300 feet, making only one stop at a shallow pool halfway down. The trees were painted in the brilliant reds, oranges and yellows of late Fall. Above the valley, the sun had turned the clouds pink and purple as it drifted leisurely over the horizon. The ring was in my camera case. I pretended to be peaceful and relaxed as we caught our breaths and watched the sun fold back its cloud sheets as it prepared for a long night's slumber.

Caroline's hair was shoulder length, worn high in a little girl's pony tail. Her bangs were mussed, and a little long, drifting over her brows. Her eyes shimmered in the fading light, and they smiled at me with infant crow's feet, giving a subtle clue that she was no longer a girl-child, but a woman. She wore blue jean shorts and hiking boots, with a red fleece under her Gore Tex. Her only jewelry was a simple cross, silver with four small diamonds, hanging just above the zipper on her fleece.

"This is amazing," she told me taking my hand and laying her head on my shoulder. I caressed the smooth skin above her knuckles, and touched my nose to her hair, holding her fragrance and letting the loose ends tickle my nostrils. As the sun rode away on its journey, the clouds gathered deep purples, with pinks off to the side and up high. "We have to get some pictures before this goes away!" she said.

"I've got something to ask you first," I said as I pulled first the ring box out of the camera case. I stepped in front of her with the ring box in my hand, and lowered myself carefully to one knee. My back foot hung over the edge of the ledge, which meant her view was as I'd planned it. She could see me on my knee below her, with the waterfall behind one of my shoulders, and the sunset above me. I opened the ring box, and said, "I want you in my life forever. Will you marry me?"

I stopped. I'm not sure what I expected. I'd practiced it a hundred times, and was sure I had practiced every possible reaction she could have over and over in my mind.

The look on her face went from peacefulness, to curiosity, to surprise, to what can only be described as terror. Lines formed on her forehead and her cheeks gathered in dozens of baby dimples that nearly pleated. Her eyes were wide and fearful and I was sure she had stopped breathing. I wanted to look over my shoulder to see what was scaring her. In my mind I was backpedaling, thinking "we could do this another time" or "I guess this wasn't a good idea" and "maybe you need some time to think before you answer". Only by force of will was I able to say nothing, and keep calm. A tear welled at the bottom of her eye, only to drop and quickly be replaced by another and another and then another.

She took the ring in her hand and said, "Oh my God," and cried some more. She held it up to her eyes to look at it, but made no motion to put it on her finger. Then she said, "It's beautiful," as she pulled it out of the box. I was still rehearsing my backpedaling, knowing while she was flattered and all, there was just no way and what was I thinking! Finally, I said, very quietly, "Well?" and she took my face in both her hands, pulled me up and said "Of course!" as she kissed me and drew me in to a hug. We both squeezed and she cried some more and I sat down next to her and kissed her salty teary lips. For the next half hour, we used the timer and remote functions of my camera to gather a few pictures of us in this picturesque little corner of the world, and she kept saying "Oh my God" and "I can't believe it."

As I began to pack up the camera, she asked me, "Do you have a flashlight?"

"Of course," I said. The sun had disappeared, but the sky was still grey as the day drifted into twilight.

"Can I see it?" she asked.

"Sure," I said, and handed it to her.

She took the flashlight, and walked to the side of the ledge where it met the valley, then disappeared over the side. I could hear her sliding down the side of the mountain as she yelled, "Follow me," laughing. I left my camera case behind and followed, collecting leaves behind my bulldozer butt as I slid down the mountain, doing my best to dodge the small trees that were in my way. When I reached the bottom, I could see the light of the flashlight fifty yards ahead, bobbing as she ran along the bank of the river.

I followed, and as I reached the clearing before the pool at the bottom of the waterfall, I saw her pull off her shirt and drop it on the rocks. I walked toward her slowly, cautiously, like a fox that is not really hungry, but is carefully considering its prey. She reached back and unhooked her bra, then unsnapped her jean shorts as her bra fell around her elbows. She stepped out of her shorts and stood before me, facing away. She kicked off her shoes, then took three steps and dove into the water in a shallow racing dive. My heart pirouetted as she disappeared, then settled into a slow spin as she came up out of the water, hair falling down her back and naked, fully erect breasts glistening in the disappearing light.

"I'm not leaving until you come in, too, and it's way too cold for me to stay long!" she yelled. I shook my head and looked at my shoes, taking only a half step forward before she yelled again, "Get in here right now, or I'll throw the ring into the waterfall!" She held the ring between two fingers, her arm cocked as if ready to pitch a fastball right down the middle of the strike zone. I stripped my clothes off as fast as they would come, and nearly tripped as my foot got stuck in my jeans leg which had turned inside out in my haste. Without thinking, I stepped off the rock and into the water, which was so cold as to be immediately painful.

"Go under," she said, and cocked her hand back farther. I shivered and shook, then mustered the courage and flung my body flat against the surface of the pool, coming up in the mist at the edge of the waterfall. She had followed me and when I came up I was in her arms and I held her for only a moment before she said, "Dang this is cold," and we both sprinted to our clothes. I had not taken off my underwear, which made for an uncomfortable ride home.

We drove home talking about all sorts of things. When she asked me when I thought to propose to her, I told her it was after she told me that I was the only one to see her Future Husband Diary. She said, "I thought so. I thought the same thing. Once I realized you were the only person I could show it to, it became obvious. I thought I was being forward when I held your hand in the car! I just wanted you to kiss me again!" She fell apart laughing at herself.

*   *   *

I dropped the bomb on her one night at dinner after we had been married for a few months. "I finished my dissertation today," I said.

She looked at me in stunned silence. Even before her first wedding, I had said I was "about a year or eighteen months" from graduating, which is what I had told her when she showed up after her divorce four years later. I finally had incentive to move on.

She asked me, "What does that mean?"

"It means I'll finally be called 'Doctor', that I'll go to a ceremony wearing a black robe and a funny hat. I'll move the tassel."

She was smiling. "And after that?"

"I won't have a job anymore, and I'll have to pay all those loans off," I paused as she gave me a puzzled, quizzical look. "I don't know what I want to do. Maybe be a father, or write a book, or volunteer somewhere."

She smiled softly. "I like the father part." She took my hand, "Have you thought who the mother might be?"

"I have a few people in mind…" She squeezed my hand and I smiled at her, and then kissed her. "You," I whispered.

We made love the next morning, and she chided me that evening that I'd made her late for her appointments all day. I would say we conceived then, but we made love every day until she missed her period three weeks later, and after that the pace dropped off only slightly.

*   *   *

Caroline grew more and more beautiful each day. Her smile broadened and everything that used to bother her—my clothes in the floor, dirty dishes and improperly placed cushions on the couch—quit being annoying. She began light calisthenics in the mornings, stretching and tensing her muscles in gentle movements, contracting and relaxing. She was keeping her level of endorphins up for the baby, she said.

She split her time between her practice and the orphanage, and sometimes came home late in the evening. I knew she was late not because she was working, but rather because some child had caught her attention, and they had spent the twilight hours throwing a Frisbee, shooting a basketball, or reading. It wasn't work for her at all, and I began to join her.

My family came to my graduation. My older brother brought his new son Forrest, who had been born since the wedding and couldn't yet hold up his head. After the ceremony, Caroline sat quietly in the corner, holding him and humming, letting his fingers curl around hers, tickling his tiny feet. She changed his diapers and once, after she had let the last drop of beer fall onto her tongue, let him play with her empty Bud Light bottle. Forrest explored her face and hair and ears with his hands, first taking hold of something and then pulling to see if it would come off, or move. She was natural with him in her arms, and grinned a satisfied, peaceful grin as long as she could see him.

Her parents had not come for the wedding, and though Hope had visited for a week, she also had to leave before the ceremony. I felt Caroline's sadness at their absence, and admired her bravery at restarting her life without them, knowing they would not withhold their love forever.

After the wedding, our life fell into a blissful routine. I met Caroline at the orphanage in the evenings to play with the kids and enjoy being with her. I had started to write my Great American Novel, set in Paris. I wanted desperately to make Madison, my main character, into a romantically tragic twenty-something who had run to Paris to flee her emotionally tormented life. Unfortunately, I placed her on a pedestal and what came out was a story of life in the fast lane as described by the desperate, self-centered waif who was too fearful to take his foot off the brakes. It didn't help that I had never been to Paris. Even I knew that, while I wanted to write with every capillary in my body, I needed a topic more stirring than teenage angst to compel the story.

For Caroline, it was a time of growing larger, and of growing more content at the same time. I've heard that the word integrity means that your actions are more in line with your words, and with your being. If so, then Caroline gained in integrity. She had a sense of becoming whole, that even though a small person was living and growing inside her who would be irreparably separated from her in a few short months, she was at the same time growing into a single whole person, more indivisible than ever before.

Chapter 10: Second Birth

Now faith is being sure of what we hope for, and certain of what we do not see.
Hebrews 11:1

The hospital was cold, hard, and filled with small noises that echoed down the halls. I awoke often with a crick in my neck and a full bladder that I had to pad barefoot down the tile floor to relieve. Once, I awoke dreaming of losing a never ending game of Pong, and only afterwards realized that it was Caroline's heart monitor sounding the bling, bling, bling of her still beating heart, sixty beats per minute as it had been for three weeks. Despite the discomfort, because it is where my wife lay, still but very warm and a part of me, the hospital had become my home.

After I walked in on Hope and Peter and found them talking, I knew I had to give them her diary. She had never asked me to keep it private, and I knew that in not asking she trusted my judgment and my love for her. I gave Hope and Peter the diary, then I left. I didn't want to be there when they read the last part where Kevin admitted to giving Caroline the morning-after pill in her hot chocolate.

I went to my room in the hospital—it felt like my room, anyway. I sat on the vinyl chair and opened my book and read. My hand drifted through the aluminum bedrail, seeking the warmth of Caroline's body. I touched her, and snuggled my fingers in under her arm. You would think I would go crazy, having monologues with Caroline, imagining her responses, and reading endless novels. For me, it was the opposite. My life—my other life—had grown too crazy for me to handle. I couldn't face the empty rooms at home, the evenings either spent explaining to the children at the orphanage where Caroline was, or at home alone. Going back would be like admitting she was gone. I had to wait for her, to not experience without her any of the life we had built. So I didn't. I ate junk food, read junk novels, occasionally held Caroline's limp fingers in my own, and spoke to her as if she could hear me and was saving up my words to respond sometime later.

I was nearly asleep when Hope opened the door two hours later and walked straight to Caroline's bed. I rubbed my eyes and lifted my book from where it was folded on my chest, and then turned down the corner of my page. She held Caroline's diary at her side. I studied her face. I couldn't find any anger, but neither did I see sadness. Instead, her feline mouth was tight with resolve below steady, forward looking brown eyes, eyes that seemed to be trying to read Caroline's thoughts.

*   *   *

Just then, a policeman stepped into the room, followed by Peter.

"A boy was there, too, on his bike," Hope said.

"Oh," I said.

"His bike was hit by the car, as well." I was silent, so she continued. "They say she knew him—a boy named Nathan."

When she said that, said his name, I knew I had to learn more about what had happened. Nathan was at the accident? Had he been hurt? Did he see what had happened to Caroline? I pictured him standing over her, her limp body contorted on the pavement, still and unmoving, bleeding, looking as if she had died. Once again, the adult he loved most had exited stage right. This time he was involved, tangled up in it as well.

I had simply forgotten our plans to adopt Nathan. We had the paperwork. Maybe Caroline had signed it already. It had been three weeks since the accident, which meant—I'd forgotten—maybe another week before his father got out of prison? Or had the month been just an estimate? Could he be getting out now? How long before he got to see Nathan?

I closed my eyes as these questions ricocheted about in my head, trying to weather the hurricane brewing there. I opened my eyes and stood.

The policeman spoke. "We didn't know who the boy was until today. He'd run off. Our only witness said she could ID him, but we didn't know where to start.'

"I spoke with Mrs. Harrington this morning," Hope said. "She said the boy had known Caroline, but ran off after the accident, leaving his bike. I told Officer Brenneman to call Miss Baldwin. She told him Nathan had lost his bike a few weeks ago."

I remember when Caroline had given Nathan the bike. He hugged her like a boa for ten seconds, then hopped on and disappeared down the street. We sat on the front porch of the orphanage for the next hour, and he returned only to zoom by at full speed, or to pop a wheelie, or wiz by with no hands, or steering with his feet. He'd had bikes before, but hadn't had one for his two years at the orphanage. It was as if we had given wings back to a crippled bird.

"Has anyone talked with Nathan?" I asked.

"No. Mrs. Harrington ID'ed him playing basketball at the orphanage. Miss Baldwin said I should get you."

"Yeah," I said. "That's right. Get me."

*   *   *

I rode with Officer Brenneman to the orphanage. On the way, he started to tell me Mrs. Harrington's story, but the logistics of the street and the car and the bike all confused me, and I convinced him to take me to the corner of Columbia and Franklin Streets, where it had happened. We parked in the public lot a block down Columbia, and walked up toward the corner.

"Evidently, she was standing here," he said, pointing at the curb on the north side of Franklin, facing across Columbia. "She had a couple of bags—"

"Birthday gifts for the kids."

"—in her hands. Nathan came down Franklin Street—"

"He shouldn't have been this far."

"—And the car came from over there," he said, pointing in front of us down Franklin Street. "And made a left hand turn onto Columbia in front of her."

"You mean into her," I said, and locked eyes with him.

"Yes. Well, into her. When I arrived, the boy's bicycle was here," he said, pointing at a place where the road met the curb a few yards down Columbia. "One tire had been run over by the car.

I looked from one place to another, trying to picture what had happened. Nathan and Caroline stepped off the curb at exactly the same time and get hit by the car? Neither one of them sees it coming, right at them? They were both too attentive for that.

"I need to talk with Mrs. … your witness," I said.

"Mrs. Harrington. Yes. Let's swing by."

*   *   *

Mrs. Harrington lived over in Carrboro, alone in a duplex down a wooded dirt road. We pulled in, and she met us at the door.

"This is Mr. Studeman, Mrs. Harrington. The husband of the woman you saw hit by the car."

"Josh."

"Yes," she said, and let us in. She sat with us, then stood up and said, "Tea? Or I could make some lemonade. Let me get you something."

"We won't be long," Officer Harrington said, then looked at me. "Josh only has one or two questions."

"Well, then, okay," she said, and sat back down.

I looked around the small living room, and out the back porch where I could hear a creek burbling on the other side of a screen door. Then I met Mrs. Harrington's eyes. "Tell me about what happened, just before the impact."

"Oh, well …" she said, looking down. Then she looked up and said, "He was a little hooligan, you know. Racing down Franklin Street like that on his bike. He could have killed her himself, without any help from anyone!"

"What? What?"

"I heard him loud and clear. 'Look Miss Caroline!' he yelled. And look she did. If he hadn't yelled that, maybe she'd have seen that car coming. Distracting a pregnant woman like that. He should have been the one hit, is all I'm saying."

"What was he doing?"

"Tricks. Kids today don't have any respect. Had both feet on his handlebars, like he was riding a big beach chair. I thought he was going to sail right past her into that car, which is how it should have happened if you ask me. I asked Officer Brenneman this morning why they don't just lock him up for what he did. It's his fault she's put out like she is."

"Then what happened?"

"Well he came on like he did, little rascal, and like I said I's sure he was going to hit the car himself. Then Mrs. Studeman—"

"Caroline."

"Right, Caroline. She yelled, 'Nathan!' and the car hit her instead of him. Must be my old eyes."

"Did the car knock her into him?" I asked.

"No, that's right. He hit her on his bike, and knocked her into the car. Little rascal should have known not to do those tricks in the first place, and surely not so close to a pregnant woman. They don't teach those children any respect, but I guess I understand now, seeing as he's from an orphanage."

I closed my eyes and imagined it. Nathan doing tricks and showing off for Caroline? Yes, no surprise. Nathan this far from the orphanage? Shouldn't be, but he's ten, so certainly possible. Nathan riding too close, and hitting Caroline by accident? No way. He could have been standing on the seat and riding on Mrs. Harrington's gravel road, and there is no way he would run into Caroline. If he was going to, he would have jumped off himself. If I knew one thing, it's that he's good on his bike, and he loves her more than Christmas ... well, that's two things, but in any case it didn't add up.

"Thank you, Mrs. Harrington," I said, and we stood to leave.

* * *

Nathan was dribbling the ball at the top of the key when we pulled up. He faked a pass left and drove to the hoop with a clear lane from the defenders. He laid the ball up against the backboard gracefully, but then it hit with a thunk and rolled off the side of the rim. The other kids looked up as the police car stopped short of their game, but Nathan grabbed the ball and said, "Come on—just take it out." The other boy checked the ball with Nathan, then started dribbling.

"You want to talk to him?" Officer Brenneman asked.

"I think I want to adopt him," I said. "Is there any chance he's in trouble?"

"Only if Caroline presses charges. Or you," he said.

"Okay. You can go then."

"You don't need a lift."

"I'll find my way."

*   *   *

I found another boy, and after the next shot said, "Jimmy, we're in. Four on four now. I'm on Nathan's team." Nobody complained. Those were the unwritten rules. Everyone could play.

Nathan took the ball out, passed it, set a screen and got the ball back, then thumped it off the rim again. Jimmy was covering me. "He's taking all the shots," he said. "Hasn't hit one yet."

I shook my head. Three more possessions, and I saw the ball only once, and managed to score on a twelve foot jumper. We were down, four to one. Nathan hadn't passed the ball to me, or even acknowledged my presence. Our normal one-two punch of his ball handling and my shooting was gone, and the bigger kids neutralized my height advantage with their athleticism.

"He's been like this for weeks," Jimmy said. "Hardly any fun to play with him anymore."

Nathan got the ball again at the top of the key, this time with me under the basket. He faked right, then dribbled between his legs and broke left past his defender, and had a clean line into the lane, with me waiting. Normally, he would just dish the ball to me, and I'd get the easy lay up. This time, however, he drove, dribbling right at me. I stood still, a wall to protect him from defensive help, expecting him to step past me and bonk another ball off the rim. Instead, he drove right into me, leaping into the air and colliding with my chest as he released the ball over my head. We both tumbled down in a tangle of limbs, mine mostly on bottom.

I peeled myself away and sat up, and he lay on the ground crying. My heart contorted and I knew he wasn't crying for himself, or the missed shot, or for me. He loved Caroline, and felt like he had hurt her. It ached.

266

Even knowing that, I wasn't prepared for what happened next.

I reached over and touched his shoulder and said, "Hey bud, let's have another try." He shrugged of my arm with an "Uuunh." I got to my knees, and reached under his shoulder to lift him and said, "Come on, I'll help you up."

I've thought back and tried to remember every detail of that moment, and all I can remember is grabbing Nathan by the arm … maybe a little roughly, but not abusive by any standards I'm aware of. I pulled him up, and then stepped toward the basket.

When I turned back around, Nathan was smashing his face over and over into the rough pavement. His forehead and nose were bleeding. I leapt to him and tried to hold his head, but he was strong and I was forced to use my hands as a cushion to soften his blows against the concrete parking lot. Over and over he drove his forehead and face into my hands. His blood was slick my palms, and eventually the backs of my hands began to bleed, too, from the repeated blows dealt by this troubled young boy.

As this was going on, one of the smaller kids who had been watching said, "No! Nathan's at it again," and then left to get help. Miss Baldwin came out and picked Nathan up and carried him away, waving me off.

Later, she told me that these tantrums had been common when he first came to the orphanage, but went away after Caroline had started visiting. She thought he'd recovered. He only stays violent like that until he goes to sleep, and then he wakes up grouchy for a few days, then goes back to normal. But he holds grudges with the offender, which in this case was me. I'd come to talk with him, but Miss Baldwin told me to stay away for a few days. I agreed, but worried about his father getting out of prison, and coming to get him. Miss Baldwin just smiled, a sad, thin smile and a slow shake of the head as if to say, "We'll be here for him when his father loses him again."

* * *

I told Hope and Peter everything when I got back to the hospital, and Hope just kept nodding her head. After I'd finished, and her nodding was nearly driving me crazy, I asked, "Why are you so agreeable with all this?"

"Hope has a theory," Peter said.

I pulled at the bandage on my hands. "Great," I said.

"She thinks Caroline doesn't want to come out of her coma."

I shook my head. "I wouldn't either," Hope said. "Dad wants her to get back with her ex-husband, who, by the way, secretly aborted her child. Her child—the unaborted one—is living some life she'll never know, and she never told the father. She doesn't know if she saved Nathan, but is sure to have heard him yell, or the bike crunch, or something. She's still scared of the guy who chased us in the ravine. And she isn't even allowed to talk with the guy who's been her best friend since she was four years old. You're her only oasis."

"Her 'safe harbor,'" I said.

"What?"

"Her 'safe harbor.' That's what she called me. Her 'safe harbor.'"

"So my theory is right. Which means my plan might work."

"What plan?"

"Hope thinks she knows how to get Caroline to come out of her coma."

"We have to make her want to come out, by making everything right for her out here. We have to fix everything."

"I'm listening," I said, and she laid out the different parts of her plan.

*   *   *

Curt was first. I pulled up at his home, after pressing the numbers in the gate at the entrance to his neighborhood, and parked my car in his circled driveway. He and his wife let me in, and I turned down an offer of a drink. His kids had gone to bed.

I didn't tell him everything, but gave him all the details about Faith— her birth, the hidden pregnancy, the adoption. They both listened, and while Curt wanted a long discussion about his rights as a father, his wife eventually realized why I was there, and asked, "How can we help Caroline?"

"Curt has to come see her. You both do, maybe. You have to tell her that you know, and that it's okay. Tell her you forgive her."

"We can do that," his wife said. She was a petite, well kept blond with chestnut eyes and erect shoulders. "I'd like for Caroline to be better, and Curt and I will do whatever it takes."

"Whatever. She can't hear us anyway."

"You have to mean it," I said.

"We will. When I get through with him, he will mean every word of it." She smiled, and after a few courtesies, I left, only imagining how the laws of their household were shifting as I drove away.

*   *   *

Kevin was a different story. He had moved back to Raleigh after the divorce, and was doing a second residency in Ob/Gyn. I pulled up to his apartment building in one of those mini-city complexes with four swimming pools and a nine-hole golf course. His apartment was on the third floor overlooking one of the pools. I never saw the view.

"Yo. Josh. Wasn't expecting you to visit."

"I wish I didn't have to."

"So don't," he said, and pushed the door closed in my face.

I rang the doorbell again. And again. Then four more times, before he finally opened the door and said, "Caroline didn't marry a rocket scientist this time, did she?"

"Nor the last," I said, and we squared off.

"She needs you," I said, and the physical pain of delivering those words to this man split my spine.

"We went through all that with our counselor."

"She's in a coma."

"I read that. Tough luck. Your baby make it? Or is she oh-for-three?"

"It'll be two-for-three after this one," I said.

"Right. Someone ought to tell Curt."

"I just left from there. He and his wife are discussing it now."

"'To be a fly on the wall.'"

"Caroline really does need you now. To get out of her coma."

"Listen—she'll have to do that on her own. You understand. You should go now." He closed the door, and I did.

Ten minutes later, I was back at Curt's house, and told his wife that I needed one more thing. She told me she would get it done.

*   *   *

Hope had had a similar meeting with her parents, and they were driving in from Brevard to see Caroline for the first time since before our wedding. Hope's theory was that, like in Matthew 5:24, Caroline had too many issues, with too many people, and they had too many with her, that she was just hiding.

"She's turtling," Hope said. "We used to play with turtles as kids. At first, Caroline said they were no fun because they just turtled up. Climbed into their shell and waited for the bad situation to go away."

"Funny," I said. "In med school, she always talked about 'going to sleep by the finish line,' like she wanted to be the tortoise."

"It's different now. Now we need to coax her out. Let her know that it's safe out here. That she won't be hurt again. After Caroline figured it out, she loved turtles. If we'd scared a one, Caroline would spend hours winning over its trust, talking to it, making it warm, offering it food. But she never kept one as a pet. She'd win its trust, and then set it free."

"So now we start."

"Now we start. Peter and I will go first."

*   *   *

I stood, and Hope pulled my chair closer to the bed and sat down. Peter stepped behind her, one arm dropping to touch her lightly on the shoulder as Hope gathered Caroline's pale, almost ghostlike hands into her own.

"I'm sorry, Caroline," she said. She raised Caroline's hands up to her lips and kissed them, then placed one hand on Caroline's belly, touching skin on skin underneath Caroline's hospital gown.

Hope spoke with a soft voice, but her tenor was resolute and steady. "I'm sorry I hated you for being unafraid, for being imperfect and yet still happy … for your bravery, and your foolishness. I'm sorry I hated you for coming back for me in the ravine, and for winning. You were so good, Caroline, so willing to sacrifice … and it made me hate myself. I'm sorry

270

I blamed that on you."

Hope broke down, leaning her head forward onto Caroline as she began to sob. Her shoulders shook and she reached around Caroline with both arms, gripping her tightly around her pregnant stomach and her shoulder. I took a step forward, but Peter stuck out a restraining arm and shook his head. "There's more," he said.

"Yes, there is, Caroline." Hope calmed herself through her tears. "I'm sorry I didn't go back and help you in the ravine; I'm sorry I ran and left you alone. I am sorry I wasn't there when you bore Faith. And I'm ... so sorry." She broke into sobs again, a tremor running through her shoulders. "I'm so sorry for Kevin, and what he did." She squeezed Caroline until her hands turned white.

"... and Caroline," she squeezed harder. "I forgive you for everything. I forgive you for being perfect, for being a nuisance, and for everything you did. You're my sister and I love you!"

She held Caroline for many long minutes, not crying or sobbing, but drawing her in and loving her with unfettered dignity. I watched, and the only sound in the room was the sound of our breathing and the rhythmic beeping of Caroline's heart monitor, beeping a steady metronome of her life.

When she finished, she stood and went to the sink and washed her face and hands, then walked over to stand beside me and Peter, and the three of us gazed down at Caroline's still figure. Hope said, "Your turn, Peter." Peter nodded, then took his seat in the chair and took her hands. I watched Caroline's face, and her mouth seemed to open a bit more as she exhaled, as if she were trying to smile.

"I'm sorry, Caroline, for letting you climb the tower for me. I'm sorry I let your father drive me away, so I couldn't be there later when you needed me. I'm sorry I didn't kill Kevin back when I wanted to, and I'm sorry I didn't let Curt kill himself. No, I take those last two back.

"I'm sorry, Caroline, for not being enough of a man to challenge you after you broke up with me, after the ravine. I'm sorry I didn't have the courage to make you be my friend then. I was such a coward. I'm sorry I was so selfish to want what I needed, not what you needed." He was calm, but his voice had begun to crack just a little.

"Caroline, I forgive you for everything. I forgive you for not loving me. I forgive you for refusing my first two proposals. I forgive you for not letting me marry you and raise Faith as our own. I forgive you for marrying Kevin six months before I was going to propose to you again. I forgive you for everything." He kissed her hand, and then stood.

Hope was the first to break the silence as we all stared down at Caroline's motionless body. "It's your turn now, Josh," she said.

*   *   *

I had let Peter and Hope interface with the police and the insurance agents. It seems Nathan had been hurt a little when he was thrown from his bike, and Hope and Peter wanted to get the driver's insurance company to pay for the expenses. They also wanted the insurance company to get him a new bike. I let them handle it, and signed whatever they put in front of me.

That morning, Peter had hit me with the part that hurt the most. "I stopped by to see Nathan today at the orphanage," he said. "He said, 'I hope her baby dies.'"

*   *   *

I wish I could describe accurately how I felt during those weeks when she lay in a coma. Less than two years earlier, she had fled from her world, leaving her husband and her family behind, and started a new life, a new world, with me. I loved that world desperately, selfishly, and wanted nothing more than to have her wake up so we could go back to it. I didn't want her family, or Peter or Hope or Kevin, back in our world with all of the baggage they brought with them. Caroline had come to me and we had started a life with no guilt, no grudges. We had each other, and the children at the orphanage, and in our life there was so much love and so much giving that her history seemed a bad story, a nether-history that could be forgotten in the way a half hour of Jay Leno can erase the fear from watching a scary movie. I was her eraser, and I loved it. Through my time alone, and my time with Peter and Hope, though, I realized how selfish I was being, and I began to fear Caroline would not come back. I was backed into a corner, and a man backed into a corner will do anything to get out.

*　*　*

The hospital room had begun to grow stuffy. Maybe it was the tears, adding salt and humidity, or maybe it was the overflowing emotion. By this time, I understood what we were doing. I stepped forward, sat in the chair, and took her hands.

"I am sorry, Caroline, I did not love you more, sooner. I'm sorry I let you fall for Kevin, that I didn't charm you away before you married him. I'm sorry I let you go, that I didn't keep up better, that I didn't force our friendship." I could feel the glands working behind my eyes, but no tears fell yet. There was a million other things to be sorry for—we were married after all—so I decided on a blanket statement.

"I'm sorry for all the little things I've done wrong Caroline, and for not loving you enough for all the little things you did right.

"I forgive you, Caroline, for not falling in love with me sooner, for making me wait. I forgive you for conceiving your first two children with someone else, and for having such poor judgment in men before our marriage. I forgive you for the nights you've left me alone, and for the times when you've been clingy. I forgive you for everything, and love you for who you are."

When I finished, I held her hands quietly, and I swear I felt her squeeze my hands back. Then I stood and joined the other two, as if to say, "now what?"

Hope broke the silence. "Mom and Dad will be here in a couple hours," she said.

*　*　*

Later that same day, Caroline's father walked in the room, took a cursory look at Caroline and shook his head, then looked at me and Peter and said, "Great, I've got the Fag and the Pussy here helping Caroline. Good thing you're here to take care of things, Hope." I waited in silence, but Peter's face turned a shade toward crimson, and a vein in his temple stood at attention.

"Dad," Hope said, and he looked at her. "For Caroline's sake, I am going to ask you to listen to us. We've got some things to say that may change how you think of people." We had brought in chairs for everyone, and Peter, Hope and I took our seats. Donna, Caroline's mother, looked tentatively at us, and then sat down beside Peter. That left only John Novak standing, and he glanced around, then looked at Caroline for a minute and sat down in the only empty chair, between Hope and Donna.

"Dad," Hope started. "You aren't going to like this." She paused, folding and unfolding her hands in her lap. "This is Caroline's third pregnancy. We're going to tell you about the first two." Caroline's mother gasped and a subtle calming come over John.

Peter spoke next. "The first one happened while we were in high school—"

"If you are the father, I'll kill you," John said, his lips white with tension.

Hope placed her hand on her fathers arm. "Peter's not the father, Dad. He was her best friend when it happened—the one who helped pull her through it."

"—so she could risk her life climbing that damned tower! So he could graduate! Do you know what that cost me?" Red faced, he glared at Peter like an angry dog, sizing up his opponent.

"Yes sir, I know what it cost you. Do you know what it cost me?" Peter glared back, the strong muscles in his neck and shoulders tense.

"Just tell the story, Peter," Hope said, and beneath the fear, there was sweetness in her voice. "He will understand, once he knows everything." I looked over at Caroline, and I could swear the lines in her forehead were a little more prominent, as if she was straining to hear.

Peter's muscles relaxed. "Curt was the father," he said, and I heard Donna whisper that he was such a nice boy. As Peter began to tell the story, I saw a change come over John, as he switched from angry father to lawyer, asking questions and getting the facts. "How do you know it was Curt's?" "Were there any complications?" "What do you mean you proposed? Did you have a ring?"

He only blew up once. Peter told John that Paul, his brother and Caroline's uncle, had arranged for Caroline to live with him when she gave birth, and also for Faith to be adopted. "That son of a bitch has known all this for the last fourteen years?" Then, very quickly, he settled down and started asking questions again.

"So what about your senior year?" he asked, and Donna took his hand in hers.

"I was in love with Caroline," Peter said. "I still wanted to marry her. I would have done anything for her … and I guess I did. I studied with her every night and spent nearly all my free time with her. I wanted to be whatever she needed."

He grilled Peter, over and over, probing. "Where did you study?" "Did you ever sleep with her?" "When did she find out about your little prank with the flag?"

Peter answered all the questions honestly, and more than once retreated, admitting he was just too young to know the right thing to do. At one point, he got frustrated, "Marriage? Abortion, even leadership? How was I supposed to know what to do?"

But in the end, John said simply, "It's okay Pete. You made a lot of mistakes. So did I. We have both made mistakes and done terrible things to each other and to Caroline—to say anything else would be a lie. We have a lot to talk about when she wakes up." Hope leaned back, smiling, and even Peter relaxed, a subtle grin settling on his face.

Without blinking an eye, John turned to me and switched the subject. "What about you? You didn't get her pregnant, that's for sure."

Even I got angry at that, but Hope stepped in. "Josh isn't going to tell his story," she said.

"Well who is?"

"Caroline," she said, producing Caroline's diary. "It's her diary. You don't get to read the whole thing—just the part about Kevin," she said, and explained why Caroline had written the diary, and who Mr. Future Husband Mann was. "Start here," she said, handing him the book, open to the part when Caroline talks about meeting Kevin in medical school.

Donna scooted her chair close to John's, and they read together, turning the pages slowly. "Oh how sweet," Donna said after they had turned only a few pages. Then, after a few more, "They were pregnant! The miscarriage must have been awful!"

I watched John's body tighten up as they turned the next few pages. His lips tensed, and his prominent forehead wrinkled above savage eyes.

275

His fingers were white against the book, and against Donna's hand.

"He killed our grandson," Donna said, very softly.

"He did," John said. "That explains why she left him. What does this have to do with you, Josh," he said to me, his voice softer than it had been before.

"She visited me after she left him—surprised me in the library. Then she showed me her diary. I loved her, and six months later I realized I was the only person she'd shown it to, so I proposed."

"Great. Donna, we didn't give our girl good judgment with men, did we?" Donna remained silent. "Why'd she choose you?" he said to me.

I started to speak, but Hope interrupted. "Because he loved her, and none of the things in that diary mattered to him. It's all in there, you know—the ravine, the pregnancy—some things none of us knew. Josh loved her, and might be the only person she knew who didn't judge her for any of that, or hold it against her. And she knew it."

"What about Peter? He proposed years ago." he asked.

"I got married four years ago. I have two little boys," Peter said.

"She showed you this, Josh, with rape, pregnancy, and a murdering husband, you didn't care?"

"Yeah, she showed me, and yes, I cared—even more. She has the purest heart I've ever met. I'm very lucky to be married to her."

"Yes, you are, son. If Donna and I had done our jobs well, you never would be."

"I am thankful for your incompetence, sir," I said, and couldn't resist a shadow of a smirk.

John leaned far back into his chair, crossing his arms and frowning deeply. He remained like that for a long moment, breathing loudly. He sat forward quickly and spoke. "What was Kevin like in med school? Was he the kind of man you wanted Caroline to be with?"

"No, he was not," I said.

"And you didn't do anything. What about later, when she came back, why didn't you fight harder when you knew we weren't seeing the whole picture? Couldn't you have told us what you knew, even if Caroline didn't want to? Or did you want her for yourself?" He paused, and his angry eyes bore deep into my soul, and I felt as if he could see my fear—of him, of Peter, of Caroline's past. I became acutely aware of my own selfishness.

I waited before answering. "I was … so happy to be living with even a fragment of Caroline … that I was scared to do anything to lose it. I drifted; I let her be in control. Yes, I hid from you." I looked at Hope. "… from you all. I knew some of you didn't like me, and I may have been scared that if Caroline took you back, she might begin to see the real me. I was a coward."

"Yes, you were," said John, and the words sunk deep into the flesh of my breast. "You are no better than the rest of us," he said, and his mouth puckered up like he wanted to spit.

Peter turned to Hope. "It worked," he whispered. "They are where we wanted them to be." Hope smiled.

"You didn't bring me here to piss me off, Hope, I know you better than that," John said.

Hope folded her hands in her lap and said, "No Dad, we need you to do something."

"What's that?"

"You've already told Caroline how you feel—I'm certain she can hear us now," she said. "Now you need to apologize to her, and ask for her forgiveness."

Donna reached up and touched John on the cheek, pulling his head to look at her. Tears flooded the bottoms of her eyes, and she nodded. He nodded, also, but then looked at Hope, Peter, and me and said, "She's our daughter—we don't need an audience." Hope nodded, and we left the room.

*   *   *

Fifteen minutes later, John and Donna joined us in the lobby at the end of the hall. Donna had obviously been crying, and they both looked exhausted. We all stood, and John hugged Hope. "Thank you, dear," he said, and then passed her to Donna, who hugged her deeply. "Listen, we're going to our hotel room. It's been a long day."

"Okay, Dad," Hope said. "Let's meet for breakfast." They agreed, and left.

"So what now?" Peter said.

"I don't know," Hope said. "Wait, I guess. I had hoped that would wake her up."

"We're not done yet," I said, and they both looked at me. "You two and her parents were only half the problem; probably the easy half. Curt is coming. His wife says she'll get Kevin here somehow."

"I may deck them both," Peter said, and his tight jaw told me he meant it.

"I may also," I said. Hope and Peter talked for several more minutes. I settled into my chair, and after a few minutes they had talked out a plan, and left. It was late evening, and I drifted to sleep in my chair, listening to the breathing of the girl I loved most in this world.

*   *   *

I woke up early, having a nightmare. The arm of the chair was pressing hard into my back, and my neck was stiff. The room was dark, the only light coming from under the door, and from the heart monitor that sounded its continual beeping. I rubbed my eyes, and prepared for the shock of light that would hit me as I opened the door and headed down to the bathroom.

My nightmare had been simple, but very disturbing. I was reliving Caroline's accident, over and over, stepping off the curb, my stomach protruding awkwardly. I saw myself, as Caroline, standing on the curb, having to go to the bathroom intensely, feeling like our daughter must be standing on my bladder and clogging to some hillbilly dance. I stepped off the curb, and then turned back when I saw the car. Then, catching one foot behind the other, I saw Nathan speeding toward me, sure to hit the car. Over and over, I willed myself—as Caroline—to step to the side, avoid Nathan and save myself. And over and over, I saw the surprise in his bright blue eyes as he recognized the car's trajectory too late, and as I saw his vision of his own death dim the lights out of his eyes, I launched myself at him, thrusting my arms at his bicycle, using my huge stomach as ballast, and pushed him out of harm's way, knowing the whole time that I would fall backwards into the car. And I did, over and over, fall into the car. I felt it slam into my hip, pain driving deep into my legs as they contorted awkwardly as I was thrown by the impact with the car. Then my head would hit the pavement first, and I would again be standing at the curb, with an intense feeling of having to go to the bathroom.

*   *   *

Curt arrived first, without his wife. Curt had said that Kevin would be coming in later. Hope met Curt down in the lobby when he arrived. The two of them walked in together, and when he saw Peter, he flinched. "What did you tell her?" he asked.

Peter nodded and clenched his lips. "Everything," he finally said.

"Is that what this is about, then?"

"It's about Caroline, Curt," Hope said.

"What about her?" he asked.

"It's about you, too," said Peter.

"What are you talking about? This is all in the past—why drag it up?"

"Tell him," said Hope.

"Tell me what?"

Peter told him about their theory, about why she was still in a coma because of all the things that had happened.

When Peter finished, Curt said, "I could never hold any of that against her. We were just kids back then. Somehow we didn't ... I didn't connect the fun we were having with anything more serious.

"You were there that night, Pete. I changed that night. I'm not saying I became an honorable man, or anything, but I've cleaned up. Caroline—well, she's the past. Inside—a place I never go—well, somewhere I might still love her. I can't go there, but sometimes I do, you know."

"What about Faith?" I asked.

"I'd like to meet her someday," he said.

"That's it?" I asked.

"Yeah, that's it. But with Caroline, I mean, I hope she could forgive me for what I did. I don't see how she could, but in that place I never go, down there I have dreams that she has forgiven me." We talked for a while more, but everything that needed to be said, had been. Curt is a clever guy, though.

"I feel like there's something you haven't told me," Curt said.

"That's all that has anything to do with you," Peter said.

279

"Maybe, Peter, if I didn't father her daughter. Now everything about her has to do with Faith, so it has to do with me." He looked from Peter to Hope, and Hope nodded.

"It's Kevin somehow, isn't it?" he asked.

"Yes," said Hope. "He's on his way."

"What did he do?"

Peter never liked Curt, and he may have been disgusted with Curt's apparent turnaround. "He slipped Caroline a morning after pill while she was pregnant three years ago," Peter said.

"He *what*?" Curt yelled.

"He put a morning after pill into her …" Peter began. As he spoke, the door opened, and Kevin walked in. "… hot chocolate, and gave it to her. He aborted her baby."

Kevin held his hands wide, his open sports coat revealing a thin waist. "Hey, wow, what have I walked in on?" he said.

Curt glared at him in disbelief, and then stood. Curt is a lot bigger than Kevin, Peter or myself, and he took three fast steps toward Kevin. I backed away, but Peter and Hope stood where they were. Curt grabbed Kevin's shirt with one hand and his long muscles flexed strongly as he raised his other hand up as if he was going to hit Kevin. I took another step back, and that's when I heard the beeping going crazy.

Caroline's heart monitor had been giving very regular, strong "beeps" at exactly sixty beats a minute for three weeks now. The doctor's regularly pointed to it and said, "Everything seems to be fine." Or, "No better, no worse." When her blood pressure had gone down, they had studied the output for minor variations in her heartbeat, and reacted strongly to the smallest change.

"Cut it out," I yelled, but no one noticed. Then a nurse opened the door and looked straight at the monitor. "Get a doctor!" she yelled. That got everyone's attention, and they disentangled themselves.

Curt stood back, and Kevin straightened his jacket, which had gone all over to one shoulder during the fray. Kevin took a look at the monitor, and strode over to look at the clipboard hanging from the foot of her bed. Two nurses had come in, and they were adjusting Caroline, trying to get her more comfortable. One of them was wrapping her stomach with a baby monitor as well. While they had occasionally looked at the baby with a monitor or ultrasound over the past several weeks, they had never given her a full-time monitor.

"Her blood pressure has been pretty normal?" Kevin asked.

"Very normal," the nurse said. "Until you came in."

"Right. What is it now?"

"One seventy over one hundred."

"Pulse?"

"Down to eighty."

"We'll watch her for an hour. If it doesn't improve, we'll have to take the baby."

"We may," the nurse said. "But you will be in the waiting room."

Curt had watched Kevin, and when it was clear that he was done with his medical duties, he took Kevin by the sleeve of his sport coat and said, "We need to go talk, Dog." He tugged him out of the room, and we followed them down the hall to the visitor's lobby. Curt pulled Kevin into the small canteen that was attached, which was currently vacant and housed only a few drink and snack machines. He pushed the doors close.

Peter and I settled into a couch in the lobby, while Hope went back to stay with Caroline. After a few minutes, we could hear Kevin and Curt yelling. "What were you thinking?" "You're dumber than a dog!" "At least we were married!" "She loved me enough to tell me she was pregnant!" I don't think it ever came to blows, but twice, someone who was headed toward the canteen with coins in her hand turned away toward the stairs, and a canteen on another floor.

After maybe twenty minutes of rising and subsiding voices, Kevin finally screamed, "So I fucked up. So did you. What do we do about it now?" Things got quiet after that.

*   *   *

Half an hour later, Curt came out. He walked straight over to Peter and me, his face red. "We need to talk for a few minutes," he said. Kevin emerged a minute later and walked past us, headed for Caroline's room. I still didn't trust him, and was glad that Hope was with her.

"Good discussion?" I asked, not hiding my sarcasm.

"Kevin doesn't think they can keep the baby in much longer," Curt said.

"Eight and a half months already. Two weeks left," I said.

"He thinks her blood pressure is going up. Preeclampsia—it means the baby might be sick. The only way to cure it is to take the baby out. C-section."

"Doctor Dansen has been pretty good so far. Let's let him take care of it."

"Kevin wants to do the c-section, Josh. As his way of making up for what he did last time."

I gaped. "Like I'm going to let him near Caroline, or the baby, with a knife in his hand. Let's just say I've got a trust issue with Kevin right now."

"Fair. It's Kevin's issue, too. And he wants to win back your trust by doing this for you. For Caroline."

"He'll do it over my dying carcass," I hissed.

Peter, who had been watching, put out a restraining arm on Curt. "Let me talk with him," he said.

*　　*　　*

Kevin came out a few minutes later with a confirmation of his original diagnosis. Preeclampsia. The baby had to come out within the next twenty four hours. Dr. Dansen—Jim—agreed. Though I knew it would be a life-changing event for me, even I couldn't disagree with the diagnosis. But I had my own opinions on who should do the final surgery. And, as everyone told me, the final decision, as well.

Before Caroline's accident, I had never considered raising our daughter by myself. Even after the accident, all I could think about was Caroline. Our daughter was still just a figment, albeit a rather large one, but not yet a real, corporeal, living daughter. To hold her, and accept her as my own, and somehow also be responsible for her feeding and her growth was outside of my comprehension. Yet, comprehension or no, it was about to become my reality.

Hope, Peter, Curt and I went down to the canteen for dinner, and talked about the surgery. They ganged up on me. "Caroline needs for Kevin to do it," Hope said.

"He was selfish then, but he doesn't have the same motivations he did then. There's nothing selfish here," Peter said.

"They're my girls," I said. "I'll cut his gonads off if I lose them both."

"I'll cut his gonads off if he loses either one," Curt said, and I heard a conviction in his voice that hadn't been there when I visited his house. In the bottom of my soul, I believed he still loved Caroline, and my heart started to turn. But they were still my girls.

"Well he's not going to get the chance," I said.

"It's your call," Hope said. "But I know that Caroline isn't coming out until we fix what's wrong. Kevin needs to make things right with her, and this is the best way."

I gritted my teeth and tried to picture my new daughter being lifted out of her mother's stomach, and tried to picture the face of the doctor doing the work. At first, it was Jim Dansen, even with his ego. Then, I saw him hand my daughter off and sew up the incision, and it was all business. I changed his face, and saw Kevin, years of remorse written in the lines around his eyes, gingerly holding the baby, cleaning and checking her himself, and finally sewing up the incision with the care he would for the woman he loved most in this world. That's when I knew.

We talked a long time after that, and I was still reluctant. In the end, it was the image of Kevin, loving and tender, which convinced me. I agreed, though I wanted Curt the room as well, to be with his best friend, and to cut his gonads off if he screwed up.

*   *   *

Whether the miracle was of modern medicine or of a more divine nature I do not know, but the doctors were able to deliver our baby daughter into the world of the living. Caroline was taken to the Intensive Care Unit, but Kevin brought our daughter to me in our hospital room a couple hours later. He placed her in my arms and she was warm and very soft and small and purple. I laid her on the bed in front of me and cradled her tiny head in both of my hands, no bigger than a small crabapple swallowed up by my gargantuan fingers, her eyes two little blue marbles, staring at me unblinking and unafraid. Her breaths were small and fast, tiny little puffs of life, and I loved her.

"She's beautiful," Kevin said.

"Yeah. A tiny little miracle."

"It's why I decided to do a second residency," he said.

"What is?"

"What I did."

"To make up for it?"

"I can never do that. Just to be a part of life, I guess, rather than the other."

"Yeah. Well, now you are."

"What will you name her?"

"Grace."

*   *   *

Caroline remained in the ICU as Hope and I took Grace home. Hope, who had done this two times before with her own kids, taught me a whole new technology mostly centered on the intake and output of her digestive system, and around making her stop crying. Then, a day later, came a rush of relatives such that I had never seen. Caroline's parents came, as did mine, and also Edward and the girls, who wanted to hold Grace endlessly, and were so gentle with her that I considered trying to hire them full time. I still made time to go see Caroline every day, but obviously could not spend as much time with her as I had—not with a newborn to take care of.

As quickly as they arrived, they left, and I was left taking care of Grace with just Hope to help me. The University was giving me paternity leave, so I had twelve weeks to figure out how I was going to adjust to my new life.

Hope stayed a total of four weeks—four weeks away from her husband, away from her daughters, away from her life. We tried bringing Grace to see Caroline, but it was too sad for us to stay for very long. Caroline's condition neither improved nor deteriorated. Her skin was pale and her eyes sank low in her head. Her muscles had atrophied, and her flesh sagged away from her bones, making her look old and haggard. In Caroline's presence, Grace was silent and pleasant, almost reverent. We made them touch, and once cradled Caroline's arms across her stomach, now much smaller, such that she held Grace, but her unmoving eyes and limp composure gave me such a feeling of stark contrast between Grace growing into life and Caroline growing toward death that I had to take her back and leave, only to return alone the next day to apologize to Caroline.

*   *   *

On the day before Hope left, I was holding Grace cradled in one arm, giving her a bottle with the other. She sucked and I wondered if the tiny blisters on her lips made eating painful. They didn't seem to slow her down, anyway. Holding her, I thought about the risk that Caroline had taken, and the sacrifice she almost made the day of her accident to save a boy who showed no gratitude, and even had enough pent up bitterness to wish death on the little angel that sat in my arms, desperately nursing the warm bottle. As I held her, I grew first disturbed and then angry at Nathan, and by the time she had finished her bottle I was positively furious.

I left Grace with Hope and went to the orphanage. I parked my car and climbed the steps to the front porch. I waved to two children who were sitting on wicker chairs reading comics, and stepped in through the front door. Miss Baldwin greeted me immediately.

"Welcome back, Josh," she said. "How is Caroline coming? And the baby?" She touched my arm and pulled herself up to kiss me on the cheek as I gave her a brief, one armed hug.

"Grace is great, but Caroline is no better," I said, pinching my lips together.

She shook her head. "Come in, then. Is there anything I can do for you?"

"Yes," I said as we sat together on a couch in the foyer. "I need to see Nathan."

She paused, her eyes rising to meet mine. "You know he won't like that," she said.

"I know. Have you heard from his father?"

"No. But we know he's out. If he ever calls, he may be able to prevent you from adopting Nathan."

"I don't think that's an issue right now. Any other family prospects for him?"

"With his history, I don't think anyone will take him."

"I suppose not," I said, and then the anger began returning. "I need to see him. I want to take him to see Caroline."

"Are you sure that's wise?" she asked.

"I'm not sure of anything," I said. "But I think they both need it."

*　　*　　*

Nathan was not pleased to see me, and sat as far away from me as he could in my Honda, hunkered all the way against the far door in the back seat. When we arrived at the hospital, I took him by the arm, not roughly, but not kindly either, and led him to the lobby, then into the elevator. When we reached Caroline's floor, he refused to come out.

I have to admit, knowing what he did the last time I had pulled his arm, I was reluctant to try that again. I stood in the elevator doorway, cautious and waiting, yet resolved, as the door hit me from behind over and over, hitting me, then retracting, waiting and hitting me again. Nathan didn't move.

Finally, my indecision got the better of his stubbornness, and he said, "I'm only going in for one minute."

"That's all I ask," I said, and he followed me down the hall.

I opened the door, and he entered slowly, cautiously. I watched him, fearing he would either have another of his self-destructive temper episodes, or run down the hall where I might lose him in all of the twisting, turning hallways. He walked slowly to her bedside and then right up to her bed where he stood with his hands on the aluminum rails, looking down on her. I gave him plenty of space, and pulled the door closed silently behind him.

"Nathan, I want you to tell her thank you, and that you're sorry," I said.

"I'm not sorry!" he screamed at me. "And I'm not thanking her for anything!" He started crying, and I backed away to the door. I had no idea what to do. I couldn't protect the door, him from a self-destructive episode, and Caroline also should he decide he wanted to attack her still figure. I mumbled "help me, God," under my breath, and waited.

The words came. "She saved your life."

"She could have let me die! It would have been better!" He screamed every word straight at her, and was crying hard in between words."

"That may be so," I said. "You were her favorite, you know."

"I was not! She hated me!" He wailed, his shoulders shaking, his knuckles pale against the handrail.

"No, she didn't. We talked about it—and you were her favorite. We even talked about adopting you."

"That was before you got her pregnant," he said, more quietly. "Now she doesn't need anyone like me. She's got her baby, so she can be happy."

"She signed the adoption papers the day of her accident, Nathan. I'm the one who hasn't signed them yet."

He didn't respond, but just kept crying, and I could see the tears falling on Caroline's sheets and on his hands as they held fast to the rails. Finally, he said it.

"I'm sorry, Miss Caroline. I never wanted this to happen to you." He cried and I could see his tear streaked face and it made me want to come up behind this poor hurt child and hold him, but I knew he didn't trust me or any other adult and I didn't know what it would do to him, so I stayed where I was and he continued to cry, alone.

"Tell her thank you," I said.

"For what!" he screamed at me, turning around to face me. I looked straight into his bloodshot eyes and my heart dropped into my stomach. Then I looked past him at Caroline's limp and useless body and my resolve returned.

"For saving your life," I said, and he wailed at me and I knew in every nucleus of every cell in my body that he would be slamming his head against the tile floor in just one second. But this time it was different. His shoulders shuddered and he reached in between the aluminum rails to touch her, and then held her hand and again his hand looked small and dirty next to her pale fingers. He dropped his forehead against the aluminum railing and sobbed, lifting her fingers up to kiss them as his last tears fell wet on her white sheets.

When he was finally calm, he turned to her. "Thank you for saving my life, Miss Caroline," he said, and then turned and walked out the door.

He called me on the phone the next day and asked me to take him to see her again, and so I did. Every day for the next four weeks I went to pick him up at the orphanage after school, or a little earlier on weekends, and we went to visit Caroline. I was an accessory, the chauffer he allowed to bring him to see Caroline. I let him hold Grace while I prayed with Caroline, and occasionally he would feed her or play with her while I changed her diaper. After a week, I signed his adoption papers, and he came to live with me, in the room Caroline had begun decorating for him.

Then, the day Grace turned ten weeks old, the charge nurse met us in the hallway as we were on our way to her room. "She's awake," was all she said. It was over.

*   *   *

NCSSM held its fifteen year reunion for the class of 1988 one year later. It was a hot June morning, and the tall trees stood sentry over a nearly empty campus just beginning to come alive with the cars and families of alumni. There were four classes there, celebrating five, ten, fifteen, and twenty year reunions. The younger alumni drove up in their VWs and Honda's, while the older alumni rode in cars and SUVs with more space, more horsepower, and basically more of everything.

"Campus has changed so much," Caroline said as we pushed our stroller around the back of Wyche. "There used to be woods here, right where that big dorm is. We turned the corner past Hunt, the new dorm, and her eyes went wide. "That used to be woods, too!" she said, pointing to a large playing field with a gymnasium complex on the side of it. We had already walked past the 1908 building, which had been redone, and now housed the school administration.

Caroline took my hand and pulled. "Come over here," she said. "There's someone I'd like for you to meet." We walked over to a picnic table which had a distinguished looking white haired gentleman in a coat and tie, and a beautiful woman with long curly hair holding two small children, a boy and a girl.

Alexander saw us first, and stood up and smiled broadly. Julia turned, then set the kids gently on the bench and ran to Caroline, embracing her in a long hug. Alexander came up and Caroline freed an arm to wrap around him. When she pulled away, she said, "I'd like to introduce you to my

288

husband Josh, my adopted son Nathan, and my daughter Grace," she said.

We sat down to talk, and told Alexander and Julia a little bit about the events of a year ago. As we were telling them, Peter walked up and joined us. Alexander was first appalled, and then warmed by the ending.

Julia asked the question, the one we all believed in while she was unconscious, but the suddenly forgot once she came back to us.

"Was their theory right, Caroline? Could you hear them when you were in your coma? Were you turtling?"

Caroline looked at her, then turned to me and took my hand. "I don't remember hearing any conversations while I was in a coma. But I am sure of Hope's intent, and certain that is why I was able to wake up. Josh was my safe harbor. I was turtling in my life with him long before the accident. Now, we're not. The rest, you can believe if you want to—it's a matter of faith. I do."

When Caroline finished, Julia said, "Peter, what was the last verse you memorized?" He gave her what I call the "Nike verse," about being doers of the word, rather than just hearers. "Here's your next verse," she said. "It comes from Colossians 3:12-14. 'As God's chosen ones, holy and beloved, clothe yourselves with compassion, kindness, humility, meekness, and patience. Bear with one another and, if anyone has a complaint against another, forgive each other; just as the Lord has forgiven you, so you also must forgive. Above all, clothe yourselves with love, which binds everything together in perfect harmony.'"

*   *   *

I'm closing this manuscript, now. The publishers say it will be on the bookstore shelves in time for Christmas. Caroline and I have prayed mightily, and have left it in God's hands whether or not Faith will ever contact us. Her eighteenth birthday is still almost two years away. After all that has happened, and after talking with Peter and Hope, we decided to put this together and place it in God's hands to publish it and, if it is His will, to guide it into Faith's arms. Maybe she will read it, wonder about her mother and come to love her as the rest of us have, and want to meet her. Or maybe not. Maybe God has another purpose, and if so, then we are glad to have been His servants.

The Author lives with his wife Mandi and daughter Alexandra in Greenville, South Carolina. He graduated from the North Carolina School of Science and Mathematics in 1985, from the University of North Carolina in 1989, and received his PhD from The Ohio State University in 1994. He is president of a company, Innegrity LLC (www.innegrity.com), which makes polymer fibers to replace fiberglass in composites. His hobbies are readin', 'ritin', and 'rithmatic … and computer gaming, and … er … when he can find the motivation, jogging. He can be reached at Brian@Morin.ws, or at 8 New Forest Ct., Greenville, SC, 29615.

The picture of the School building on the cover, known affectionately to older alumni as the "1908 Building," was taken by Joe Liles, Instructor of Art, North Carolina School of Science and Mathematics. The building has since been renovated, and is called Watts Hall. In the early days of the School, the building was surrounded by a chain link fence and filled with wonderful discoveries and crannies to wile away the time in much needed solitude. While we were not allowed to enter, the place was filled with footprints.

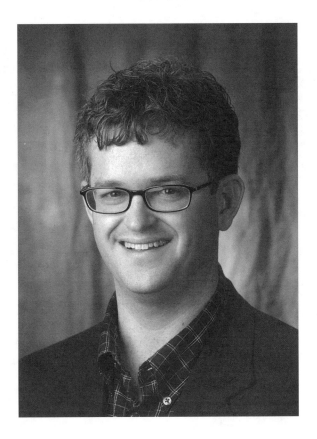

The cover was designed by Peter McRae '85. Peter received a BA in Fine Arts from the University of North Carolina at Chapel Hill ('89). Looking for a way to use both sides of his brain, Peter embarked on a career as a graphic designer. He worked for several creative firms, spent six years as a freelance designer before establishing Peter McRae Design (www.mcraedesign.com). Peter currently lives in Charlotte, NC with his wife, Lisa, his stepson Sam, and his three children, Megan, Seth & Quinn. He is active in the community serving on several non-profit boards.

The photo of the author's daughter, Alexandra Denise Morin, on the cover, and the photo of the author and his wife on p. 290 were taken by Steve Verdell, www.verdelldesigns.com. Steve and his wife Beth are close friends with the author and his wife. We recommend Steve's services for weddings, portraits, and of course, baby pictures.

The website, www.amatteroffaith.org, was designed by Gina Norman '86. Gina is the manager of Intranet Governance at Nortel Networks, where she is responsible for information architecture and intranet policies. In her spare time she's a confessed craftaholic (http://www.lintqueen.com/craft) and can usually be found knitting, sewing or making jewelry.